The
MARKET DRIVEN
ORGANIZATION

Understanding, Attracting, and Keeping Valuable Customers

GEORGE S. DAY

THE FREE PRESS

*f*P

THE FREE PRESS
A Division of Simon & Schuster, Inc.
1230 Avenue of the Americas
New York, NY 10020

Designed by Carla Bolte

Manufactured in the United States of America

10 9 8 7 6 5 4 3 2 1

Library of Congress Cataloging-in-Publication Data

Day, George S.
    The market driven organization: understanding, attracting, and
keeping valuable customers / George S. Day.
        p.   cm.
    Includes bibliographical references and index.
    1. Marketing—Management.   2. Sales management.   3. Consumer
satisfaction.   4. Customer relations.   I. Title.
    HF5415.13.D367   1999
    658.8—dc21   99-16155
                                                          CIP

ISBN 0–684–86467–3

Contents

Part II
Building the Capabilities

Part III
Aligning the Organization to the Market

Introduction

Move to the Market

It is in vogue to aspire to become market-driven. CEOs exhort their employees to get closer to customers, stay ahead of competitors and make decisions from the market back. While this rhetoric is now commonplace, successful market-driven organizations still are rare. Too often, even the best-intentioned senior managers have been unable to translate their aspirations into action. Their organizations haven't grasped what it means to be market-driven or they lack the commitment to make the deep-seated changes that are needed.

Why should organizations strive to become market-driven? Our answer is that in an era of increasing market turbulence and intensifying competition, a robust market orientation has become a strategic necessity. Only *with superior skills in understanding, attracting and keeping customers* can firms devise strategies that will deliver superior customer value and keep this strategy aligned with changing market requirements. Even firms with world-class technology and innovative business models have to stay close to their customers and ahead of competition to realize their full potential.

The power of a market-driven organization can be seen in the success of companies such as Intuit, Wal-Mart, Virgin Airlines, Disney, Gillette, and many others who have used a superior relationship to customers to gain advantage over rivals. In contrast, the stories of IBM's loss of control of the PC market, Motorola's stumble in shifting from analog to digital cellular systems, and Sears, Roebuck's difficulties in the early 1990s show how a failure to align the organization to the market can quickly and seriously erode competitive performance. In fact, a growing body of research supports the insight that market-driven organizations outperform their peers.

Given the benefits of becoming market-driven, why do so many organizations fail to do so? The first reason is confusion about what it means to be market-driven. Some companies have become "customer compelled," jumping to meet every customer whim without a clear strategy. As a backlash, a growing group of firms argues that there are times when it is better to "ignore the customer." As discussed in Chapter 2, both these views are misconceptions with unfortunate consequences.

The second reason is that the culture, capabilities and configuration of most organizations are more a hindrance than a help. In working with executives to apply the concepts of my 1990 book, *Market Driven Strategy*, it became clear that most firms lacked the means to implement such an approach to a strategy. Their internal processes, structures, incentives and controls were in the way. As one 3M manager summed up their problem, "The fact that we are a: multi-dimensional, multi-functional, multi-regional and multi-plant organization is not the customer's fault."

What does it mean to be market-driven? How does this orientation to the market improve performance? How can companies build successful market-driven organizations? I have spent the better part of the past decade pursuing these questions. This work began in earnest with a conference on "Organizing to Become Market-Driven" I coordinated as executive director of the Marketing Science Institute in 1990. It continued in executive programs and consulting with more than a thousand senior executives around the world. Through this work and through my research I have developed insights into distinguishing features of the market-driven organization.

Part I of this book examines the many organizational elements that work together supportively in a market-driven organization. Those with the greatest leverage on performance are an externally oriented culture, capabilities for market sensing and market relating, and a configuration that aligns vertical functions and horizontal processes. All of these elements work together to foster a market orientation. We will study each element in turn and then show how best to integrate them to support the chosen strategy.

Part II then explores the distinctive market-sensing and market-relating capabilities that are at the heart of market-driven organizations. These firms stand out in their ability to continuously sense and act on events and trends in their markets. They also are better at anticipating how their markets will respond to their actions. Not surprisingly, these organizations also have superior capabilities for relating to their markets. They develop intimate relationships with their customers, instead of seeing them as a means to a series of transactions. These capabilities are built upon a shared knowledge base that is used to gather and disseminate knowledge about the market. We show how these capabilities are developed and applied to gain a competitive advantage in consumer and business-to-business markets.

Finally, Part III offers a road map to managers who want to align their organizations to the market. How do companies navigate from an internal focus to a market focus? The first step is to reshape the organization to create a stronger market focus. Second, we explore the strategic thinking used to set the direction by combining top-down guidance and bottom-up market insights. Finally, we describe the six conditions needed for a successful change process. We illustrate this process through case studies of three companies (Owens Corning, Sears and Eurotunnel) who transformed themselves into market-driven organizations, and turned around their fortunes in the process.

How does your organization measure up? At the end of the book, we offer a diagnostic questionnaire to help you assess the progress of your organization in becoming market-driven. These tools can help you identify specific strengths and weaknesses, to guide your efforts to strengthen a market orientation. If you prefer to start with an assessment of your own situation, you might want to flip to the back of the book and work through the questionnaire now. Then you can pay particular attention to areas of weakness as you move through the book.

Although becoming market-driven still is challenging, the path toward improvement has never been clearer. Many pioneering firms have already broken the trail, and the insights of their experience are distilled in this book. Advances in network technologies—including the Internet, intranets and extranets—have created new opportunities to develop a market-driven organization more quickly, efficiently collect and disseminate information and build relationships with customers. This technology brings us closer to realizing the ideal of an organization that is continuously responsive to the changing requirements of customers.

Your organization can gain tremendous benefits from becoming more market-driven. Whatever your industry and current level of market orientation, aligning your organization more closely to the market can give you enduring advantages over rivals, provide insights into new opportunities and help avoid costly missteps, contributing to overall performance. While there are no simple recipes for creating a market-driven organization, this book offers frameworks and proven strategies that can help you achieve the advantages, performance and profits that accrue to such organizations.

PART I

UNDERSTANDING MARKET ORIENTATION

Chapter One

What It Means to Be Market Driven

First Direct was the world's leading telephone-only bank, and the fastest growing bank in Britain during the 1990s. It had overcome the notorious inertia of the retail customers of the four big chartered banks to attract 650,000 affluent customers in less than seven years. These customers called 24 hours a day, seven days a week to pay bills, trade stock, arrange mortgages or buy any of 25 financial services.[1]

The concept of a bank with no branches originated in the convergence of improvements in call center technology, the availability of an automatic teller machine network to provide cash, and a high level of dissatisfaction with the service in the established banks. Meanwhile, research by First Direct revealed a substantial segment of bank customers who didn't want to visit their branches or found the hours inconvenient.

Traditional banks ignored phone banking at first. However, the explosive growth of First Direct soon caught their attention. Within five years, there were 14 direct competitors with another 15 rivals using different technologies such as touch tone–based services. How did First Direct keep up with rapid growth and beat so many well-funded imitators? One answer is that they had very low operating costs, which meant low customer charges, while their highly trained banking representatives delivered the best customer satisfaction ratings in the industry.

First Direct's most observable advantage was a prototypically market-driven organization. Their culture contrasted sharply with the formality of the established banks and emphasized openness, being right the first time and responsiveness. The 2,400 banking representatives saw themselves as problem solvers providing trouble-free banking with a personal touch. They were supported with extensive investments in information technology and training. These systems also enabled the firm to learn a great deal about their customers and cross-sell other products. Yet there was no complacency within the management team. They realized they would have to do more to tighten relations with customers while providing Internet-based banking services to stay ahead in the future. By working hard to build a market-driven organization, First Direct has stayed on top in the intensely competitive U.K. market for telephone banking.

Failing to Monitor Vital Signs

In contrast, Johnson & Johnson's cardiology unit squandered its lead in a new market by failing to react to market changes. Like First Direct, J&J was a pioneer in defining a new market in 1994 when it introduced a revolutionary device called a stent, which held open obstructed heart vessels with a tiny metal scaffold. The benefits of this new device were so compelling that cardiologists adopted it en masse. Within two years, J&J had sold a billion dollars worth—at 80 percent gross margins—and held 91 percent of the market. Yet, by 1999, their share had collapsed to 8 percent and they faced two entrenched competitors.[2]

How did this highly regarded marketer of Tylenol and Band-Aids lose what they thought was an insurmountable lead? At the head of a long list of shortcomings was a failure to listen to the market and keep innovating. Perhaps because they were new to the cardiology marketplace, they weren't sensitive to the needs and frustrations of the doctors. The first version of their stent had limitations that doctors soon found annoying: it was hard to use in some situations, came in only one size and couldn't easily be seen in the X-rays that were used to locate and then guide the stent through the arteries.

J&J was slow to address these problems because the small unit had its hands full just meeting demands. Also their ability to innovate was impeded by a culture with a pharmaceutical company mind-set that was unused to the speedy development cycles of medical devices firms, and a traditional organization with strong functional departments that created obstacles to a customer focus. Their challengers had an advantage because they were configured into teams that were adept at getting products to market quickly. When J&J finally made improvements, their rivals had already beaten them to market with products that were easier to use and less expensive.

These rivals also benefited from J&J's inflexibility in pricing as hospitals struggled to cope with the unexpectedly high cost of stents. Initially insurers wouldn't pay these costs, but they relented in the face of compelling evidence of the lifesaving and cost benefits. While the stent ultimately won the support of insurers, J&J's higher-priced products didn't. The company's lack of empathy for the cost pressures of the hospitals alienated influential luminaries in the field who instead welcomed the new competition.

UNDERSTANDING THE ORIENTATION TO THE MARKET

How did First Direct stay on the top of its market while Johnson & Johnson lost control of the market it helped to create? Both firms launched breakthrough innovations, but the difference was that First Direct was more market-driven. It demonstrated *a superior ability to understand, attract and keep valuable customers*. This is the definition of a market-driven firm.

By putting "superior" into this definition we remind ourselves that winning in a competitive market means outperforming competitors. Our abilities cannot be judged without reference to the "best of class" competitor or competitive alternative. I am frequently asked who are the most market-oriented firms. This is not the right question, because there are no absolute standards. What matters is being closer to your market than your rivals.

The definition also incorporates Drucker's dictum[3] that the purpose of a business is to attract and satisfy customers at a profit. But satisfaction is not sufficient, for customer acquisition is costly, so real profitability comes from *keeping* valuable customers by building deep loyalty that is rooted in mutual trust, bilateral commitments and intense communication.

Market-driven organizations know their markets so thoroughly that they are able to identify and nurture their *valuable customers*, and have no qualms about discouraging the customers that drain profits—those that are fickle and cost a lot to serve. Thus, being market-driven is about having the discipline to make sound strategic choices and implement them consistently and thoroughly. It is not about being all things to all people.

Three Elements of Successful Market Driven Organizations

How do market-driven organizations achieve their superior ability to understand, attract and keep valuable customers and consistently win in their markets? What is it that sets apart exemplars like the brokerage house Edward Jones, upscale retailer Nordstrom, discounter Wal-Mart, or supercompetitive MCI and Dell Computer from their rivals? Why was Nike able to prevail over Adidas and Reebok for so long and why are these rivals starting to close the gap? A decade's worth of research and the careful dissection of best practices has banished the myth of a simple answer. Reality is found in the artful combination of the defining elements shown in Figure 1–1.

- An *externally oriented culture* with the dominant beliefs, values and behaviors emphasizing superior customer value and the continual quest for new sources of advantage.

FIGURE 1–1

The Elements of a Market Orientation

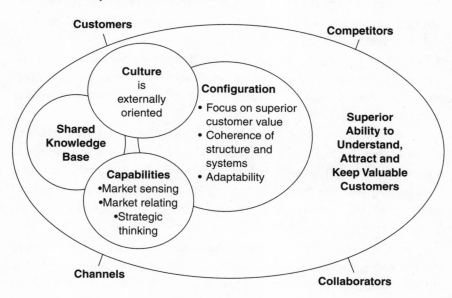

- *Distinctive capabilities* in market sensing, market relating, and anticipatory strategic thinking. This means market-driven firms are better educated about their markets and better able to form close relationships with valued customers. The clarity of their strategic thinking helps them devise winning strategies that anticipate rather than react to market threats and opportunities.
- A *configuration* that enables the entire organization continually to anticipate and respond to changing customer requirements and market conditions. This includes all the other capabilities for delivering customer value—from product design to order fulfillment, plus an adaptive organization design and all the supporting systems, controls, measures and human resource policies. All these aspects of the configuration are aligned with a superior value proposition.

Supporting these three elements is a *shared knowledge base* in which the organization collects and disseminates its market insights. This knowledge builds relationships with customers, informs the company's strategy and increases the focus of employees on the needs of the market. Advances in information technology present new opportunities to build this shared knowledge base, but only if the technology is applied with a clear market focus.

These elements reinforce one another in a market-driven organization. They don't simply add together; instead they are multiplicative, so a weakness in one area afflicts the others. A rigidly functional organization with fiefdoms that carefully protect their turf will thwart the sharing of market learning and undermine efforts to introduce an open, participative culture. Each of these elements must be at least as good as the best of the rivals if the overall market orientation is to ensure the strategy gains an advantage.

The Role of Culture

A market-driven culture is much more than a market mantra. We are all familiar with the sort of market-orientation slogans to which most firms nowadays pay lip service:

> *The customer is at the top of the organization chart* (Scandinavian Airline Systems).

Our mission is to find needs and fill them, not make products and sell them
(Colgate).
Do business the way the customer wants to do business (US West).
If we're not customer-driven our cars won't be either (Senior Officer,
Ford Motor Co.).
Customer satisfaction is the basis of our legitimacy (Tektronix).

Although slogans may be useful as reminders on wallet cards or rally-
ing points in speeches, they seldom pervade or motivate an organization.
Some reflect an underlying organization that is tightly aligned to its present and prospective markets, but others are mere facades that mask an
internally focused culture but do not truly change it. Because they give
the appearance that something is being done, they can actually be obstacles to real cultural change. The true test is not in what the organization
says about itself but whether it acts in a way that reflects a culture aligned
to the market.

In a market-driven firm, a pervasive market orientation is woven into
the fabric of the organization. It is seen in what Jan Carlson, then CEO of
the Scandinavian Airlines System, called the "million moments of truth"
that determine the collective experience of customers as they interact
with cabin staff, ticket agents, baggage handlers, and ticket takers.
Whether these front-line people actually deliver superior customer value
depends on their having the right incentives, tools and organizational
setting. When they are part of a culture that insists on putting the customer first, while staying ahead of competitors, they have a reason for
doing their jobs. Then "quality" becomes a collective dedication rather
than an imposed dictum, "customer retention" a meaningful motivation
rather than a mechanical metric, and "cross-functional teams" are mechanisms for improvement rather than a time-consuming indulgence.

On the other hand, a lack of a market-driven culture was one of the
factors that contributed to Motorola's downfall in the cellular telephone
market. Its failure to develop digital systems and address customer service
problems led to the decline of its share of the cellular phone from 60 percent to 34 percent between 1994 and 1998. Motorola was focused on
making a better analog phone while the market was marching toward digital technology. It mishandled relationships with key customers operating
cellular networks and underestimated the challenge from rivals such as
Nokia, Qualcomm, and Lucent.[4]

The signals from its main customers couldn't have been clearer. In the early 1990s executives from McCaw Cellular (now AT&T Wireless Services) decided the future of cellular was digital. Over the next few years, they met repeatedly with Motorola managers who said they would work on it. Yet in 1996, just as AT&T was rolling out its digital network, Motorola unveiled its Star TAC phone—a design marvel, light, smaller than a cigarette pack, and analog! AT&T had no choice but to turn to Nokia and Ericsson for digital handsets. Why did Motorola miss or ignore the signals from its customers and rivals? Some argue it was hubris; that the company was blinded by its success in creating the cellular phone market. However, Christopher Galvin, the CEO, also attributed the problems to a culture that was engineering and product-driven and distracted by internal rivalries.

Contrast Motorola's aloofness with the behavior of John Chambers, the CEO of Cisco Systems, the networking giant that provides the routers, hubs and switches that make the Internet feasible. He is passionate about avoiding the arrogance that makes technology-driven companies unresponsive to their customers. Before his first board meeting as chief executive, he insisted on staying to sort out a customer problem and was half an hour late for the meeting. It was a clear sign that customers were a top priority. Every evening he goes through voice mail from managers who are dealing with customers on the "critical list." He insists on voice mail because he wants to hear the emotion in the voices, which is undoubtedly amplified because these managers' pay is closely tied to customer satisfaction levels. These signals from the top contribute greatly to the distinctive "feel" of Cisco that sets the company apart.

Markets eventually punish firms with arrogant and unresponsive cultures. When this happens, the shock to the system is so great that the dysfunctional values and beliefs can finally be challenged and displaced. Motorola was forced to attack its problems by consolidating its feuding fiefdoms under a common umbrella and then making a concerted effort to patch up relations with customers. One customer reported, "We are finally seeing Motorola acting like a hungry vendor who needs our business rather than an arrogant vendor entitled to our business."

The Role of Capabilities

In addition to culture, a market-driven organization has superior capabilities in market sensing—reading and understanding the market. It also excels in market relating—creating and maintaining relationships with customers. Finally, the market-driven organization has capabilities in strategic thinking that allow it to align its strategy to the market and help it anticipate market changes.

Intuit offers a powerful demonstration of how these superior capabilities contribute to a company's success. How did Intuit's *Quicken* gain a near monopoly in personal finance software despite fierce competition from Microsoft and others? When Intuit launched *Quicken* in 1983, it faced 43 competing products and soon found itself staring down Microsoft, which had bested rivals in word processing, spreadsheets and presentations.

Yet Intuit managed not only to survive but to dominate. By 1998, *Quicken* held 75 percent of the market because it was easier to use than the alternatives. The vast majority of *Quicken* customers simply buy the program, load it into their computer, and begin using it without reading the manual. This delights customers who then tell their friends. It also pleases the makers of the program, who believe "we are successful when the customer is successful," in the words of Scott Cook, the founder.

An essential ingredient of Intuit's success is its highly tuned market-sensing capability. Teams of software developers watch for small hints of where the program might be difficult or confusing to find ways to make *Quicken* progressively easier to use. Intuit listens not only to current customers but also noncustomers, who make up 80 percent of the subjects in its usability labs. Intuit employees visit customer homes to see how they organize their finances and install their software. Customer service is a rich source of insights into potential problems and latent needs to feed the development process. When employees on the help line started hearing about the problems small businesses were having when using *Quicken* to keep their books, the company developed *QuickBooks*. They learned that the smallest companies had turned to *Quicken* because all the other packages were designed to be used by an accountant and were much too complicated and sophisticated for their needs. If you didn't know what an audit trail was, it wasn't necessary to have the feature in your software.

The new product was so well received that it captured 70 percent of the market within two years of introduction.

The Role of Configuration

The third element of the market-driven organization is a distinctive context in which the culture and capabilities of a market-driven organization are embedded and activated.[5] This *configuration* is the nested relationship of the firm's culture, capabilities and processes in the structure of the firm. It includes the capabilities for market sensing, market relating and strategic thinking discussed above, as well as other capabilities and assets of the business plus the organizational structures and supporting information, control, and reward systems. Competitive success comes when all these elements are aligned with a compelling value proposition.

The depth and impact of a configuration and the connections among elements can be seen in the workings of General Motors' Saturn program. The early success of Saturn shows how a market-driven company was able to break away from its parent to create "a different kind of company." Saturn was conceived in 1985 as a world-class compact with a strong quality culture, outside the oppressive General Motors system and free from the confrontational culture of the UAW. Although the car was well designed and had good quality, the technology and styling were soon dated, and its performance and features were merely acceptable. It was not the product but rather a market-driven configuration—supporting a vibrant quality culture and market-relating capability—that set the company and car apart.[6]

The organization's capabilities were built into cross-functional teams that formed the basic organizational structure. The team focus was reinforced with extensive training, empowerment, and incentives based on team goals with an explicit quality component. The emphasis on delivering high customer-perceived quality was heightened with an unusual money-back guarantee. The distinctive culture and configuration of the company became a selling point in advertisements that stressed its teamwork, values and beliefs and enthusiasm of employees as "a different kind of company." This showed a deep appreciation of the market realities and the futility of trying to position the car in a crowded market where its competitors had long since preempted most of the credible quality claims.

Instead, prospective buyers were persuaded that the employees stood behind the car.

The most sustainable advantage came from Saturn's organization of its dealers to create a distinctive market-relating capability. Its retail system used low-pressure selling by salaried sales consultants that eliminated price haggling. The consultants were recruited from outside the car industry, so the old, bad habits of high-pressure bargaining would be discouraged, and group rather than individual sales effort would be encouraged. Meanwhile, price competition among dealers was minimized by giving dealers large market areas to serve, in contrast to the usual practice of swarms of independent dealers fighting for the same market.

The results of the Saturn experiment were gratifying. After a successful debut in 1991, it was the tenth highest selling car in the United States, despite having only 20 percent as many dealers as its competitors. By 1994, it achieved the highest J. D. Power customer satisfaction rating after Lexus and Infiniti. But the reality remained that the company was part of a larger corporate configuration. Saturn's ability to capitalize on its strengths was hurt by spending cutbacks by its parent company, so it was disadvantaged in features such as passenger air bags and a quieter ride. In addition, the company lacked product line breadth. By 1998, the momentum had not been regained but the firm's culture, capabilities and configuration had kept it in the race.

Saturn's later decline in performance shows how important it is to view configuration as an ongoing concern rather than a single event. Management's job is to maintain the integrity and stability of the basic configuration while pushing the organization to stay ahead of rivals through superior execution.[7] If and when the configuration falls out of alignment with the market and can't deliver superior value, then it is time to begin a transformation. But the most successful market-driven organizations don't wait and then belatedly react—they keep their antennae up constantly so they can anticipate the need for change and initiate moves on their terms.

What are the distinguishing features of the configurations of market-driven organizations?

- *Strategic focus on the market.* The organization is configured to focus on delivering superior customer value. This strategic theme is the central tent pole around which all the elements are orchestrated and connected. This ensures that all functional activities and investments are part of an overriding business model focused on the market.

- *Coherence of elements.* This is achieved when all the elements of the organization—culture, capabilities and configuration—complement and support each other. Conversely, incoherence leads to disconnects in strategy and implementation, creating lapses that the customer is usually the first to see. If the service department can't follow through on the warranty promise and its systems can't talk to the rest of the organization, you have a recipe for confusion. The sales force won't hear about complaints until too late, billing is haphazard and the customer is forced to play telephone tag as everyone passes the buck.

- *Flexibility.* Markets change, so the configuration should not be a straitjacket that inhibits trial-and-error learning and continuous improvement. The challenge for a market-driven organization is to devise a structure that can combine the depth of knowledge found in a vertical hierarchy with the responsiveness of horizontal process teams. Otherwise, even the best-aligned organization will ultimately find itself out of step with the market and face expensive "retooling" of its organization to meet the new demands.

As in the case of Saturn, the focus, coherence and adaptability of the market-driven organization offer a powerful advantage over rivals. The configuration of the organization itself gives it the ability to forge closer connections to the market and respond quickly or anticipate new customers' needs.

ADVANTAGES OF A MARKET ORIENTATION

Why is it important to be market-driven? The superior abilities of the market-driven firm lead to bottom-line benefits from improved performance. Although managers have been exhorted to "stay close to customers," and "put the customer at the top of the organization chart" for at least forty years, this advice had to be taken on faith until recently. Now, a growing body of research has found that market-driven firms usually are more profitable than their rivals, a conclusion that has been sustained with a variety of measures and methods.[8] One illustrative study found that market-driven businesses were 31 percent more profitable than self-centered firms, while those that were customer-oriented and didn't pay attention to competitors were 18 percent more profitable than those that were self-centered.[9]

Although these studies have not been able to trace the precise reasons why a market orientation enhances profitability, clues from other sources indicate several benefits of a market orientation:

- *Superior cost and investment efficiency.* Not all customers are equally attractive, and loyal customers are considerably more profitable than others. A market-driven firm is better able to identify and keep its profitable accounts, and understands the payoff from its marketing investments.
- *Employee satisfaction.* Satisfied employees are both a cause and consequence of customer satisfaction. They are also more committed and enthusiastic about the firm, more productive, and because they are more loyal, the costs of recruiting, selecting, and training are lower.[10] The cost of employee turnover is also lower—not only the direct costs of hiring replacements, but the indirect costs of lower productivity as replacements learn their jobs and broken relationships are repaired.
- *Price premium.* A market orientation contributes to a more powerful value proposition, which translates into greater value that usually is rewarded with a price premium.
- *Revenue growth.* Here the evidence is not so conclusive, but we expect that a superior ability to anticipate changing market requirements and target innovation efforts more effectively should have top-line benefits.
- *Competitive preemption.* With highly satisfied customers, the firm has erected switching barriers that competitors cannot easily breach. These could be psychological (the customer is comfortable in the relationship and resists changing) or economic (there is a large perceived cost or risk to making a switch).

These bottom-line benefits are derived from a set of inherent advantages market-driven firms have over more internally focused rivals. These advantages, summarized in Figure 1–2, are drawn from a superior ability to understand markets, and attract and retain customers. The market-driven organization is better able to understand markets by sensing emerging opportunities, anticipating competitors' moves and making fact-based

FIGURE 1–2

How a Market Orientation Enhances Performance

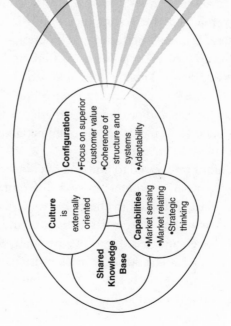

Superior Ability to Understand Markets

- sense emerging opportunities
- anticipate competitors' moves
- make fact-based decisions

Superior Ability to Attract and Keep Customers

- deliver superior value
- encourage loyalty
- leverage market investments

Bottom-Line Benefits

- cost and investment efficiency
- employee satisfaction
- price premium
- revenue growth
- preemption of rivals

Configuration
- Focus on superior customer value
- Coherence of structure and systems
- Adaptability

Culture
is externally oriented

Capabilities
- Market sensing
- Market relating
- Strategic thinking

Shared Knowledge Base

15

decisions. It is also better able to keep customers by delivering superior value, encouraging loyalty and leveraging its market investments.

Superior Ability to Understand Markets

Being able to sense opportunities, anticipate moves of competitors and make fact-based decisions are all part of market understanding.

Sensing Emerging Opportunities

Market-driven firms are adept at anticipating and acting on market shifts and emerging opportunities ahead of competitors. Thus, General Electric saw the potential in augumented services earlier than its rivals in markets as diverse as locomotives and factory automation, and British Airways became a leader in providing an in-flight experience that reduces the burdens of long flights. Both firms recognized that their offerings were susceptible to the inexorable forces of commoditization as competitors catch up, and that customers buy the expectations of benefits and solutions to their problems.

This ability to anticipate opportunities comes from a more creative view of the market. Former British Airways chairman Sir Colin Marshall[11] firmly rejected the commodity mind-set as misguided thinking "that a business is merely performing a function—in our case, transporting people from point A to point B on time and at the lowest possible price." Instead, British Airways goes "beyond the function and price to compete on the basis of providing an experience." Similarly, Disneyland provides an enjoyable and predictable experience for families, and American Express offers a card with a sense of financial security and cachet that tells the world you've arrived.

Organizations motivated to find and offer better solutions and experiences to their chosen customers have a different mind-set and culture. That is particularly reflected in the priorities of their leaders. Employees instinctively know that customer satisfaction and retention are the first priority, and this encourages them to continually seek new ways to excel in serving customers. The strongly market-driven culture of British Airways can be traced to the behavior and example set by Sir Colin Marshall. For this he was admired and respected by the organization he led.

Anticipating Competitors' Moves

Market-driven firms are focused not just on sensing needs of customers, but also on anticipating the moves of rivals in the market. A continuing point of contention is whether a firm can be both customer and competitor oriented. Can the marketing concept, which calls for putting the customer first in all decisions, coexist with the aggressive competitive posture of Jack Welsh of GE who advises his managers to "hit your competitors before they are big enough for it to be a fair fight?"

Of course a myopic focus on simply beating competitors at all costs is destructive, and a sure recipe for a profit-sapping price or promotion war. On the other hand, superior customer value can only be assessed in relation to the offerings of rival firms. This is why market-driven firms are so intensely competitive; they watch their rivals closely to see why they may be gaining an edge, become paranoid about disclosing moves prematurely, calibrate their performance against the "best of class," and celebrate wins against competitors. In short, they integrate a customer and competitor orientation.

Competitive rivalry has been likened to a multidimensional game of chess where the board keeps changing size and shape, new players emerge and the rules change as customers' requirements change. Market-driven firms are especially adept at anticipating the moves of their competitors, both the moves they initiate and their reactions, and spreading this information throughout the organization. Firms that lack this capability are often caught by surprise when attacked by a competitor. The early indicators may have been scattered throughout the organization but no one pulled the clues together to sense a pattern.

A major discount footwear retailer recently paid a high price for following a predictable promotion strategy when its biggest rival made a number of damaging attacks. During peak buying periods such as back-to-school, the rival surprised the firm with heavy television spending and "buy one, get one free" offers that drew away up to 20 percent of its customers in some markets. In retrospect, these moves were predictable; a new and aggressive CEO combined with an improved cost structure gave them the weapons they needed. Had the victim been more market-driven, it would have been prepared to counterattack or even take preemptive actions.

Making Fact-Based Decisions

Rather than basing decisions solely on gut instincts or qualitative research, the market-driven organization has a superior ability to make decisions based on the facts. It can base its strategy on the actual behavior of customers and competitors, or information that provides insights into future opportunities and risks. This requires knowledge bases that capture what is known about (a) market structure—how are the competitive boundaries shifting and market segments evolving? (b) market responses—what are the drivers of customer value and how will consumers, competitors and channels respond to these drivers? and (c) market economics—where is the firm making money, and what moves will improve profitability?

Firms are increasingly using technological advances to manage and exploit the knowledge in these databases. Three different technologies are needed: database management systems to capture the information, communications and messaging to help retrieve and transmit information independent of location, and secure search procedures that allow people to access databases and obtain immediate answers to their queries without relying on intermediaries. These technologies have been greatly facilitated by Internet-based standards and architecture.

Ability to Attract and Keep Valuable Customers

In addition to an ability to understand markets, the market-driven firm is better able to attract and retain valuable customers and leverage its market investments more efficiently.

Delivering Superior Customer Value

Within a market-driven organization, there is a pervasive understanding and commitment by all functions to a well-defined positioning theme that emphasizes superior value. These firms know their target markets intimately and focus obsessively on the things that customers value most highly. This is true of firms as wide-ranging as Wal-Mart with its promise of "always the low price," to Dell Computers with its ability to tailor personal computers cost-effectively to individual requirements, and Hertz which excels in no-hassle, speedy rental car service for the business traveler.

A clear focus on customer value is also a hallmark of the *Mittelstand*, the small and midsized companies that are the export engine of the German economy.[12] They dominate the global markets for highly specialized products such as labeling machines for beverages, metal filters, bookbinding textiles and sunroofs for cars. They concentrate their energies on the areas customers in these markets value most: product quality, closeness to customers, service, economy, quality of employees, technological leadership and innovativeness. Employees know what their customers want by staying in close and frequent contact. This ensures that the people with the technical knowledge have a deep and realistic understanding of the customers' situation and are not likely to underestimate application problems.

Keeping Customers

Market-driven organizations recognize that customer satisfaction alone is not enough. Satisfaction must be converted to relationships and loyalty.

In 1987, Xerox made customer satisfaction its highest priority, in the belief that meeting or exceeding customer expectations was necessary before market share and profitability could be improved. To act on this belief management implemented a famously elaborate customer satisfaction program that featured highly visible top management involvement, a restructured organization with multifunctional teams at the local district level, formal complaint resolution procedures, rewards tied to achieving customer satisfaction targets, and ambitious objectives for improvement. All these elements were tied together with a comprehensive measuring and monitoring system.

In the course of tracking customer satisfaction, Xerox made a startling discovery. If satisfaction is rated on a 1-to-5 scale, from completely unsatisfied to completely satisfied, the 4s—though reporting they were satisfied—were six times more likely to defect than the 5s. This challenged the prevailing assumption that satisfaction and loyalty move in tandem.[13] At about the same time Frederick Reichheld of Bain Consulting was also finding that loyalty was an important driver of profitability, and could be greatly increased if managed properly. Armed with these insights into the behavior and underlying economics of the copier market, Xerox in 1996 changed its objectives:

From	*To*
1. Customer satisfaction	1. Customer retention
2. Market share	2. Employee satisfaction
3. Profitability	3. Market share
	4. Profitability

Many other market-driven firms have followed the Xerox lead to make customer retention and loyalty the centerpiece of their strategy and objectives.

Leveraging Market Investments

Market-driven firms achieve higher profitability by making better long-run investments. They understand the cause-and-effect connections between what they spend on marketing and revenue. These firms know that the process of developing a loyal customer takes time: from creating awareness through generating interest and trial to inducing loyalty. They focus on the long-run returns from their marketing investments relative to competitors, understanding which customers are profitable to pursue, and knowing how to encourage loyalty by reducing customer acquisition costs.

Many expense-oriented managers, by contrast, implicitly behave as though projected sales revenue determines the marketing budget. One result is the common practice of setting advertising budgets or sales force expenditures as a percentage of anticipated sales. Their thought process emphasizes cutting marketing expenditures, or comparing spending ratios with industry norms to decide what to spend. Because these managers don't understand where and how they make money in their markets, much of this spending is ineffective.[14]

With a mind-set that market development activities are investments, not just expenses, it is natural for market-driven firms to view their brand portfolios as assets to be leveraged.

Properly cared for, a brand is a symbol that can bestow credibility and attract attention in new markets. Companies with strong brand names have more loyal buyers, get greater leverage from their marketing investments and are rewarded with handsome price premiums. In recognition of the strength of brands that communicate a meaningful image, General Motors has hired marketing managers from packaged goods industries to enhance its car brands, while Intel and Microsoft are investing heavily to build their brand identity and visibility. Further evidence of the power of brands is the demise of Eagle Snacks in 1996 at the hands of PepsiCo.'s Frito-Lay brand. Although known for its quality snacks, Eagle never had the resources to establish enough of an identity with consumers.

To manage a brand as an asset, it is necessary first to have a deep understanding of why the brand provides benefits to customers; second, to know how to keep the brand strong in the face of attacks by competitors; and third, to be able to leverage the brand by extending it to new products while protecting it from dilution or damage through inappropriate usage. This requires the deep market insights, organizational commitment and reasoned investment decisions that come naturally to market-driven organizations.

IS BEING MARKET DRIVEN FOR EVERYONE?

Do these advantages of being market-driven apply to all firms or just to particular types of firms? Can't firms be successful without being market-driven? What about Shell? Dell? Honda? Intel? Boeing? Nucor? Merck? Each of these firms and other market leaders would point to different sources for their enduring advantages.

For Merck it would be superior science, Intel keeps obsoleting its own chips with superior design, Dell has mastered the mass customization of personal computers and Shell would cite its decentralized structure that enables its 100 operating companies to take on local colorations. Each would recognize the payoff from being market-driven but would not credit superior skills in understanding, attracting and retaining customers as a primary factor in its success.

Yet these companies are actually more market-driven than they might think. If we could objectively dissect these and other creators of superior shareholder value, we would find they outperform their rivals on some or most of the elements of a market orientation. Their cultures, capabilities, structures and strategic thought processes interact with and reinforce the other sources of advantage. These enhancing and enabling effects may be obscured from view because they are woven into the complex fabric of the organization.

A good example is Nucor, which has successfully beaten its slower-moving integrated rivals in the steel business. It might point first to its mastery of mini-mill manufacturing, its egalitarian culture and exceptional productivity as the key sources of its advantage.[15] But this company, through the leadership of Ken Iverson, who perfected an unconventional "trust your instincts" management style, is also much more market-driven than the competition. Nucor's culture puts a premium on information sharing and tapping into collective wisdom. This is essential to the functioning of a flat, highly decentralized structure that gives managers unusual autonomy—and keeps them close to their diverse markets. Relations with customers are open and straightforward—there are no special discounts from posted prices as is the practice with other companies.

Strategic choices are guided by intimate knowledge of its competitors. Nucor entered the flat-rolled steel market with a low-cost, thin-slab casting technology because managers had confidence in their ability to innovate, and they knew their competitors wouldn't be able to imitate their technology. In short Nucor manifests all the attributes of a market-driven organization—but these attributes are not grafted onto a resistant organization, they are an integral feature.

STAYING AHEAD IN TURBULENT MARKETS

A market-driven organization promises to become even more valuable in today's environment of rapid and unpredictable change. Organizations are buffeted by centrifugal, divisive forces—such as globalization, intensifying competition, technological change, channel proliferation and fragmentation of consumer requirements. These forces are overwhelming the centripetal, stabilizing forces such as economies of scale and scope and entrenched consumer habits. This makes it increasingly difficult to sustain the alignment of the capabilities and energies of the organization with the market, making the advantages of the market-driven organization more pronounced.

Five transitions in particular are having—or will have—especially disruptive effects on the ability of companies to stay aligned with their markets and keep delivering superior customer value. These changes also are magnifying the benefits of a market orientation:

• *More Supply and Less Differentiation:* From consumer electronics to aluminum cans, automobiles to textiles, the world is awash in production capacity. Weak demand, trade liberalization that encouraged companies to expand output to enter new markets, cheap financing and regulatory changes have all contributed to an increase in supply. As a result of deregulation, for example, many U.S. cities have six or more wireless telephone providers. This abundance of supply leads to price pressures as competitors try to sell more to better utilize capacity and lower unit costs. Eventually weaker players are bought up or shaken out.[16] At the same time, rapid imitation and diffusion of technology have eroded differentiation. Companies imitate one another quickly, as can be seen in the many look-alike designs in the athletic shoe market. In this environment, the market-driven organization has a greater advantage because it should understand its market better than rivals. It can stake out early positions in growth segments and generate new sources of customer advantage through superior capabilities in relating to the market, which are much more difficult for competitors to copy than product features.

• *More Global and Less Local:* The continuing progression from a world of distinct and self-contained local or national markets to linked global markets is being fueled by the persistent forces of the homogenization of customer needs, gradual liberalization of trade, and the recognition of the competitive advantages of a global presence. Network technologies are accelerating this shift by moving us from "marketplaces" to "marketspaces" in global arenas where needs are communicated, transactions occur and value is extracted. From books and CDs to mortgages, customers can shop across the globe or country, dramatically undercutting the advantage of local presence that is the mainstay of many retailers. As geography and real estate become less important in connecting with customers, the sophisticated strategies for market connection of the market-driven organization—which are not tied to geography—are increasingly essential. In addition, the complexity and differences among global markets mean companies will have to challenge the strategies and approaches that worked in their home markets. The only way to create effective approaches to is to develop deep insights and strong connections to these new markets.

• *More Competition and More Collaboration:* The intensity of competition will not abate in the future, but what will have to change is the mind-set that is used to think about competitors and the consequences of competitive behavior. Corporate leaders increasingly realize that the self-defeating tendencies of a purely competitive orientation need to be counterbalanced with the ability simultaneously to see prospects for collaboration. Relationships with customers are not a zero-sum battle to see who can walk away with the lion's share of value but should focus instead on increasing the value to divide. Sometimes companies would benefit from replacing rivalrous relationships with competitors—triggering destructive behavior such as price wars—with more collaborative relationships. There are many markets in which a firm can be a customer, supplier and rival at the same time. As the distinctions between these roles are increasingly blurred, it is often better for rivals to seek to collaborate. For example, Sony and Phillips are working together to develop common optical media standards and supplying components for one another.

• *More Relating and Less Transacting:* There has been a major shift in emphasis from capturing new customers to keeping and growing the valuable ones. This transition is being propelled by the growing recognition that keeping customers pays handsomely and creates enduring advantages. Some indicators of this transition are the large numbers of companies planning to organize around customers rather than products or geographies, and the adoption of customer retention and profitability as critically important measures of performance. Although the Worldwide Web would appear at first glance to weaken relationships, because it facilitates searches for alternatives, it also can enhance relationships. It increases stickiness by creating switching costs as customers streamline their search-and-purchase process by giving the company more information about themselves. To switch companies, the customer would have to go through this process again.

• *More Sense-and-Respond and Less Make-and-Sell:* Traditional make-to-forecast firms with the familiar hierarchical structure, economies of scale, and vertical command-and-control systems were suited to a simpler time when demand was predictable and large segments of the market could be expected to behave alike. As markets change more quickly and behave less predictably, fleet-footed "sense-and-respond" organizations that compete one customer at a time have an increasing advantage.[17] These market-driven companies win by establishing a dialogue with each customer and providing personalized responses to their unpredictable requirements. They have the ability to search out, capture and intercept clues about emerging customer requirements, and then build to order by deploying modular capabilities that can be combined and reused in many different ways. These firms also learn from each interaction with individual customers and communicate with personalized messages that take account of each customer's unique response. The relationship created through these interactions keeps getting smarter.

MARKET DRIVEN WINNERS

Who will prosper in the markets shaped by these turbulent changes? Some would say that newcomers have an advantage because they have no history to overcome or earnings to protect. There are many examples of upstarts like First Direct and the firms that opposed J&J in the stent market, who have used a superior market orientation to gain significant advantage over incumbents with far greater resources. Yet there also are established firms such as Schwab, Dell and Procter & Gamble that have been able to stay connected to their markets during a time of tremendous change.

It is not size or history that counts, but their ability to understand, attract and keep their valuable customers and a willingness to keep reorienting themselves as markets change. In other words, the winning firms—whatever other advantages they may have—will also be market-driven.

Becoming market-driven is not something that is done quickly or easily—the transformation may take years. It cannot be delegated to the marketing department for it requires the willing involvement of all functions. Many firms will take up the market-driven banner but will not succeed, either because of a shortage of knowledge or a lack of determination.

This book can help make up for that shortage of knowledge. We begin with a discussion of misperceptions about what it means to be market-driven and then examine the culture, capabilities and configuration of the market-driven organization and how companies have used them to advantage. We also offer insights into how to make the transition to a more market-driven organization.

While this book can provide knowledge, addressing the second challenge—a lack of determination—is up to you. There are many obstacles to overcome, which may be why so few companies are successful in building truly market-driven organizations. It is a far-reaching and fundamental change for many organizations, often requiring them to abandon the very traditions that contributed to their past success. But because creating a market-driven organization is challenging, it also means that the field will be less crowded for those that succeed.

There has never been a better time. The benefits of market orientation are clearer, the knowledge about how to achieve it is more refined, and information technologies keep opening up new ways to compete for customers. With determination, and the insights and strategies outlined in this book, you can increase the market orientation of your firm, creating opportunities for increased profits and enduring advantages for many years to come.

Chapter Two

Misconceptions About Market Orientation

In 1996, while he was the head of Asea Brown Boveri, Percy Barnevik participated in a panel of global business leaders at the World Economic Forum in Davos, Switzerland on the prerequisites for corporate leadership. His top items were:

- Create a customer focus and ensure this is present from top to bottom
- Make the organization regard continuous change as a way of life—not an exception
- Exercise leadership through deep understanding, coaching and empowerment, and a willingness to intervene when necessary.

As the audience nodded its agreement, a fellow panelist, Helmut Maucher, the CEO of Nestlé, responded that he couldn't agree with Barnevik. He asked "why is this a revolutionary idea in a market economy?" In his view, "A customer focus is simply a necessary condition." He went on to list a number of qualities he thought a global leader needed, including courage, good nerves and composure; the ability to continually learn, communicate effectively and create an innovation culture, and an understanding of other cultures.

In some industries, a market orientation is as natural as breathing. In others, it is a sharp departure from their history and instincts. ABB is a decentralized, engineering-driven maker of heavy industrial equipment, while Nestlé is a global food giant with a well-deserved reputation for close integration into each of its diverse domestic markets. For Nestlé to be market-driven is much more natural, whereas other priorities frequently prevail in the diverse ABB businesses.

WHY DON'T MORE FIRMS BECOME MARKET DRIVEN?

ABB and many other companies are discovering that a robust market orientation can enhance the effectiveness of any strategy, and serve as one of the few sustainable sources of advantage left in an environment of rapid technological change and aggressive competitive imitation.

But given its proven performance benefits, why do some companies choose not to adopt a market orientation? Often it is because of a set of misconceptions about what it means to be market-driven. These traps lead some companies to either dismiss a market orientation or stumble in trying to implement it. Three of the most common pitfalls are:

- *Being Oblivious to the Market:* Some *product-centered* firms become so internally focused that they can no longer see the market. They may have been market-driven at one time but don't realize until they encounter trouble that they have lost their focus.
- *Becoming Compelled by the Market:* In an overreaction to an internal focus, these companies bend over backwards to do whatever customers want. The *customer-compelled* companies fundamentally misunderstand the market-driven concept and fail to exercise discipline in their strategy. Instead of a clear focus, the energies of these organizations are diluted by the uncoordinated efforts of different parts of their organizations.
- *Feeling Superior to the Market:* If customer-compelled companies make the mistake of blindly following customers, companies that believe they should "ignore the customer" make the opposite mistake. Managers in these firms, particularly technology-driven firms, contend that customers never come up with the most valuable innovations. Did customers ask for the Walkman or the minivan? These skeptical executives fail to see that a market-driven focus can be used to support and inform research and product development without blindly following customers.

Each of these misconceptions is a form of organizational myopia that prevents the company from becoming market-driven or dooms its change efforts to failure. Recognizing these possible pitfalls can help managers avoid them and realize the full potential of the market-driven organization.

Oblivious to the Market: IBM in the 1980s

Successful firms are especially susceptible to the trap of being blind to the market. These firms achieved prosperity because at one time they had a clear and widely shared concept of how to deliver superior customer value. As successive generations of managers refined this positioning concept, it became easier for them to take their market setting for granted and put growing emphasis on squeezing out greater returns. The dire consequences of this inward focus may be obscured for years until the value proposition loses touch with changes in the market or the original meaning is distorted beyond recognition by the original target market.

Few firms fell into this trap harder than IBM. By the early 1980s the company that taught large corporations how to use computers to solve their business problems had earned exceptional access to the senior managers.[1] The rewards were handsome: IBM revenues almost tripled from $23 billion to $63 billion between 1979 and 1989; profits were growing apace and the company was the dominant player in its served markets. This performance obscured a loss of focus as Big Blue became progressively more distant, arrogant, and unresponsive toward its customers. Meanwhile, IBM placed greater emphasis on pushing hardware—often not the best and rarely priced competitively—rather than meeting the customers' needs. A revealing indicator of the change in thinking was the statement of goals IBM announced in 1983:

1. To grow with the industry.
2. To exhibit product leadership across our entire product line—to excel in technology, value and quality.
3. To be the most efficient in everything we do—to be the low-cost producer, the low-cost seller, the low-cost servicer, the low-cost administrator.
4. To sustain our profitability, which sustains our growth.

One could quarrel with the conservatism of the growth goal, but at that time IBM did equate itself with the industry. What is noticeably absent is any direct mention of customers or competitors. The obvious internal orientation was even then being exacerbated by an unwillingness to migrate customers away from mainframes for fear of cannibalization of their fat margins, which sometimes exceeded 80 percent.

Although customers were locked into IBM's protocols and operating systems—which further masked their discontent—they were becoming more difficult to persuade as newly aggressive competitors educated them about alternatives. Meanwhile, the move toward distributed processing was decentralizing the buying process. By 1990, the company had largely squandered its position of trust with customers and access to the highest levels in the organizations.

IBM salespeople, accustomed to selling to the corner office, found they were being referred first to the CFO, then to data processing executives and finally to the data center manager. This was also due to an erosion in the quality of the sales force. In the mid-1980s, management believed growth was slowing because their competitors had many more "faces in front of customers." Curiously, all competitors were treated alike for this analysis. To tackle this problem, and preserve their vaunted full-employment policy, large numbers of maintenance people and programmers were transferred into the sales force. The customer saw more IBM faces, but very few could add value because they lacked an intimate understanding of either the customers' business needs or IBM technology. Cost went up, while customer satisfaction went down.

Symptoms of Market Blindness

In retrospect the IBM of the 1980s exhibited many of the worst features of a self-centered organization. Of course, it would have denied the allegation by pointing to its exceptional financial results and apparently loyal base of customers. So, what clues are there to help managers spot when they are falling into this trap? The symptoms can fall into three areas:

• *Weak ability to capture market signals:* The organization is poor at capturing and sharing market signals. Customer relations and contracts are the job of the sales force while customer insights come from the market research group. Senior managers spend little time in the field, and so are shielded from complaints, changing requirements and emerging opportunities. Meanwhile, a strong sales force consolidates its power by cutting off market signals to the rest of the organization. It believes it "owns the customer," and should protect its clients by restricting access to them by other functions.

• *Product-focused organization:* Competitive advantage is achieved by controlling assets or achieving functional excellence. IBM had outstanding hardware and software developers, program managers and salespeople, and some of the most advanced factories and facilities. But these were disconnected islands of excellence, for the integrating logic needed to tie them together had been lost. As a result, IBM was increasingly unable to put together complex systems for global firms. There were no incentives for the European product groups to work on an opportunity in the Asia-Pacific region, and vice versa.

• *Short-run, cost concerns dominate:* An emphasis on controlling costs and managing short-run earnings dominates long-run concerns about erosion of market position or diminishing technological advantages. Of course a low-cost position—although not necessarily the lowest cost—is an essential ingredient of superior profitability. But this becomes dysfunctional in a self-centered organization when across-the-board cutting is done without recognition of the long-run consequences for the customer, or that other costs may rise to compensate for an ill-advised cut. Reducing customer service, for example, may shift the problems to the sales force, which then has little time to sell or prospect for new accounts.

As late as 1990, IBM was regarded by outsiders—and many insiders—as a first-class marketing organization. In reality its prowess was in sales, whose job was to get the customer to buy what was being made. The sales force understood individual customers and their business needs for the purpose of crafting persuasive sales presentations, but were not identifying emerging requirements that would help the other functions better understand the customer. Only slowly did it become apparent that they didn't think in terms of market segments—groups of customers with distinct needs—and didn't fully recognize IBM's declining position in important growth segments. Instead all their data were about products or sales by geographic territory which further obscured the market from view.

Compelled by the Market: P&G's Line Extension Madness

Becoming self-centered is not a malaise contracted only by big bureaucratic technology or regulated companies, although it seems to flourish in these settings. Even firms with the sensitivities and pedigree of Procter & Gamble (P&G) can fall into this trap and lose sight of the interests of the consumer and trade. P&G's problems started in the 1980s as sales flattened, retailers consolidated, the rate of meaningful innovation slowed, and competitors began to narrow the performance and quality lead that P&G had achieved.[2] Important categories such as disposable diapers suffered significant declines in share, from 50 percent in 1988 to 38 percent in 1994, because of private label competitors and the innovations of Kimberly-Clark.

It then overreacted and fell into the second trap, being compelled by the customer. The way for P&G to win, it was decided, was to give the consumer more choices, use heavy promotions to stimulate buying activity and load the channels, and then give the sales force large quotas so they kept up the pressure on the retailers. By clogging supermarket shelves, they also hoped to squeeze out their competitors. The results were costly and unproductive. A blizzard of line extensions and variants was launched, with only minor differences—Bounce fabric softener, for instance, had 35 variants.

This led to consumer confusion and clogged supply channels. P&G then pushed so many complex promotion and price changes that almost a quarter of all orders contained mistakes that had to be corrected at high cost. The aggressive sales reps, backed by the power of heavy advertising and couponing, antagonized the trade, and relations became adversarial. At the height of this absurdity, the progress of P&G products through the complex supply chain was so slow that ingredients had to be altered so products would stay usable longer—but doing so often degraded taste and other attributes.

Similarly, after IBM realized it was disconnected from the market, it overcompensated by moving to the other extreme. When John Akers became chairman of IBM in 1986, he was acutely aware the company was losing ground in key markets and relations with major accounts were deteriorating. As one step toward recovery he approved the following executive instruction in 1989 as part of a Market-Driven Quality Campaign:

If we can be the best at satisfying the needs and wants of customers in those markets we choose to serve, everything else important will follow.

Market-Driven Principles

- *Make the customer the final arbiter*
- *Understand our markets*
- *Commit to leadership in the markets we choose to serve*
- *Deliver excellence in execution across our enterprise*

The emphasis on choices among markets was both refreshing and demanding for a company that used to say, "we've never met a market we didn't like." Tellingly, no one ever said what it meant to make the customer the final arbiter—so everyone had their own interpretation.

Unhappily, when these ideals were put into practice, they created chaos instead of clarification, resulting in an organization that was customer-compelled. Each function felt empowered to get its own inputs and insights from customers and then tried to act separately on what it learned to find new segments, features or points of difference. Instead of the sales force filtering customer inputs, the development people talked to their contacts, marketing managers visited those they knew and manufacturing talked to their counterparts in different customer organizations. Because IBM sold to virtually every large and medium company in every industry, the result was a cacophony of voices. The decision-making units within each company were made up of different functions with different requirements; there were few common themes in their responses. The avalanche of conflicting information created varying degrees of confusion, analysis-paralysis, and unfocused product initiatives. Each initiative may have been valuable on its own, but the total offering often lacked coherence. Meanwhile, response times lengthened and organizational conflict mounted. IBM had lost its way so completely that between 1990 and 1993 it had losses of nearly $18 billion.

What was missing was the discipline needed to set priorities for which markets to serve with which benefits and features. Instead the floundering company tried to be all things to everyone—and singularly failed in most markets. Good intentions are not enough; they must be given meaning by changes in rewards, measures, and processes. Otherwise, hard choices can't be made.

Organizations that are customer-compelled mistakenly believe that every customer is worth pursuing, and they should be given whatever they want. Customers soon learn to exploit this, threatening to switch if the latest move by a competitive supplier isn't matched. Costs mount and prices come under increasing pressure.

Eventually, customer-compelled companies become disillusioned, and may reject the value of a market orientation. They may argue that "we tried to get close to our customers and it didn't work." One manufacturer of advanced medical devices felt that because it spent all its time catering to the needs of a diverse set of surgeons, it was late with the next generation of technology and wasn't well prepared to deal with the unfamiliar pressures of managed care. This firm had a history of technological leadership and was strongly tempted to use the bad experience to justify going back to using its own judgment about what to make and then letting the sales force figure out how to sell it. This is an especially seductive path for technology companies, but ultimately a flawed one.

SUPERIOR TO THE MARKET

A curious backlash is forming against giving the customer primacy in decisions. Instead, a growing set of influential voices counsel that sometimes it is better to ignore the customer. Hamel and Prahalad assert that customers are unable to envision breakthrough products and services.[3] The companies that slavishly follow their customers "may be able to protect their share of existing markets but won't be able to lead customers where they want to go, but don't know it yet." To justify their position Hamel and Prahalad resort to the correct but misleading observation that customers seldom ask for new products they eventually come to value.

This criticism fails to recognize the difference between asking customers to identify problems and expecting them to develop solutions. It is true that fifteen—or even ten—years ago most customers weren't clamoring for books and CDs over the Internet, 24-hour discount brokerage accounts, cars with on-board navigation systems, or the Home Shopping Network. Yet there were recurring problems to be solved, or deep-seated needs to be satisfied by these offerings—otherwise the innovations would not have succeeded.

Another reason given for ignoring the customer is that the constant effort to get in better touch through more focus groups and surveys leads to new offerings that are safe but bland.[4] Robert Lutz, the vice-chairman of Chrysler, is especially dismissive of heavy reliance on consumer inputs into the auto design process.

> Let's face it, the customer, in this business, and I suspect in many others, is usually, at best, just a rear-view mirror. He can tell you what he likes about the choices that are already out there. But when it comes to the future, why, I ask, should we expect the customer to be the expert in clairvoyance or creativity? After all, isn't that what he expects us to be?[5]

These thought leaders don't deny the need to listen to customers; they simply find listening deficient as a guide to action. On closer examination each is posing a false dichotomy:

- that you must either lead or follow customers
- that you can't stay close to both current and potential customers
- that technology push can't be balanced with a market pull

These dichotomies are misleading because they confuse inept implementation and poor interpretation with best practices. In fact, what the critics present as an alternative to being customer-led is what we mean by market-driven. Let us examine each of these false dichotomies in turn.

False Dichotomy #1: Following Customers versus Leading Customers

Peter Drucker once observed that "one can use market research only on what is already in the market." He supported his point by saying that American companies failed to put fax machines on the market, "because market research convinced them there was no demand for such a gadget." In other words, following the customer doesn't lead to important innovations.[6]

In reality Xerox knew by 1974 that the initial potential market for the fax machine was about one million units. The company based its estimates on the extent and frequency of urgent written messages, their time sensitivity, and the form and size of the message and contrasted the anticipated fax capability with existing alternatives. Unfortunately, Xerox chose the wrong technology path to meet this need. It developed a system of sending facsimile messages from one computer to another, with the receiving computer printing out a copy with a standard imaging technology. This turned out to be a much less attractive approach than having dedicated machines linked by telephone lines.

Customers never asked for the fax machine per se but insightful research by Xerox did identify the underlying problem that the fax machine was designed to solve. They saw that new forms of decentralized organizations would require numbers of copies far greater than was possible with carbon paper. The dichotomy between following and leading customers is not as simple as it initially appears.

Three primary reasons are given for not following customers. First, customers respond most positively to what is familiar and comfortable. Chrysler found this in testing designs for its 1996 minivans. Two-thirds of focus groups rated the then-current 1991 model a "nine" or "ten" out of ten, while only a third rated the proposed 1996 design as highly because it was seen as too extreme and aerodynamic for their tastes. Yet, given the advance of competitors like Toyota, Chrysler management knew their 1991 look would be dated in the showrooms of 1996. And they were right.

A second complaint is that research methods are incapable of sorting out customers' contradictory requirements, and are further flawed because customers in a survey don't mean what they say because they aren't choosing with their own money.

Third, customers view the imperfections and high cost of the early versions of a new technology or service from the standpoint of the more refined established products. Thus, pictures from electronic cameras lack the resolution of chemical emulsion film and personal digital assistants were shunned because of the limitations of the Apple Newton. Motorola got very discouraging initial customer feedback on cellular phones because the crude early models worked so poorly they were no improvement on existing ways of doing things.

These criticisms are often valid, but they miss the point. Management insight and conviction that a market exists for a new product or service must be grounded in intimate understanding of customer behavior, latent needs, changing requirements and deep-seated dissatisfactions with current alternatives. Such keen insight comes from having the key decision makers literally living with customers, observing them in their natural habitat, and seeking out lead users who have needs well in advance of the rest of the market.

To be market-driven means seeing past the shortsighted and superficial inputs of customers, to gain a deep-down understanding that gives managers confidence their judgments are right. Because leading customers to where they want to go is inherently risky, firms must be willing to continually learn and refine their judgments through broad scanning and experimentation. So if a company truly understands its present and prospective customers, it knows when to ignore the superficial reactions to a survey.

Market Driven vs. Market Driving? A variant of this false dichotomy is the argument that market-driven firms are only reactive, and simply respond adroitly to events and trends in their markets, rather than driving change by breaking the rules of the game and conceiving new ways to compete. In short, market-driven firms are not market-driving. This is a distinction without a difference.

Was Medco Containment Services being market-driven or market-driving when it provided prescription drugs through the mail rather than through retail drugstores? What about Dell Computers when it bypassed intermediaries to sell PCs directly to end buyers, or Swatch when it conceived an economical and fashionable timepiece? A firm cannot be legitimately market-driven without a strong guiding point of view of how it wants to shape the market to its advantage. Managers recognize early the potential for delivering new forms of value from technology development or the emergence of complementary products because they have deep insights into the latent needs of customers and can anticipate their responses. In short, a market-driven organization stays ahead because it is a change agent and not because it is content with protecting its position.

False Dichotomy #2: Current Customers versus Potential Markets

Another concern about becoming more market-driven is the fear that focusing inordinate attention on current markets might result in a failure to see emerging markets. Companies will become so fixed on meeting the needs of their current customers that they dismiss or overlook new technologies or approaches that seem applicable only to small or emerging markets they do not serve.[7] This makes them vulnerable to an unexpected attack by outsiders who use the emerging technology or business model as their entry platform.

Thus, the large copying centers that were the core of Xerox and Kodak's served market could not appreciate the value of small, slow table-top copiers. This opened the way for Canon. Machine tool manufacturers dismissed the early versions of linear induction motors because they were much less powerful than hydraulic systems. Sears ignored the threat from Wal-Mart's discounting strategy because it was first implemented in small and apparently uneconomic local markets that could not support conventional stores.

Why are firms reluctant to participate actively in potentially disruptive technologies or business models that initially attack low-priority markets on their flank? The mental models that guide managers give known customers disproportionate attention. These mental models are reinforced by past experience that tells them they have to keep ahead or close to direct competition with the technologies that sustain their position. Meanwhile, the "disruptive" technology often offers a different package of benefits that may not be as highly valued by existing customers. This is why the manufacturers of 5.25-inch hard disks, attuned to the demands of PC manufacturers for increasing memory capacity, underestimated the appeal of 3.5-inch disks that were smaller, lighter, and more rugged and enabled the market for laptops to emerge.

Often the potential for improvement of the "disruptive" technology is underestimated, until the mainstream market starts to migrate from the established technology. At this point, the reluctance to participate is easy to overcome, but the pioneers of the new technology are too entrenched and have too much of a lead to overcome.

One conclusion is that it is risky to stay too focused on the immediate needs of known and familiar customers when there is a disruption in technological capabilities or market behavior. This, again, is a failure to understand what it means to be market-driven.

Being market-driven does not mean focusing on current markets. Managers know that their current served market is only a portion of the total market, and will be watching for the emergence of unserved segments with different requirements and growth rates that might be attractive to serve. Being market-driven also requires a point of view on how the industry structure will evolve. This means tracking new entrants and understanding their capabilities, intentions and strategies. Seldom is a dominant firm attacked frontally; instead a stealth attack is mounted on unprotected flank markets or low-end segments that serve as a beachhead for moves into other segments.

Finally, for industrial companies operating at one stage of a complex, multistage value chain, it is important to see past the immediate customer to understand the end user. Thus a supplier of fine paper to a business form manufacturer needs to know how the digital transmission of orders, invoices and payments will supplant paper forms. A market orientation facilitates this broader view.

False Dichotomy #3: Technology-Push versus Market-Pull

Should the market drive technology or technology drive the market? Drug manufacturer Amgen makes a persuasive case for the technology-driven view. Its emphasis on lab research rather than market research has earned it a 68 percent average annual return over the past decade. Like all drug companies, its success depends on a few blockbuster drugs. The company has a pair of billion-dollar drugs—one helps dialysis patients and the other is an immune system booster that helps people fight infections. The economics are compelling. The question is how should development projects be chosen?

In the pharmaceutical industry, the prevalent market-driven approach is to identify diseases with many sufferers and assign a team of scientists to work on it. However, Amgen believes the opposite strategy is superior—start with brilliant science and find unique uses for it. Its scanning is focused on developments in science, relying on about two hundred collaborative efforts with colleges and universities to identify new research.

The greatest resistance to a market-driven, outside-in orientation is found in technology-driven, inside-out firms such as Amgen. Their development starts with the pacing technologies they have mastered and takes into account the prospects for improvement in cost and performance to decide the product requirements that can be met. The job of the sales force is to sell the product to the target market, and marketing's job is to help the sales force. Customer benefits are dictated by the technology, with secondary input from customers as the development process proceeds. Testing with end users is highly valued, but the emphasis is on technical feasibility and acceptance. This is very different from a market-driven development process that combines an understanding of the mar-

ket situation and technological possibilities with deep insights into customer problems and requirements, and then seeks new opportunities to
deliver superior customer value.

While it is hard to question the validity of this strategy, the real issue
is whether this technology-based strategy precludes a market orientation.
Could Amgen have been even more successful if it integrated its technology strategy into a market-driven organization? Why does a company
have to choose one over another?

On the evidence, high-technology firms win more frequently by
adopting a balanced approach that rejects the market-driven versus
technology-driven dichotomy. One study of six high-technology firms,
including Hewlett-Packard, Motorola, and General Electric, found that
successful projects exploited the organization's core competencies, were
closely aligned with the competitive strategy, and were continually
immersed in timely, reliable information about customer and user preferences or requirements.[8] By contrast, when the development team didn't
collect and use extensive market information the project rarely succeeded. Technology leadership was a necessary condition for success but
had to be married with a market orientation if the opportunity was to be
fully realized.

So why do most high-technology companies behave differently than
these leading firms? An in-depth, long-term study of a large computer systems firm identified several impediments to a market orientation:[9]

• The first impediment was an *engineering-driven culture* that encouraged beliefs that "customers don't know what they want," and that
marketing inputs just reflect what the competition is doing. Marketing
was also widely believed to lack technical expertise, and to be out of
touch with the leading edge of the technology. It was faulted for not being
able to identify the design assumptions in competitors' products, for
example.

• A second impediment was the *organization structure*, in which most
traditional marketing tasks such as product management and strategy
development were largely done within engineering groups, which also
had responsibility for profitability. This broad accountability was beneficial to the extent it motivated the engineers to get out and visit
customers, but was just as much of an impediment to developing an ef-

fective launch strategy or positioning the products to meet competitors' responses.

• Finally, the unremitting *time-to-market pressures*, driven by rapidly changing price-performance improvements in computer components, placed enormous demands on design teams to make decisions quickly to meet demanding delivery schedules. One result was for the engineers to bypass marketing entirely to make contact with customers in whatever time they had available. These engineers naturally tended to seek out technically oriented customers because they shared values and backgrounds and were easy to communicate with. Meanwhile an increasing share of sales was coming from commercial rather than familiar technical customers, so there was a gnawing fear that unless practices changed the product development process would be out of touch with this part of the market.

High-technology companies are beginning to appreciate that being market-driven complements rather than competes with a technology orientation, and entails much more than just listening to current customers. It is less obvious how they can overcome the ingrained culture and structural constraints to achieve a better balance.

These three dichotomies that lead companies to ignore markets are false. Market-driven organizations can follow customers in identifying potential problems and lead them in presenting solutions. They can serve current customers and remain vigilant for unserved emerging markets. They can join the finest laboratory research with the finest market research. The only true choice is whether to be market-driven or not.

AVOIDING THE PITFALLS

If your organization has spurned a market orientation in the past for any of the reasons described here, this may be the time to rethink your position. Are you falling into one of these traps? Could a true market orientation benefit your organization?

If your organization already has made a strong commitment to a market orientation, understanding these pitfalls can help you be more successful. You can avoid being lulled by your success into being blind to market. You can also avoid being so anxious to be responsive as to become customer-compelled. Between these two extremes lies the path to a successful market-driven organization.

For companies seeking to develop or improve their market orientation, the path is more clearly defined than ever. Pioneering companies have created the distinctive culture, capabilities, structure and strategies that contribute to the success of market-driven organizations. Researchers have explored the impact on performance. These insights from the best practice and research, pointing the way for other firms, are the focus of the rest of this book.

Chapter Three

Market Driven Cultures

There are no market-driven organizations with shallow or forgettable cultures. Market-driven organizations are held together by a pervasive, externally oriented culture designed to provide superior quality and value on the customers' own terms and create advantage over rivals. For Federal Express that means the package is "absolutely, positively" delivered when it was promised. At Home Depot—the paragon of low prices and low frills, but legendary service and help with home repairs—a strong value ethic dominates the culture. This means giving customers more than they expect at lower prices than they can find elsewhere. Employees are continually encouraged to spend as much time as necessary to educate their customers, who keep coming back for more. This is culture in action.

A strong culture represents an organization's shared beliefs, mindsets, and understanding—and defines what is appropriate and inappropriate behavior. It is often summed up simply as "the way we do things around here." Because cultures are pervasive and intangible they have also been defined as "things people take for granted." Those that inhabit a strong culture benefit from its liberating value, but it usually takes a newcomer or an outsider to fully appreciate its worth.

A culture has many levels and facets.[1] At the deepest level are *values* that express enduring preferences or aspirations for specific outcomes or modes of conduct. These may be so deeply embedded that they exist only as tacit assumptions that are difficult to talk about and even harder to change. The more accessible parts of a culture are *norms*, which are shared beliefs about appropriate or expected behavior, and the *mental models* people use to simplify and make sense out of a confusing, fluctuating reality. Thus, a culture plays a big role in how information is sought and turned into usable knowledge. The most obvious outcroppings of a culture are the *behaviors* that top managers and employees exhibit as they make choices about how to spend their time. If top management prefers to spend time with security analysts rather than make visits with distributors and customers, they have sent a strong signal that reinforces the culture.

No Two Cultures Are the Same

Every culture is unique—shaped by the character of the industry, past strategic choices, important events in the heritage, and the remembered personality and beliefs of the leader or founder. Strong cultures are often embodied in the stories told about the leader that are used to teach newcomers and provide guidelines. Hewlett-Packard, Marriott, and IBM are still influenced by David Packard, Bill Marriott, and Tom Watson. Wal-Mart is still an expression of the persona of Sam Walton. Store associates are empowered to be advocates of the customers' interests because Sam Walton insisted frequently and forcefully that he wanted them to be "agents for the customer."

A culture expresses what is different about an organization; what gives it a distinctive atmosphere, feel, or climate. The Disney culture, where employees are "cast members" who are "onstage" while working, speaks volumes about the organization's approach to service. Those immersed in this culture would feel like aliens in the Intel culture, which prizes "constructive confrontation" at all levels. This is not a feel-good environment, and even Andy Grove concedes there is "ferocious arguing with one another while remaining friends."[2] Strong cultures are also captured in mission statements. Nike's mission is to "serve the athlete." There is no ambiguity here. There is a clear signal that they are not a shoe or apparel company but a sports company that is committed to making the sports experience better.

MARKET DRIVEN CULTURES

Given the distinctive flavor of every organization's culture, what distinguishes a market-driven culture? As summarized in Table 3–1, the market-driven organization has beliefs, values and norms that are quite different from its more self-centered peers. Here are some of the characteristics that set the culture of a market-driven organization apart.

All Decisions Start with the Customer

Within market-driven organizations every decision begins with the customer and anticipated opportunities for advantage. The entire organiza-

TABLE 3–1

Illustrative Differences in Values and Norms

Market-Driven Organization	Self-Centered Organization
• All decisions start with the customer and opportunities for advantage	• We'll sell to whoever will buy
• Quality is defined by customers	• Quality is conformance to internal standards
• The best ideas come from living with customers	• Customers don't know what they want
• Employees are customer advocates	• Customer relations are problems for the marketing department
• Customer knowledge is a valuable asset and channels are value adding partners	• Customer data are a control mechanism and channels are conduits
• Customer loyalty is key to profitability	• New accounts (conquests) are what matters
• No sacred cows—cannibalize yourself	• Protect the existing revenue stream
• Learn from mistakes	• Avoid mistakes
• Market research is decision insurance	• Market research is a justification tool
• Paranoia about competitors is healthy	• We can live with our competitors
• The behavior of competitors can be anticipated and influenced	• Competitors are unpredictable
• We know more than the competition	• If competition does it, it must be good

tion follows through to insist on providing superior quality and service on the customer's own terms. At all levels in the organization, employees ask "How will this decision enhance our value proposition? How will competitors react? How will customers and consumers react?"

These organizations are also highly tuned to changes in customer requirements and priorities or signs of value migrating to different parts of the value chain, and keep modifying their value propositions with these changes in mind. These cumulative insights may have profound impacts on the thrust of the strategy. Charles Schwab succeeded in discount brokerage by breaking away from the traditional product-centered, "customer as sales target" approach prevailing in financial services. He saw that investors had varying needs for advice and disliked pressure selling and bundled service when all they wanted was low cost trades.

Given their attachment to the market over the company's own products and services, market-driven companies have a willingness to cannibalize a current product to meet or shape the emerging demands of the market. They will obsolete a successful product with the next generation or even a new technology. Can the strong temptation to protect the short-term profitability be resisted by the longer-term recognition that the competition will seize on any delay to wrest away market leadership?

In contrast, the self-centered firm is focused on selling a product or service to the market. Success is defined by sales performance compared to last year, or perhaps share of a carefully delineated and unchanging market. Quality is defined by degree of conformance to internal standards rather than calibrating the product against the "best of breed" rivals, or the ability to satisfy customer requirements. These firms are so dominated by the historical success of their traditional way of doing business that they are slow to respond to changes in customer requirements. The problem for these firms, as one manager put it, is "we don't see things as they are, we see things as we are."

Listening to Learn Versus Listening to Sell

There is a belief in market-driven firms that real understanding comes from living with customers—both the easy-to-please and the most demanding.[3] This doesn't mean scheduling a few perfunctory visits to tame customers, making obligatory appearances at trade shows or sitting through one or two focus groups—although not much harm will be done by these practices unless the results are wholly unrepresentative.

Instead, living with customers should be a continuing and painstaking effort to share the details of customers' experiences and problems in the buying and using context. Ideally, these customers should be the most demanding and sophisticated, because they stretch the organization's capabilities. This effort should not be captured or filtered by front-line customer contact people; everyone in a market-driven organization should be able to relate to customer experiences and learn from them. Thus, Procter & Gamble requires its top officers to spend one day a month with a consumer or retailer—no exceptions permitted.

Within self-centered organizations the main listening posts are the customer relations department and the sales force. Customer relations in this setting is usually a euphemism for customer complaint handling. Their job is to placate aggrieved customers at the least cost. Because they are always reacting to problems, important insights are usually lost. Meanwhile the sales force tends to be protective of the customer relationship, and carefully controls who has access. Unfortunately, many salespeople are poor listeners and behave as though a customer complaint or mention of a change in their situation is an interruption to a well-rehearsed sales message. We hasten to add there are many good salespeople that have empathy for their customers, but these are more likely to be found in market-driven organizations because they know this is valued.

Customer Knowledge Is Treated as a Valuable Asset

A market-driven organization is distinguished by the way it creates, shares and uses knowledge about present and prospective markets—including consumers and channel members. What is Nike without the extraordinary fashion sense and ability to create designs that appeal to the fickle athletic footwear market? Cargil goes to great lengths to nurture and protect its commodity buying expertise. Swatch bucks the trend to outsourcing by keeping its low-cost manufacturing skills in high-cost Switzerland because they are integral to its competitive position. The ability of these firms to leverage their knowledge is strongly influenced by the mind-set of their culture. There are three kinds of connections at work.

First, culture shapes assumptions about what knowledge is important and useful and how it is to be interpreted. In some organizations, information about prospects and new account acquisition is more valued than information about loyalty or the pattern of lost accounts. Often these organizations don't even seek such information because it is not deemed worth the effort, and thus its potential value cannot be appreciated—in effect, there is no knowledge.

Second, cultural norms influence who is expected to have knowledge and whether they are obliged to share it. Some cultures are very open with information, while others condone hoarding it to enhance power. Status hierarchies that create a silo mentality are one of the greatest obstacles to collaborative knowledge use. This was one of the dysfunctional features of the IBM climate of the 1980s.

Third, the culture also shapes how knowledge is used, through the pattern of rewards and punishments. Does it support or discourage people from seeking out expertise and knowledge across boundaries? This is a particularly pointed question for global organizations that set up information systems designed to tap into the collective wisdom of different people in different places in the organization on how to deal with a particular fault or problem or share knowledge about competitors or opportunities.

The combined effect of culture on knowledge development is seen most painfully in databases built to capture enterprise-wide customer knowledge. Many multimillion-dollar databases start to lose value almost from the day of installation unless everyone updates customer files religiously as information about changes is obtained via phone calls, reservations, visits, or feedback. If the culture denies the value of this information or believes it should be the responsibility of specialists there will be neither the energy nor the discipline to keep the database fresh and useful.

Research Is Decision Insurance

Market-driven firms view market research as decision insurance: a premium that is paid to widen and deepen the understanding of customer, competitor, and channel factors; anticipate changes in market requirements; and eliminate poor decision alternatives. To get the most value from this market research, these firms involve the researchers early in the decision process, so they are aware of the alternatives being considered. Why are researchers being asked to assess the potential of a market? The approach will depend on whether management is thinking of acquiring a competitor in the market, or the lab is exploring a new technology that might be applicable to the needs of that market.

Within self-centered organizations, we find market research studies are more likely to be used to satisfy curiosity—"we really should find out how the market is segmented"—or to increase the salability of a decision. This "security blanket" research is conducted after the decision has been made. Such studies are designed to buttress political positions and gain support rather than assess whether the idea was worthy of investment in the first place. This has the corrosive side effect of biasing the choice of research design and shading the question wording to favor the chosen alternative. The scope of the inquiry is likely to be constrained, since there is no incentive to seek disconfirming evidence or troubling but inconsistent trends. When market research has been widely misused in this way no market study will have much credibility and little learning will happen.

Time pressures are often used as an excuse to avoid going to the market for insights and reactions. As one disgruntled manager in a packaged good firm put it, "Concept tests are viewed as obstacles by our product managers. They are rewarded for keeping their products moving ahead." This is just one more aspect of the "ninety-day syndrome," which pushes inquiry toward issues of momentary tactical significance and crowds out attentiveness to subtle and gradual signals about future trends.

Paranoia (About Competitors) Is Healthy

Market-driven firms watch competitors closely, calibrate performance against the best of breed and celebrate wins against competitors. Rubbermaid makes a fetish of listening to competitors for new product ideas, but to avoid disclosing its plans it never uses test markets. Instead, it relies on user panels, awareness studies, and diaries that consumers fill out with notations on their problem and usage behavior.

Just because these firms are paranoid about their competitors—present and prospective—doesn't mean they are immobilized. Instead they channel their nervous energy into studying these rivals so they can try to anticipate and influence their actions. They send signals to discourage their competitors from attacking core markets, or use capacity announcements to dissuade others from adding capacity, or discipline an errant competitor who has ignored a signal to raise prices (all legally, of course).

Self-centered firms are more inclined to accommodate their rivals than try to manage them. There is an implicit mind-set that believes if a competitor makes a move it must have been for a good reason, and it should be worth emulating. Now imitation is often necessary to neutralize a competitor's advantage, but this should be based on a clear-headed understanding of the intentions behind the move and its likelihood of succeeding.

Learning from Mistakes

An organization focused primarily on itself will view mistakes as problems to be avoided at all cost. In contrast, a market-driven organization believes that more can be learned from the careful examination of failures than from successes. A failure in a market-driven organization is seen as an opportunity to uncover and eliminate the mistakes, and if done quickly there may be time to recover without suffering too much damage. An important part of the 3M culture is the tolerance of "well intentioned failure." Managers are willing to go out and interview defectors who were once good customers to find out why they switched to a competitor and what could be done to salvage the relationship. The lessons are widely distributed throughout the organization. By contrast, in less supportive cultures, risk takers that lose are the first to be punished.

Top Managers Are Role Models

The tone of the organization is set at the top. The signals that top managers send in meetings, how they spend their time and the questions they ask in strategy review sessions are much stronger cues about the real culture than their slogans and exhortations. To get meaningful culture change there has to be a visible change in the behavior and priorities at the top.

Consider how IBM extricated itself from the various traps described in Chapter 2. By 1993, the bloated and struggling computer maker had suffered through wrenching restructurings to rein in costs and was about to be divided into a number of autonomous operating divisions. The idea was to mirror the newly disaggregated industry that was breaking into horizontal pieces. However, this plan made no sense to Lou Gerstner when he arrived from Nabisco in 1993 to become chairman.

While Gerstner knew relatively little about the diversity and complexity of IBM businesses, he did have one advantage. As he says, "I came with the mind-set of a customer." From this viewpoint the disintegrated computing industry was deeply confusing. Companies had no idea how to tie different computing platforms and applications into a network. In short, they were looking for solutions—and only IBM had the resources to provide them. But could IBM overcome the persistent conflict between providing the right solution versus promoting individual products? Gerstner confronted the cultural impediments by invoking new priorities: the customer comes first, IBM comes second, and the business unit comes third. Specifically, customers were entitled to best of breed solutions, and if an IBM unit couldn't offer it, then it was okay to go outside the company. These new priorities were pushed deep into the company to ensure the culture was congruent with the strategy.

UNDERSTANDING THE CULTURE

A clear-headed diagnosis of the functional and dysfunctional elements of the prevailing culture is a necessary prelude to efforts to change or sustain a culture. This section reviews ways of getting insights into the culture as an input to the overall change program in Chapter 12.

A good place to start is with the questions posed in "Overall Orientation," the first section of the assessment form in the Appendix. Each question is designed so the right-hand side represents superior if not "best" practice, while the left-hand side is deficient practice. Few firms will be purely one side or the other of this scale; most will be somewhere in the middle so the problems are not overwhelming but there is abundant room for improvement. Of course, the presumption here is that there is a distinctive culture, with broadly shared beliefs, and norms and mind-sets. It is always advisable to test this assumption by having this assessment form filled out by a variety of people from different levels and functions. Wide variance in judgments is troublesome for it indicates a weak culture with lack of cohesion and plenty of potential for conflict and misunderstanding.

Deeper insights into the culture come from surfacing the mental models, contrasting the prevailing culture with other cultures, seeing the customer from the employees' perspective and testing for sustainability.

Surfacing Mental Models

Mental models are the part of the culture that comes closest to the surface.[4] These are simplifying frameworks that include the vocabulary used to talk about customers and the prevailing assumptions about how markets work. Without mental models to impose order, the sheer volume of ambiguous and fragmentary information about market trends and conditions would overwhelm the limited capacity of managers to extract meaning and make decisions.

Mental models don't announce their existence. Instead, you have to go looking for their outcroppings. This takes ingenuity. Not long ago, a major life insurance company used content analysis to examine a sample of reports, memos and e-mails to see what words were used to describe their customers. It discovered that the one word that was scarcely used was "customer." Instead, each product division had developed its own vocabulary, which spoke volumes about the prevailing mind-set:

Pension	Group Insurance	Personal Insurance
• active lives	• claimants	• insureds
• deferred lives	• eligibles	• policyholders
• certificate holders	• dependents	• orphans
	• lives	• annuitants
		• participants
		• contract holders

This kind of dispassionate terminology got in the way of employees thinking of customers as people with needs, problems and lifestyles. Instead, customers were reduced to paper contracts, digitized records and obliga-

MENTAL MODELS ARE NOT ALWAYS WHAT THEY SEEM

The vice president of development couldn't fathom why she was having so much difficulty getting senior management to accept aggressive proposals for developing and launching new beverage products. She viewed them as vital to the long-run health of the company, and was concerned that their biggest rival was preempting them in emerging segments and investing more heavily in technologies for formulating new product types.

To clarify the picture she worked with her staff to identify the prevailing beliefs and assumptions that seemed to be influencing the behavior of the organization. A list of 37 items was grouped into categories. Some illustrative elements were:

1. Market Behavior and Market Research
   - the market is tired of new products
   - the acceptable taste spectrum is in a narrow band
   - research is more a justification tool than a learning tool
2. Competition
   - if competition does it, it must be good
   - first in the market with a meaningful proposition wins
   - all competitors will match each other's moves
3. Strategic Priorities
   - we prefer acquisition to retention strategies
   - cannibalization is bad
   - we have too many SKUs
   - we cannot effectively micro-market
   - our emphasis is on safe products with minimal impact on operations
4. Organization
   - "Quick ROI or walk away." Once the product is launched it is too late to fix mistakes
   - lack of success is deemed a failure—not a learning experience
   - leadership is expected to come from the top

Since these were just hypotheses based on what her group had observed or experience she decided to test them individually with the senior management team. Initially they rejected the picture of a defensive, play-it-safe company, but then reluctantly agreed that there was a lot of validity to the hypotheses. Finally, the president agreed to address the issue directly with the executive committee and consider how to overcome the disconnect between the avowed growth strategy and the constrained vision that seemed to pervade.

tions—not opportunities. The company also faced huge problems in developing coordinated strategies for its customers. Because each division was looking at contracts and not people, they had no way of knowing when they had a pension contract and group and personal life policies with the same person. Valuable opportunities to cross-sell were being missed.

Our mental models help us to process information and make decisions quickly. However, rigid and constraining mental models can hinder strategic thinking because we pay attention to what supports our existing beliefs and ways of operating. Compare the enabling power of a more expansive definition of strategic reach with a more myopic concept. Are we in the business of selling seeds versus caring for lawns? Selling toothpaste versus oral care? Or selling gaskets versus helping customers find solutions to sealing problems? The choice of mental model has a great deal of influence on the organization's self-concept.

These mental models are often like water to a fish. They are difficult for the members of the organization to see. For example, as described in the box, a beverage maker had no idea that its stated commitment to innovation actually masked a more conservative mental model. Mental models are such a part of the thinking process that they are almost invisible, so there may be a disconnect between how an organization thinks it is acting and its real, underlying culture.

Contrasting Different Types of Cultures

In addition to identifying underlying mental models, the company can also examine the type of culture it has and the culture it needs. One useful model, illustrated in Figure 3–1, distinguishes culture along two dimensions: whether the organization is more internally or externally focused, and whether responses to change are flexible and spontaneous or tightly controlled and orderly. There are trade-offs in different types of organizational cultures, and each has different mechanisms for processing and acting on information about the changing market environment.[5]

An *adhocracy* is most congruent with a market orientation because it values flexibility and adaptability while maintaining a primary focus on the external environment. Companies like General Electric, British Air-

FIGURE 3–1

*Cultural Types**

ORGANIC PROCESSES
(flexibility, spontaneity)

CLAN	ADHOCRACY
Dominant Values: Cohesiveness, participation, teamwork, consideration, fairness, openness	**Dominant Values:** Entrepreneurship, creativity, adaptability, autonomy, experimentation
Leader Style: Mentor, facilitator, parent figure	**Leader Style:** Entrepreneur, innovator, risk-taker
Information Processing Style: Discussion, participative consensus	**Information Processing Style:** Insight, invention, flexibility
Strategic Emphasis: Developing human resources, commitment, morale	**Strategic Emphasis:** Innovation, growth, new resources
HIERARCHY	MARKET
Dominant Values: Cautiousness, logic, obedience, economy	**Dominant Values:** Competitiveness, goal achievement, initiate, diligence
Leader Style: Coordinator, administrator	**Leader Style:** Decisive, achievement-oriented
Information Processing Style: Measurement, documentation, computation	**Information Processing Style:** Goal clarification, individual judgment, decisiveness
Strategic Emphasis: Stability, predictability, smooth operations	**Strategic Emphasis:** Competitive advantage, market superiority

INTERNAL MAINTENANCE (smoothing activities, integration)

EXTERNAL POSITIONING (competition, differentiation)

MECHANISTIC PROCESSES
(control, order, stability)

*Adapted from Deshpandé, Farley and Webster (1993) and McDonald and Gandz (1994).

ways, and Citibank seem to fit this profile. A *market* type of culture emphasizes competitiveness and goal achievement as well as productivity and market mechanisms. The aggressive style of PepsiCo. in both the beverage and Frito-Lay Snack Division fits this culture type. These two cultures contrast with *clans*, where cohesiveness, participation and teamwork matter more than financial and market share objectives, and *hierarchies* which stress order and value control over flexibility. Unfortunately, AT&T and General Motors have historically been hierarchical and internally oriented and are finding change difficult. Although progress is being made they find it difficult to even stay up with fleet-footed rivals like Sprint and MCI or Chrysler and BMW.

The contribution of culture to financial and market performance was rigorously studied in five countries.[6] Additional questions were used to assess the *climate*—the way the culture determines which behaviors are rewarded, encouraged and expected—plus the extent of *market orientation* as measured by specific beliefs and behaviors—and *innovativeness* in the sense of continuous problem solving on behalf of customers. Innovativeness included whether the firm was usually first to market, and at the cutting edge of technology. An important feature of the research design was the use of both managers and customers to make the judgments. This helped to overcome the well-known biases of self-assessments.

In explaining performance differences, innovativeness mattered most, followed closely by culture and climate. This held whether the managers were in Japan, the United States, France, Germany, or England. As expected, a market culture exhibited the highest performance, while the clans performed worst. The influence of specific market-oriented behaviors and beliefs was modest because their effect was captured by the culture measures. These results demonstrate that culture does matter, and that Drucker got it right when he wrote more than forty years ago, "There is only one valid definition of business purpose: to create a customer. . . . It is the customer who defines what the business is. . . . Because it is its purpose to create a customer, any business enterprise has two—and only these two—basic functions: marketing and innovation."[7]

Seeing the Customer from the Employee's Perspective

Market-driven firms are not oriented only to the external customer, they give equal emphasis to the employees who define and deliver the customer value. They follow the dictum of Sam Walton who exhorted his employees to be "advocates for the consumer." Wal-Mart has found that most of their best ideas for improvements come from the ongoing dialogue of customer and employees. This requires employees who are enthusiastic about what the company is doing and are given incentives to behave in the best interests of customers.

There is direct evidence from service firms such as fast-food chains that employee satisfaction is closely correlated with customer satisfaction. A disgruntled employee with a bad attitude toward service will trigger negative reactions from the customer, but trying to placate unhappy customers can also be very dispiriting for employees. When this vicious circle is replaced by a virtuous circle where enthusiastic employees exceed the expectations of customers, the customers will reciprocate with appreciation and loyalty.

A powerful enhancer of supportive customer and employee relations is continuity and stability on the employee side. Rapid turnover of the kind found in large firms that have restructured and downsized corrodes mutual understanding and commitment and hurts customer relationships. By contrast the managers and technical contact people in the midsized German firms called the *Mittlestand* know they probably will be working with the same customers for many years, and so are highly knowledgeable and committed to them.

Managers disclose their beliefs about the importance of employees in many ways: performance feedback, compensation and training. Surprisingly, what employees seem to watch most closely is the care and resources the company devotes to recruiting and hiring. When researchers asked employees at three financial services firms about the climate or culture of their organizations and the role of service in it, they found that no variable was as highly correlated with passion for service as employee views of who gets hired and how hiring gets done.[8]

Can the Culture Be Sustained?

A market-driven culture takes an agonizingly long time to build—but can be dismantled in a matter of months. A deeply embedded hierarchical culture may take five or more years of sustained effort to transform, judging by the experiences of the regional Bell operating companies. Not only is change very stressful, because it foments resistance at the threatened middle levels, but the rivals keep progressing. A lot of energy is being expended, but the gap never seems to close, which can be dispiriting.

Once an appropriate culture is in place, it must be constantly nurtured and adapted to keep it from being lost. The big threats are complacency and conflicting priorities. Delta Airlines once had a reputation for stellar service and committed employees. Granted it was an expensive, ingrown, and paternalistic culture, but it delivered a high level of customer service that engendered strong passenger loyalty.[9] Complaints were much lower than average for airlines, and passengers would willingly wait to take Delta flights, so load factors were higher. This was not enough to overcome the dismal conditions in the industry in the early 1990s, so the airline accumulated over a billion dollars in losses between 1991 and 1994. With the growth of low-cost carriers like Southwest Airlines, Delta foresaw continuing losses unless costs were cut by 16 percent. This would mean the elimination of 15,000 jobs. The cost cutting program did return the airline to profitability, but it also erased its service edge. Fewer baggage handlers meant more lost luggage. Customers complained about loss of amenities, and employee morale fell much further than costs. One survey in 1996 found that only 22 percent of employees rated leadership as "effective." The enthusiasm that had once prompted the employees to buy the company a new Boeing 767 was gone. Although Delta was able to achieve the lowest operating costs of any big carrier with a hub and spoke route network, their aggressive cost goal had to be abandoned in 1997 and the long-time CEO was forced to step down.

As Delta also found, it takes years to rebuild a damaged culture. A renewal was launched by a new CEO from outside the industry who combined immediate fixes of the worst problems with patient efforts to regain trust with employee groups. Just to deal with the scheduling problems that were the source of many flight delays meant attacking seventy different issues. Other changes reached deeply into the configuration to replace antiquated systems. Because they had such unreliable information on loads, Delta led the industry in bumping passengers off full flights. As each step succeeds, management will gain further credibility and the distrust that pervades the culture slowly will give way to healthier attitudes.

Delta is one of many companies that embraced cost cutting, restructuring and reengineering in the early 1990s, and achieved impressive short-run savings but eroded the beliefs and values that sustained their long-run performance. The long-run cost in customer dissatisfaction and diminished competitiveness will be paid for years.

SUMMARY: THE DEFINING ROLE OF CULTURE

Some organizations are market-driven, but many more aspire to be. The aspirants believe it is "a good thing" but are hesitant to proceed or have been disenchanted because of failings with past efforts. Most often their frustration is due to unrealistic expectations. They thought that marginal changes, a few management workshops and proclamations of good intentions would suffice when they should have been mounting a wide-ranging and fundamental change in their culture. The degree to which market-driven behavior is embedded in the culture—those shared values, norms and beliefs that give members of the organization meaning and provide them with rules for behaving—is increasingly being recognized. No meaningful effort to undertake cultural change can proceed without a broad agreement on the orientation and defining beliefs of the current culture.

Chapter Four

Configuring Around Capabilities

The Corning, Inc. division that manufactures fiber optic products faced a dual challenge: It needed to balance demands for increased product customization and faster delivery while reducing costs to stay ahead of aggressive competitors. Its original objective was to be the most efficient mass producer of standard fiber optics. But as the fiber optic market evolved, customers began demanding more specialized products, making efficiency more difficult to achieve. Corning had to convert its manufacturing process from a rigid, standard-production system to a flexible manufacturing platform capable of building customized fiber optic products to order. This transition required the ability to produce the custom products on a timely basis at a competitive price and a capability for understanding its customers' evolving requirements and energizing the organization to respond to them.

Corning had to develop new capabilities in customized manufacturing and exercise them through a new set of organizational processes. No matter how market-driven its culture, Corning would not have been able to meet the shifting market demands without the right capabilities and processes.

Market-driven organizations recognize the power of organizational processes and how superior processes deliver value to the customer. In contrast, more self-centered firms focus on the hierarchical structure of the organization, which often obscures the underlying processes. The market-driven organization creates a configuration that exploits its capabilities for superior market sensing and market relating. The whole configuration includes the structure of the organization, the other capabilities of the business and supporting information, control and reward systems.

It is the combination of these interlinked elements that produces a strong market orientation. A market-focused culture would only create tension and frustration if it were grafted onto an internally focused structure. No matter how strong the culture, the organization would not be able to implement a market-driven approach without the capabilities and processes to do so.

CULTURE, CAPABILITIES AND PROCESSES

Culture and capabilities have a symbiotic relationship; one can't function without the other and they have to be in alignment to get superior results. Capabilities are needed to direct the shared values, beliefs and behaviors embedded in the culture toward the delivery of superior customer value. Capabilities—bundles of closely integrated skills, technologies and cumulative learning—are exercised through organizational processes.[1]

Wal-Mart's mastery of cross-docking logistics illustrates a capability in action. This is part of a broader "customer pull" system that starts with each individual store placing its orders on the basis of its own sales data. Orders are gathered from many stores and filled by suppliers in full truckloads. The loads are delivered to Wal-Mart's warehouses, where they are sorted, repacked and dispatched to stores. The transfer from one loading dock to another takes less than 48 hours, sharply cutting the usual inventory and handling costs. Wal-Mart's capability rests on the integration of a broad range of underlying skills and technologies, including network management, inventory control, bar-code technology, and systems modeling, to name a few. It is the integration that is the hallmark of a capability.

Capabilities should not be confused with assets, which are the resource endowments the business has accumulated. Investments in the scale and scope of plants, patents or computer systems cannot be capabilities because they are things, not skills. Capabilities are the glue that brings these assets together and enables them to be deployed advantageously. Capabilities also don't wear out over time; indeed, the more a capability is used, the better it becomes because it incorporates more learning. Also, capabilities are so deeply embedded in the organization that they cannot be traded or readily imitated.

Capabilities and organizational processes are closely entwined, because it is the capability that enables the activities in a business process to be carried out. The business will have as many core processes as needed to carry out the natural business activities defined by the stage in the value chain and the key success factors in the market. The core processes of a life insurance company will be different from those found in a microprocessor fabricator. Each process has a beginning and end state that facilitates identification and implies all the work that gets done in between. Thus, new product development proceeds from concept screening to market launch, and order fulfillment extends from the receipt of the order to payment. To fully appreciate capabilities, we need a new way of thinking about an organization as a collection of linked processes that span levels and functions.

The capabilities that distinguish the market-driven organization are market sensing, market relating and strategic thinking. We will examine these in more detail in Parts II and III. To build and strengthen these capabilities, the organization needs a structure that supports these capabilities, which also will be examined in Part III.

IDENTIFYING CAPABILITIES

Because capabilities are deep within the organization, they can be hard to identify. Marriott Hotels consistently receives high ratings from business travelers and meeting planners for quality service. Marriott is certainly as capable as Hyatt, Hilton and others at selecting good sites, opening new hotels smoothly, and marketing them well. What sets them apart and reveals a distinctive service capability (actually a set of linked capabilities each performed outstandingly well) is a "fanatical eye for detail." This begins with a hiring process that systematically recruits, screens, and selects from as many as 40 applicants for each position and continues through every hotel operation; for example, maids follow a 66-point guide to making up bedrooms. The effective management of these linked processes, within an organizational culture that values thoroughness and customer responsiveness, creates a distinctive capability that gives Marriott employees clear guidance on how to provide excellent customer service.

As with the case of Marriott, it is often difficult to identify capabilities, particularly if the organization is viewed functionally rather than as its component processes. A functional lens obscures key linkages between activities. Another problem is the temptation to confuse capabilities with a vague omnibus concept like "strengths" which may surface 30 or more "capabilities." These are more likely to be the constituent skills, activities and technologies that have been mastered rather than true capabilities.[2]

Capabilities are further obscured because much of their knowledge component is tacit and dispersed. This knowledge is distributed along four separate dimensions.[3] First are the accumulated employee *knowledge and skills* that come from technical training, and long experience with the process. The second dimension is the knowledge embedded in *technical systems,* comprising the information in linked databases, the formal procedures and established "routines" for dealing with given problems or transactions, and the computer systems themselves. Third and fourth are the *management systems* and the *values and norms* that define the content and interpretation of the knowledge, transcend individual capabilities and unify these capabilities into a cohesive whole. Thus the organization's culture is embedded within each capability.

What Are Distinctive Capabilities?

Every business acquires many capabilities that enable it to carry out the activities necessary to move its products or services through the value chain. Some will be done adequately, others poorly, but a few must be superior if the business is to outperform the competition. These are the distinctive capabilities that support a market position that is valuable and difficult to match. They must be managed with special care through the focused commitment of resources, assignment of dedicated people, and continued efforts to learn, supported by dramatic goals for improvement.

A workable definition of a distinctive capability is: a tightly integrated bundle of complementary skills, technology and knowledge that enables a team or group to execute one or more critical processes *much better than the competition.* Sony has a distinctive "miniaturization" capability that enables it to bring innovative consumer electronic products to market ahead of formidable competitors such as Sharp and Matsushita. This capability combines superiority in three complimentary processes:

- Integration of multiple technologies (microprocessors, power controls and electronics packaging)
- Intimate understanding of user-friendly design, ergonomics, and customer needs and life-styles
- Quick-to-market product development.

Each of these is managed at world-class levels, but superiority comes from the rapid sharing and use of information about market opportunities and technological possibilities. Speed is of the essence for consumer electronics, where the average product has a life of eighteen months and most of the profits are made in the first three or four months before the competitors arrive.

Despite the appeal of the concept of distinctive capabilities (and its corporate-level counterpart, core competencies), it has proven elusive and hard to use. The difficulties are often traceable to sloppiness in specifications or unjustified assumptions about the competitor's level of capability. One packaged goods firm, with a reputation and self-concept as an excellent marketer, believed it was superior in all aspects of marketing. In reality, it was not especially competent at making pricing and promotion decisions, was average in managing channel relations and getting distribution coverage, and had underperformed in new product development for several years. Its distinctive capability was narrowly defined as demand stimulation through image-based advertising.

Evaluating Distinctive Capabilities

Distinctive capabilities are embedded in two types of processes.[4] One type yields superior foresight or insight that can be used as the basis of a first-mover advantage. This includes market sensing (as described in Chapter 5). It also can be seen in the ability to invent and create that is the hallmark of Disney or the ability to create proprietary scientific knowledge or uncover patterns such as those Citibank uses when screening for creditworthiness. The second type arises from a superior ability to implement front-line processes that consistently deliver quality comparable to what the best craftsman could achieve. The market relating and partnering capabilities mastered by market-driven organizations, described in Chapters 7, 8 and 9, are in this category. Nordstrom's prowess in merchandising and building customer loyalty, enhanced by a culture that provides socialization and incentives, is an example.

To qualify as a distinctive capability that is a fundamental source of competitive advantage, four tests have to be satisfied:[5]

1. *Does it matter to the customer?*

The most defensible test is whether a capability makes a disproportionate contribution to superior customer value—as defined from the customer's perspective—or permits the business to deliver value to customers in an appreciably more cost-effective way. For example, Honda's prowess with fuel-efficient, reliable and responsive small displacement engines and drive trains adds a great deal of value and helps to set its cars apart from the competition. Other examples are Motorola's mastery of continuous quality improvement and rapid product development and Federal Express's ability to manage integrated transaction processing systems.

Customers are unlikely to be aware of or interested in the underlying processes that yield the superior value they receive. Thus a critical task for top management is to decide which capabilities to emphasize, which depends on how they choose to compete.

2. *Are we truly superior?*

If a distinctive capability is to be the basis of a strategy, the business must be demonstrably better than all or most of its present—and prospective— competitors. Too often, particular capabilities or skills are singled out because they are important to the business without any independent verification of superiority based on comparisons with competitors or customer judgments. This step is often skipped because the data are hard to acquire or would take too long to collect. This is myopic since new or transformed competitors may be closing the gap—or creating their own distinctive capabilities that are more highly valued by customers.

3. *How long can superiority be sustained?*

This test asks whether rivals can readily match the capability. Because distinctive capabilities are difficult to develop, they resist imitation. Kmart knows full well what Wal-Mart has accomplished with its logistics system and can readily buy the hardware and software, but it has been unable to match the underlying capability. First, Wal-Mart's capability is embedded in a complex process that harmonizes an array of skills and knowledge and involves considerable learning over many years. Second, Wal-Mart's processes are not readily visible because they cut across different organizational units. Third, because much of the collective knowledge that makes up the coordination skills is tacit and dispersed among many individuals, a competitor could not acquire the requisite knowledge simply by poaching a few key people.

Barriers to imitation are created by three conditions:

- It is unclear to the competition how the distinctive capability works. This ambiguity about capabilities arises because they embody *tacit knowledge* acquired through experience and refined by practice, require *complex patterns of coordination* among diverse skills and resources so a rival cannot grasp the functioning of the capability by direct observation, and employ *transaction-specific assets* that cannot be used elsewhere so they cannot easily be disentangled or imitated.
- Even if the competitors understand the advantage, they still can't duplicate it, either because the needed resources are scarce or immobile, or there is little or no reliable information available on the productivity of the needed resources.
- The early movers are able to deter efforts at imitation with a *credible threat of retaliation*. Procter & Gamble has discouraged direct attacks on its core detergent markets by publicly signaling its intention to defend these markets. Erstwhile invaders believe these signals because they are backed up with a long history of retaliation against aspirants and frequent public reminders that defending market share is a high priority.

4. *What will be needed in the future?*

Distinctive capabilities are robust and can be used in different ways to speed a firm's adaptation to environmental change. Honda has been able to apply its company-wide mastery of engine and drive train technology development and manufacturing processes to create distinctive capabilities in a variety of related markets such as generators, outboard marine engines, and lawn mowers. It is less clear whether Honda's distinctive capability in dealer management, which was used to develop a network of better managed and financed motorcycle dealers than the part-time deal-ers of competitors, also aided its entry into new markets.[6] On the one hand, Honda's skill at managing dealers has been of value in the auto market, where Honda dealers consistently receive high ratings for cus-tomer satisfaction. It is harder to say whether the logic of Honda's diver-sification into related markets was really guided by a desire to exploit this dealer management capability. More likely it was the ability to gain a multiplier effect by integrating both distinctive capabilities that shaped its moves into new markets.

The question of what capabilities will be needed to win in the future is both the most difficult and most important—especially if there is a dis-ruptive technology or innovative business model on the horizon that devalues current capabilities. Established firms are often at a disadvantage here, because they have momentum and commitment to an old model. We will return to this issue in Chapter 11, when we look at the strategic thinking ability of market-driven organizations that enables them to anticipate such disruptions.

MANAGING CAPABILITIES

Managing horizontal processes, such as order fulfillment or new product development, so they become distinctive capabilities that competitors cannot readily match, is very different from managing a vertical function in a traditional hierarchical organization.

Process management emphasizes external objectives.[7] These objec-tives may involve customers' satisfaction with the outcome of the process, such as quality, delivery time or installation assistance, or may be based on competitive performance benchmarks (e.g., cycle time, order process-ing time). This helps ensure that all those involved with the process are focused on providing superior value to external or internal customers. These objectives become the basis for a measurement and control system that monitors progress toward the objective.

In coordinating the activities of a complex process, several jurisdic-tional boundaries must be crossed and horizontal connections made. These interactions require an identifiable owner of the process who can isolate sources of delay and take action to eliminate them. When no one understands the total flow of activities in an order-entry process, for example, critical time-consuming steps such as credit checks may be undertaken separately in sequence when they could have been done in parallel to save time.

With process management, information is readily available to all team members, unfiltered by a hierarchy. If a question arises concerning order requirements, delivery status or parts availability, everyone who is affected by the answer can get the information directly without having to go through an intermediary.

The order fulfillment process in Figure 4–1 illustrates both the problems and benefits of managing a process so that it becomes a distinctive capability rather than simply a sequential series of necessary activities. Often this process is obscured from top management view because it links activities that take place routinely as sales forecasts are made, orders are received and scheduled, products are shipped and services are provided. Things can go awry if unrealistic promises are made to customers, these promises are not kept and blame is passed around. Meanwhile inventories expand as each function seeks to protect itself from the shortcomings of another (in part because no one incurs a cost for holding excess inventories).

Furthermore, the order fulfillment process has a wealth of connections to other processes. It brings together information from the market relating and market sensing processes, and depends on their ability to forecast and generate a flow of orders. It depends even more on the man-

FIGURE 4–1

Managing the Order Fulfillment Process

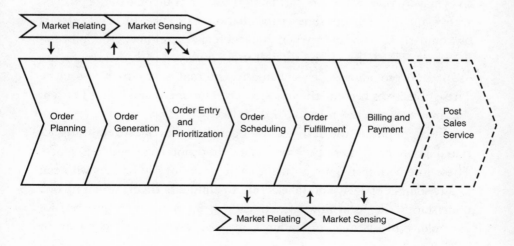

ufacturing and logistics processes to fulfill the scheduled orders and ensure there is capacity in place. Finally, there is the allied process of cost estimation and pricing of orders. The management of this activity will significantly improve profitability, if the customer value of each order is clearly recognized and the costs of filling each order are known.

Organizing Around Processes

When processes are brought to the fore, the premises underlying traditional organization structures are seriously undermined. Managers have to turn their organizations on their sides and take a horizontal process view rather than a vertical function view. This horizontal mind-set is needed to see the entire collection of activities that taken together create value for the customer rather than individual functional activities in isolation. Because these processes and capabilities cross organizational boundaries, and team members are drawn from different functional groups, they require new organizational arrangements.

Each business will have its own configuration of processes depending on past commitments, the capabilities needed to deliver customer value, and anticipated requirements. Nonetheless, certain generic processes can be recognized in businesses as diverse as Xerox, Chemical Bank, Unilever, and Astra-Merck.

If a business is defined by its customers, then each process should be classed according to its contribution to the creation of superior customer value. There are usually 20 or so core processes and 120 or more subprocesses, which can be grouped into five different types, as shown in Figure 4–2.[8]

The value-defining and value-developing processes yield strategic insights and foresights that are linked to the resource allocation and control processes to build the rest of the organization. The value-delivery and value-maintaining processes are where front-line execution matters, because they come into contact with the channel members and end consumers. Their objective is to satisfy and retain the most valuable customers.

Market-driven organizations are noteworthy for their superior market sensing, market relating and strategic thinking processes, and these are the basis for their related distinctive capabilities. They are concerned with the "outside in" processes that look beyond the organization's walls, and connect the value development and delivery processes to the market.

FIGURE 4–2

Organizing Around Processes: A Value Delivering Perspective

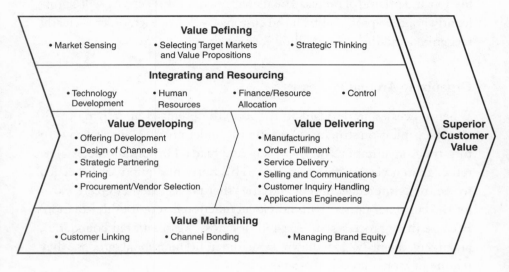

They enable the business to compete by anticipating market requirements ahead of competitors, interpreting them better, and creating durable relationships with customers, channel members and suppliers. In these organizations all processes have an external orientation because of the relevance and credibility of the outside-in processes.

Even the integrating management processes are shaped by this orientation. When human resources are managed by the belief that customer satisfaction and loyalty are both a cause and a consequence of employee satisfaction, key policies look different. Rewards are based on measurable improvements in customer satisfaction and loyalty, employees are empowered to resolve customer problems without approvals and recruiting emphasizes customer problem-solving skills.

Interactive Processes: From Value Chains to Value Cycles

Although Figure 4–2 suggests a linear sequence of linked processes moving from the company to the customers, the reality is that organizations are more like loops of interacting processes. Instead of a value chain, a linear process, we have a value cycle, which is a self-reinforcing process, as shown in Figure 4–3. Value is defined, developed, and delivered to customers. The response to this value from the market leads to activities to

FIGURE 4–3

Value Cycle

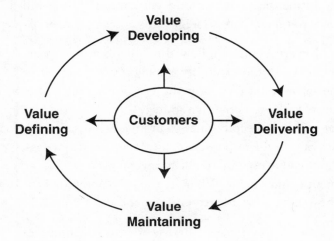

maintain and strengthen it, which ultimately lead to a renewal of the value proposition. As firms move from a make-and-sell to a sense-and-respond model, these loops and value cycles will become even tighter.

Instead of viewing the process as a chain that delivers value *to* customers, the market-driven firm views the process as an interaction *with* customers. The value chain is not merely a steady progression from order planning to post-sale service. There is a market-sensing capability interacting with all the steps of the value chain. This interactivity creates a radically different view of organizational processes.

Interactivity represents a sea change in the way companies relate to their markets. The essence of interactive marketing is the use of information *from* the customer rather than *about* the customer. This is entirely natural for those firms selling large capital equipment to a few sophisticated buyers. Manufacturers of aircraft engines, digital switchgear, or packaging machinery already have close collaborative relationships with their customers that are mutually informed. However, interactivity is a radical departure, with exhilarating and potentially threatening prospects for those in financial or travel services, publishing, apparel, or white goods that have traditionally used broadcast marketing.

This interactive view of processes has implications for the evolution of the structure of the organization. One view[9] is that firms will follow a "probe and learn" progression that begins with ad hoc committees, and increasingly formalize and institutionalize the organization effort until there is a distinct business unit or department with key skills in place to implement an interactivity strategy. This raises a number of questions:

- Should every business follow this progression—especially if only a modest degree of interactivity is sought?
- Is the separate business unit the best way to align the organization structure with an interactive strategy?
- What will help keep businesses from achieving the necessary alignment? Successful responses require changes in processes, mind-set, and innovative organizational arrangements as well as sustained management commitment. What are the traps and pitfalls to avoid as the business moves toward greater interactivity?

As these questions suggest, there is no "one size fits all" organizational template. The appropriate choice will be crafted to fit each specific situation through a process of trial-and-error learning, and astute borrowing from other firms.

The Legacy of Reengineering

The biggest impetus for a process view of organizations came from the once fashionable pursuit of reengineering,[10] "the radical redesign of business processes for dramatic improvements." The initial surge of enthusiasm for the promise of delayering and restructuring was soon followed by disappointments because of unrealistic expectations, flawed understanding of its profound consequences and serious implementation problems. Reengineering became a quick fix for managers seeking to cut costs and head-count, who were persuaded by early successes with mundane claims handling, purchasing and invoicing processes to believe it could be applied everywhere. In most cases, only a few of the twenty or so core processes in an organization were tackled, and these were redesigned with little consideration for the surrounding and enabling processes.

These reengineering initiatives seldom began with a view of the market. Most often, they were initiated with a view to improving the internal organization. Even when the individually reengineered processes were optimized they didn't come together as an optimized whole. And they didn't necessarily optimize value to the market. Most often, the missing ingredients were an integrating strategic logic and external orientation that are the hallmarks of a market-driven organization.

Like all management fads and fashions where excitement is inevitably followed by disenchantment, reengineering is now seen in a harsher light. There is now a realistic sense for when it is appropriate to apply the full-scale approach. The positive legacy of reengineering is that managers began to view organizations from a process perspective rather than through a traditional functional lens. And through trial-end-error learning we now have a much better idea of what is needed to implement this approach and coach people through the traumas of change.

The insight from market-driven organizations is that an inward-looking restructuring of processes will probably fall short. If companies can instead begin redesigning processes from the outside in, the results should be more closely linked with the creation of customer value and profits. This approach will also help ensure that the organization is not only executing its processes well, but is focused on the right processes.

INTEGRATING CULTURE AND CAPABILITIES: HOW VIRGIN ATLANTIC FLIES ON ALL ENGINES

Configuration creates the context for the capabilities. The more *congruent* the elements of culture, capabilities and configuration, the more effective the strategy can be at delivering superior customer value. Here congruence means not only that there is internal consistency among the facets of the culture and its activities but that they are mutually reinforcing.[11] Although it is important for the individual sources to be well executed, what matters more is how well they are combined and integrated to support the positioning.

Consider how Virgin Atlantic Airways has prospered in the face of intense competition from British Airways on the London to New York route.[12] When Virgin Atlantic launched its first transatlantic flight in 1984, it was viewed as an unwanted upstart because it flouted so many airline conventions and practices. Much of the freewheeling, entrepreneurial culture was a reflection of founder Richard Branson. His exuberant personality, flair for publicity and innate business sense spawned a diverse empire of businesses ranging from soft drinks to record stores. All these businesses carried the Virgin name which consumers associated with quality, fun, innovation and low prices.

From the beginning, the goal of the airline was to give the best possible service while staying original, spontaneous and informal. It saw itself as a passenger-carrying airline that was also in the entertainment and leisure business. The airline excelled in passenger service—garnering the "airline of the year" award for three consecutive years—and was renowned for its recovery from service problems where its goal was to be proactive, not defensive. To keep passengers stimulated, Virgin pioneered many service innovations including an individual video screen for every seat, on-board beauty therapists or tailors on some flights, and a motorcycle chauffeur service for Upper Class passengers. A real point of difference was Virgin's Upper Class service, marketed as first class service at business class fares. Meanwhile, economy class promised the best value for money, targeting price-sensitive leisure travelers who sought comfort.

The results were impressive. By 1994, Virgin Atlantic had carved out a 20 percent share of the New York–London route, and expanded into five other markets including London to Orlando, Florida where it had a 33 percent share. Despite its small size, it was perceived as the strongest brand name in transatlantic travel by 24 percent of United Kingdom executives (versus 2 percent for American and United respectively).

How did VAA achieve such a distinctive and valuable position at a time when most airlines were becoming indistinguishable? There is no single strength that stands out. As Figure 4–4 shows, the assets, culture and capabilities of Virgin Atlantic work together and reinforce each other. The most distinctive feature is a strong market-oriented culture that is an exemplar of an adhocracy—starting with the leadership of Richard Branson. The operative values of creativity, adaptability and autonomy enable and enhance strong capabilities in service delivery and innovation. This is an organization single-mindedly devoted to making flying a memorable experience. The dynamic culture also attracted high-quality staff, who were willing to go out of their way to help customers, despite relatively low salaries. Staff were encouraged to take the initiative and given the means to do so. Everyone took responsibility for providing insights into what customers wanted or needed and often anticipated their expectations better than the customers themselves. The overall philosophy was set out by Richard Branson:

> We aren't interested in having just happy employees. We want employees who feel involved and prepared to express dissatisfaction when necessary. In

FIGURE 4–4

How Virgin Atlantic Airlines
Integrates Culture and Capabilities

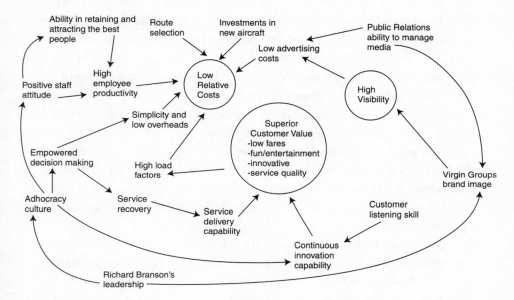

fact, we think that the dissatisfied employee is an asset we should encourage and we need an organization that allows us to do this—and that encourages employees to take responsibility, since I don't believe it is enough for us to simply to give it.

These sources of advantage collectively contribute to the three themes that define Virgin's competitive advantages. By offering superior customer value, it operates at higher load factors, which helps offset the adverse revenue effects of lower fares and more spacious seating arrangements. Costs are further reduced by high employee productivity and low advertising spending of 2 percent of sales compared to 5 to 7 percent for the competitors. All these elements must work in harmony. If any one of them broke down, the economics of the airline would be jeopardized. But this insight applies to all organizations. The effective execution of a strategy requires ongoing discipline and shared understanding of how value is created for customers so that employees know how to behave in their day-to-day choices. A market-driven organization is more likely to achieve a harmonious congruity.

TOWARD A NEW CONCEPT OF THE ORGANIZATION

All the elements of a market-driven organization must work together. The power and enduring advantage of the market-driven organization flow from these interrelated elements. Becoming more market-driven requires rethinking all the elements that contribute to the organization's success. This complexity is the challenge of creating a market-driven firm, but when all the elements come together as with Virgin Atlantic, it is a tremendous source of competitive advantage.

The essence of a market-driven organization is the capabilities used to direct the culture and resources toward the strategic objective of delivering superior customer value. Because these capabilities are exercised through processes, the organization design question is how to align these processes with the market. Which functions, processes and capabilities should steer the structure and how should the functions and capabilities be aligned?

The usual steering mechanisms are the strategic thinking process and the resource allocation/budgeting process. For example, one telecommunications firm has given funding authority to the marketing organization. The aim is to ensure that the "factories"—the telephone network and information systems that control the switches—focus improvements on areas where there is a demonstrable customer demand. This is a clear signal that a marketing capability is to have primacy. A recurring challenge is balancing traditional concerns of the value delivery process (engineering, manufacturing, purchasing and logistics) with efficiency and cost control, with the need to support the overall value proposition and stay responsive to changing market requirements.

The preferred solution for improving the alignment of the organizational structure with the market is to adopt a flatter structure and organize around processes. As will be discussed in Chapter 10, market-driven organizations are rethinking their structures to combine elements of horizontal, process-focused structures and more traditional vertical functional specialization. The focus on horizontal processes facilitates the organization's capabilities for market sensing and market relating. The remaining functional structures, however, facilitate its ability to function effectively and flexibly to meet market changes and reshape its processes. This combination creates an organization that can remain aligned with the market.

PART II

BUILDING THE CAPABILITIES

The superiority of market-driven organizations in understanding, attracting and keeping their valuable customers is due to their distinctive capabilities for market sensing and market relating. The former capability allows the market-driven firm to continuously anticipate market opportunities and respond to them before competitors. The latter capability keeps the organization closely linked to its market, creating a two-way street for interacting with customers. These two capabilities also help keep the culture and overall configuration completely aligned with the market.

To be effective at market sensing, companies first need to be looking in the right direction. For example, managers need to engage in open scanning, remaining open to insights from the periphery, closely examining competitors and actively seeking out latent needs. Fixating on the existing needs of existing customers, ignoring rivals and listening to the same voices lead to blindness toward the market.

In addition to effective approaches to sensing the market discussed in Chapter 5, the organization also needs to be able to make sense of the information it gathers. The company's mental models—the filters the organization uses to interpret the world—shape this sense-making process. Mental models are necessary for organizations to make any sense of the welter of information in which they exist, but they also limit the focus of the firm. When these filters are ineffective, they can become blinders that prevent the organization from recognizing or anticipating important market threats or opportunities. When these mental models are effective, they can help the organization to use its information to deepen its knowledge of the market.

All this sensing will be for naught if it is not held in an organizational memory that can be accessed throughout the organization. This "shared knowledge base," discussed in Chapter 6, organizes and disseminates market knowledge throughout the organization. The shared knowledge base is strengthened through market sensing activities, and it also helps to shape and contribute to these activities by giving the organization the perspectives it needs to interpret market information and identify areas where information is needed.

In addition to market sensing, market-driven organizations also have a superior capability for market relating, as discussed in Chapter 7. The relationships that were a natural part of small businesses were lost in an age of mass production and mass markets. Companies focused on transactions rather than relationships with customers and developed arms-length relationships with suppliers to capture the efficiencies of mass markets. But new technology and organizational structures now allow companies to rebuild close relationships with customers and supply-chain partners while retaining the advantages of scale. In Chapter 8, we examine a spectrum of different relationships, from transactions to value-adding exchanges to collaborative exchanges and discuss when each is most appropriate. In Chapters 8 and 9, we explore in more detail how this market-relating capability is shown in both consumer markets and business-to-business channels.

In consumer markets, market relating is seen in the strength of customer relationships designed to increase customer loyalty, as discussed in Chapter 8. As companies increasingly recognize that retaining loyal customers results in significant profit advantages for the company, they are more focused on creating strong and enduring relationships with their most valuable customers. Companies need to identify why customers switch, which customer relationships are worth investing in and how these relationships create advantage. As companies build these relationships with customers, customers become more closely tied to the company, creating a virtuous cycle. But to sustain this cycle, the company needs to continue to deliver superior value, demonstrate trustworthiness and tighten its bonds with customers.

What is the impact of electronic commerce on these relationships? Some see the Internet as leading to more transaction-oriented relationships, as customers use smart agents to track down the lowest prices around the world. But this technology, particularly when coupled with technology for mass customization, *can also facilitate a two-way interaction between the customer and the firm, strengthening relationships.*

In business-to-business markets, the market-relating capability is seen in collaborative relationships with channel partners. Chapter 9 examines ways that companies have shifted their adversarial relationships with suppliers and other partners to closer linkages. These relationships reduce the costs of moving goods to market and increase the flow of information from the market to producers of goods and services. Given the more enduring relationships with suppliers, companies must take more care in selecting partners and managing the ongoing relationship to align the firms. The second issue in building collaborative relationships is effective ways of "channel bonding," using technology to link the channel more closely to create advantages for all channel members. This again takes skill to execute effectively and to ensure that plans for cooperation do not lead to coercion.

EDWARD JONES: BULLISH ON CUSTOMER RELATIONSHIPS

Stockbroker Edward Jones quietly rose to become one of the largest U.S. investment firms through its capabilities for market sensing and market relating. When Jones, founded in 1871, began its expansion in the 1960s and 1970s, it concentrated on building personal relationships with its clients.

Unlike many large brokerages, Jones from the outset made a commitment to serving individual investors with one-man offices in rural towns that allowed customers always to deal with the same broker. It established 4,000 offices, more than any of its rivals. Jones strengthened these direct customer relationships with heavy spending on information technology, building the largest client-server computer network outside the U.S. military.[1] This allowed the firm to collect and rapidly disseminate information to support its brokers, creating a shared knowledge base.

This formula of close, personal relationships with customers built Jones into the eighth largest investment firm in the industry with more than 2 million clients. It achieved pre-tax returns of at least 29 percent each year from 1992 to 1997. Jones's solid relationships with customers also made its arbitration awards the lowest in the United States, just $8 per broker, compared with $370 per broker at second-place Morgan Stanley Dean Witter. Jones's capabilities in market sensing and relating gave it an advantage by driving its growth and profits, while reducing the costs of conflicts with clients.

The rise of Internet trading has posed the most serious challenge to the strength of Jones's relationships and its business model based on face-to-face service with higher margins. Jones initially dismissed the threat posed by electronic trading, but the on-line trading services of respected firms such as Charles Schwab—offering advice as well as inexpensive transactions—raise the question of whether customers will continue to be willing to pay extra for their relationships with Jones.

There are a variety of ways Jones could use the technology to launch new services or strengthen its existing relationships. For example, by providing more information to customers about their portfolios on-line, it could make clients more informed in their discussions with brokers. But the challenge is to add these capabilities without undermining the company's margins and current relationships. Here Jones's customer relationships continue to be the firm's strongest asset and its market sensing capability shapes its future actions.

As the Jones case illustrates, the capabilities for market sensing and relating can provide a tremendous advantage to the firm that develops them. The battle for superior market sensing and relating capabilities is shaping up to be one of the key competitive contests among firms in market after market. These capabilities, always essential to small, local firms, are now a key source of advantage for large, market-driven organizations. Enduring relationships with customers can lead to enduring advantages over competitors in the market. The following chapters examine how to build these capabilities for sensing and relating to establish market-driven advantages.

Chapter Five

Market Sensing

The market data of a major pet food manufacturer seemed to give managers little cause for alarm or new initiatives. The company appeared to be holding its dominant share in a market with relatively flat growth. In reality, the company was losing share in a total market that was growing at a healthy rate. What managers overlooked was the emergence of scientific pet food formulas sold through nontraditional specialty outlets and veterinarians. They were missing a major growth opportunity. In trying to pinpoint why this new segment was missed, managers cited their own complacency and the restrictive scope of their market data. They relied on sales data that were readily available, and lacked curiosity about events at the periphery of their served market. This weakness in their market sensing ability cost them a significant opportunity.

Why do firms lose touch with their markets? Why are they surprised by shifts in customer requirements, slow to react to emerging competitors, and unprepared to use innovative channel arrangements? Without an effective capacity to anticipate, they continually miss opportunities and never seem able to do more than catch up. Even their reactions are liable to be slow and ill-advised, or counterproductive because of flawed assumptions, misinformation or internal disagreements.

Market-driven firms, in contrast, stand out in their ability to continuously sense and act on events and trends in their markets. They are better equipped to anticipate how their markets will respond to actions designed to retain or attract customers, improve channel relations or thwart competitors. In these well educated firms, everyone from first-line sales and service people to the CEO is sensitized to identify and seize market opportunities as they arise. For example, the boxed insert describes how Intuit's superior market-sensing abilities, briefly discussed in Chapter 1, helped it to become the leading personal financial software company.

Market-driven organizations also excel in their ability to make sense of the information that they draw from the market. They have a highly refined capacity to turn this information into knowledge and then share it across the organization. Without this sense-making ability, the avalanche of data generated by new information systems often swamps the organization. The Unilever Fabrics Business discovered that in just five years between 1989 and 1995, its data base swelled by 20 times (70 gigabytes of hard data were coming in every year) but the company could profitably use only 10 percent of it.

A Learning Process

As shown in Figure 5–1, the linked activities of market sensing and sense-making allow organizations to learn continuously about their markets.[1] Market sensing depends upon open-minded inquiry rather than looking for information to confirm preexisting beliefs about the market. The next stage in this learning process is disseminating the information generated by these inquiries and absorbing the insights into the collective mental models of how the market behaves. These mental models help make sense of information, ensuring that everyone pays attention to the essence and potential of the information. A hallmark of a market-driven firm is broadly shared assumptions about their markets that assures the coherence and timeliness of strategies that anticipate rather than react to market events.

This process of learning about markets may be triggered by an impending decision, an emerging problem, or a belief that effective innovation requires deep insights into latent customer needs. This spark begins the active *collection* and *distribution* of information about the needs, expectations and requirements of customers, how the market is segmented, how relationships are sustained, and the intentions and capabilities of competitors. Before the information can be used it has to be *interpreted* so patterns can be revealed and understood. Further learning comes from the feedback about what actually happened.[3] Did the market

HOW INTUIT LISTENS TO ITS MARKETS[2]

When Intuit launched Quicken into the personal finance software market in 1983 they faced 43 competing products: By 1997 they had gained a near-monopoly with 75 percent of the market, despite fierce competition from Microsoft Money. Sales in 1997 exceeded $550 million, although aggressive acquisitions and investments in new business often kept the firm in the red. What set Intuit apart was the realization that people buy their products to make their life easier. From the beginning, Quicken was among the easiest to use, resolutely focused on the daily lives of ordinary people. The praises of their happy customers created such strong word of mouth that the firm has spent very little on advertising or sales.

Why did Intuit prevail? Begin with the leadership of Scott Cook, who left his job as a product manager with Procter & Gamble to found the firm. He embodies and continually articulates the market-driven culture of the firm; such as the belief that "we win by creating products that function well and feel good to the senses" and "we are successful when the customer is successful." Another widely shared belief holds that most of the best ideas came from customers. A true "listening" organization has been created to act in these beliefs. This organization is guided by three principles:

First, listen continually to the needs and wants of consumers.

Noncustomers play a large role in this process. These people make up 80 percent of the participants in the company's usability labs where their reactions to new features and products are closely studied. Intuit employees often visit their homes to see how they cope with the need to organize their finances. When they do buy the software, employees follow them home to see how they fare in their attempts to get the software installed and running.

Second, create products that satisfy needs.

Many insights have come from their slavish attention to customer experiences, including the discovery that many small-business owners were using Quicken home-finance software to keep their books. This led to the development of Quick-Books, now used by thousands of small businesses. Such products are developed by multifunctional teams where each person has extensive face-to-face contact with customers. This helps reduce barriers between functions. Once the

(continued)

(continued)

product is launched the software engineers listen to customers' calls to get first-hand feedback on their efforts.

Third, put listening posts in place at each point of customer contact.

Here the central artery for the sensing process is the customer service function. The representatives receive thousands of calls daily, each being an opportunity for learning. Patterns in problems and questions are carefully studied for insights into latent needs that are fed back into the development process. The culture supports and motivates all employees to seek out and share customer insights so there is complete immersion at all levels.

Despite its successes with customer data, Intuit is gravely threatened by the explosive growth of the Internet. Sooner or later the era of stand-alone, feature-rich software will give way to on-line services where personal finance tools will be developed by content providers with specialties in banking or real estate and distributed piecemeal via the Net. In response they have a Web site that guides users to an array of services provided by financial planners, brokers, banks, and insurers. Intuit hopes to make money by selling ad space and getting a share of each transaction. However, many others aspire to provide the same services, ranging from Schwab, Microsoft and Yahoo to American Express. Against this formidable array of competitors Intuit has the advantage of intimate understanding of the market, a strong brand name, an installed base of 10 million users, and the objectivity that comes from being a disinterested facilitator rather than a service provider.

---

respond as we expected, and if not, why not? Were our judgments confirmed or disconfirmed? What should we have known that we didn't? The cumulative insights are then lodged somewhere in the sprawling *memory* of the organization, ready to be retrieved (we hope) when needed. This begins a new cycle of sensing and sense making.

Mastery of the complete market-learning process is rare. Most firms suffer disabilities at one or more stages of the process. Their inquiries may be constipated, their mental models myopic, the circulation of information constricted, or the collective memory afflicted by amnesia. The cost of these disabilities is high and mounting rapidly in markets experiencing accelerating rates of change. Yet organizations can learn to better sense

FIGURE 5–1

Market Driven Processes for Learning About Markets

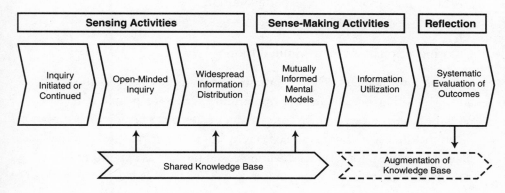

their markets, by understanding each step in their process, critically assessing their market-learning capability; and then correcting the learning disabilities.

This superior market learning capability is supported by a knowledge base that is accessible to the entire organization, which is the topic of the next chapter.

As the half-life of usable knowledge shrinks in the face of compressed life cycles, fragmenting markets and proliferating media and distribution channels, it is becoming much harder to stay well educated. This process of sensing and sense making has to be continuous, with knowledge flowing throughout the organizations like the circulatory system in the human body.

SENSING THE MARKET

Market-driven organizations use many devices to open their collective "mind" to new information that can help anticipate emerging opportunities and competitive threats and more accurately forecast how the market will respond to changes in strategy:

- Creating a spirit of open-minded inquiry
- Carefully analyzing rivals' actions
- Listening to staff on the front lines

- Seeking out latent needs
- Active scanning of the periphery of the market
- Encouraging continuous experimentation

Creating a Spirit of Open-Minded Inquiry

Throughout a market-driven organization there is an openness to trends and events that present market opportunities. Service people don't get upset because their schedule is thrown off by a customer request for a modification to meet a changing need. Front-line contact people hear complaints or requests for services the firm doesn't provide as opportunities for new businesses, rather than as nuisance calls to be avoided. Salespeople are motivated to report on customer developments and competitive moves within their territory, for they know their intelligence-gathering efforts will be rewarded and the information they supply will not disappear into a corporate "black hole."

The inquiry activities are often threatened by an insidious closed-mindedness, that blinds management to emerging possibilities and latent threats by narrowing the scope of the inquiry. This learning disability is often hard to detect, being masked by arrogance ("We know what the market wants because we're out there selling to them"), complacency ("The information was good enough for my predecessor, so it's good enough for me"), and an inward orientation that focuses attention on readily available internal measures, activities and standards of performance.

Close-mindedness was almost fatal to a maker of high-performance radio transmission equipment. The firm was once a strong second in its market, with a product that was costly and built to order with the flexibility to accommodate thousands of features and options, but took twenty weeks to deliver. Management became concerned about a new competitor with a "cherry-picking" strategy based on three models of transmitters and immediate delivery through existing dealers. They responded with a cost improvement program that took out most of the extra functions. The decision was based entirely on internal data about the costs of complexity and order reports. Only after the new line was launched—to the dismay of the sales force—did management realize that the distributors were modifying the product in the field and needed lots of flexibility in the base equipment. The absence of direct information about customer preferences and responsiveness to product changes was blamed for a 30-point dip in market share.

Carefully Analyzing Rivals' Actions

Most firms routinely do tear-down analyses of their competitors' products, and monitor news sources and call reports for sightings of unusual competitive activity. Often the outcome of these efforts is an undigested mass of news clippings, and some comparisons of the price and performance of their own products with the competitors' products that most closely resemble their own. Meanwhile, important information may never come to the attention of those who can act on it: how do manufacturing executives know what to do with evidence that a competitor is ordering large numbers of high performance processing machines? Thus the first step in improving competitor analysis is to develop an organization-wide appreciation of the need for competitor intelligence, and provide a visible and easily accessible focal point in the organization for receiving and interpreting the information and making sure it is acted on quickly.

Benchmarking takes competitor analysis somewhat further, by comparing costs and performance at every step in the firm's value chain against the best rivals. This reveals developments in capabilities and processes that could be used to increase their competitive lead. Firms like Xerox often use the outcomes of these benchmarking studies to shake up complacent manufacturing and service groups with the news they are slipping behind.

Market-driven firms go further to study the attitudes, values and management processes of nonpareils in different industries that share the same challenges. They recognize they can always learn to improve their methods and the way individual functions work together. These firms also study their direct competitors so they can emulate successful moves before the competition gets too far ahead. This requires thoughtful efforts to understand why the competitor succeeded, as well as further research probes for problems and shortcomings to identify improvements that would be welcomed by customers. The masters of informed imitation are the Japanese electronics firms that quickly rush their versions to market just in case the pioneer's product is a success. With a target to aim at, they know the innovation is at least technologically feasible and their ongoing marketing research tells them where improvements would be welcomed by customers.

Listening to the Front Lines

In most organizations, front-line contact people—who handle the complaints, hear requests for new services, cope with lead users, or lose sales due to competitor initiatives—are seldom motivated to inform management on a systematic basis. They may fear having their job loads increase, suspect the information won't be used, or not know where it should be sent. Unblocking this valuable upward flow requires organizational changes that begin with a recognition of the value of this source of information. Upward flowing channels of information need to be established and incentives need to be offered for useful insights. Information technology can play a strong supporting role. For example, Ford is able to electronically forward complaints that have come to the customer service representatives directly to the dealers who are supposed to settle the problem. The same information goes to marketing research and then to engineering, where the need for changes can be readily appreciated.

Service people who are motivated to listen carefully are an especially valuable resource. Hewlett–Packard intercepted an emerging problem when several technicians heard unanticipated negative comments about an innovative program that offered four levels of service: "priority plus" meant a service response in two hours or less at a premium price, with successively lower prices for same day, next day or regularly scheduled service. Meanwhile the service organization was pushing hard to be able to respond to most calls in two hours. Unhappily this confused customers, and made those paying extra for the two-hour service contract quite angry. HP has now learned to manage customers' expectations much better by aligning their service promises and service delivery.

Seeking Out Latent Needs

A whimsical definition of latent needs as "evident but not yet obvious" has a serious message. It addresses the shortcoming of structured research methods that impose fixed attribute descriptions and scaled response categories to obtain standardized and comparable responses from large samples. Although these methods are helpful for understanding manifest needs that are close to the surface, they obscure latent needs. Focus groups are not much better for this purpose. As one critic noted, "they spend two hours competing with ten strangers for five minutes of our time." A good focus group can be rich in insights if the participants stimulate each other, but the odds are that a dominant personality will sway everyone else's opinions.

A number of techniques have been devised to help firms surface latent needs and sharpen their ability to anticipate market requirements:

1. *Problem identification.* These are straightforward efforts to get prospective or current customers to describe their problems and frustrations with a product or service or the barriers to adoption. H&R Block has invested heavily to appreciate the difficulties people face when preparing tax forms to identify ways to serve them better. A variant of problem identification is to elicit the ideal purchase and usage situation— what they wish they had rather than what they got. These become good targets for focusing technology development efforts.

2. *Story telling.*[4] Another kind of dialogue asks customers how they behave and how they truly feel. Kimberly-Clark listened over and over to stories from parents before they realized that parents viewed diapers as clothing that signals particular stages of development, not as waste-disposal fodder. Armed with this insight they developed training pants that look and fit like underwear, yet still keep accidents on the inside. Such finely detailed stories and case experiences help surface unanticipated purchase criteria. There are formal techniques such as "laddering" that have the same objective, by probing ever deeper for underlying beliefs and motives, such as why many people view soft drinks as rewards.

3. *Observation.* The advantages of observation over direct inquiry are, first, that it occurs in a natural setting and doesn't interrupt the usual flow of activity; second, that people give nonverbal cues of their feelings as well as spontaneous, unsolicited comments that are stimulated by an actual product or prototype; third, trained observers with knowledge of technical possibilities can see solutions to unarticulated needs or problems which users could not conceive.[5] This is why firms like Sony and Sharp have set up "antennae shops" so they can watch prospective customers pick up and try to use their new products. The salespeople are trained to delve into the reasons for the observed reactions. Similarly,

most auto firms have design studios in southern California to see how the leading-edge car owners are modifying their cars to meet special needs or make personal statements, that can yield clues for design. Reebok, Nike, and others employ "cool hunters" to watch what teens and street youths are wearing and buying because they are the ones who set the coolest fashion trends.

4. *Customer economics*. Most customers don't know the full costs of acquiring a product or service; including the costs to use, store and dispose of it; the time consumed in the buying process or ongoing maintenance, insurance, energy and training costs. A firm buying a PC may spend eight to ten times as much on the support costs of maintenance, upgrades and training. These costs are hard to identify, and are often hidden in functional silos that don't share information. Spending "a day in the life of your customer" is a way to surface these costs and find latent opportunities to deliver superior value.

All this deep digging will be fruitless if the listeners impose their judgments and biases to interpret what they are seeing and hearing. Remember the definition of latent needs—it still takes attentive listening to decode the messages in the stories and observed behavior.

Actively Scanning the Periphery

All managers scan! They are continually exposed to a wealth of data ranging from the fuzzy imprecision of trade rumors to harder evidence from trade association statistics, product movement data, syndicated market studies, and sales reports. The difference in market-driven organizations is that managers actively scan the periphery to look for new opportunities.

Scanning gives managers an illusion of being fully informed that may obscure important shifts in the market. Because most of the data that are scanned come from familiar sources, they tend to reinforce existing frameworks that define the boundaries of the market, how it is segmented, who the competitors are, and the benefits customers are seeking.

As shown in the case of the pet food manufacturer in the opening of the chapter, companies commonly fail to ask for or receive the data they need to understand the full market. They become reliant on outsiders to define the market by virtue of the categories they use to sort the data. In the pet food case, the supplier of the syndicated sales data had no way to access some of the new segments—but also had never been asked. This narrowing of vision means the managers pay attention only to what the data suppliers provide, and the suppliers provide only what they are asked for.

Encouraging Continuous Experimentation

True learning organizations are serious about continuous experimentation.[6] This process of active, ongoing experimentation is where original insights into the market are developed. For example, American Airlines identified the true drivers of customer satisfaction through a series of real-time experiments, as described in the boxed insert.

How is experimentation encouraged? First, the organization needs an experimental mindset. General Electric's Quick Market Intelligence ini-

---

OPEN MINDS OPEN DOORS FOR AMERICAN AIRLINES

American Airlines used a set of natural experiments to improve customer perceptions of on-line arrival performance. It found that these perceptions improved markedly if the plane doors were opened less than 16 seconds after gate arrival. The key to this insight was their ability to measure how quickly they opened the doors and then follow up with telephone surveys of the passengers on the flight. Another airline used a tool of statistical process control called "fishbone" analysis to isolate all the reasons for delays in pushbacks from the gate. The biggest single cause of delay was accommodating late passengers. These weren't passengers who had connection problems, they were simply casual about being at the gate on time. Individual gate agents were making their own decisions to delay the plane, so the airline wouldn't lose the fare, but also out of sympathy. The second cause of delays was because motorized pusher tugs weren't available at the time of "pushback." This was solved with better scheduling and the addition of more tugs. As with American Airlines, the raw data were already available—what was added was a desire to improve, a methodology to identify successful and unsuccessful activities and the willingness to monitor the results and act on them.

tiative creates a culture and process for encouraging continuous curiosity and experimentation. In the words of Chairman Jack Welch:

> Quick Market Intelligence is GE's term for the magnificent boundary-busting technique pioneered by Wal-Mart that allows the entire company to understand, to touch the changing desires of the customer and to act on them in almost real-time. The rhythm of the Wal-Mart intelligence-action cycle encourages experimentation, because whatever doesn't work is never in place for more than a week. The secret of Wal-Mart is that it keeps its small company speed and behavior as it grows bigger. QMI is a chance for us to get bigger—by acting smaller. The QMI rhythm—that weekly pulsing of customer needs—will become the rhythm of GE in the years to come and one of the key drivers of our top-line growth.

More formal approaches are being used by pharmaceutical firms who are experimenting with creative approaches to communicating with notoriously hard-to-reach physicians. The different approaches are evaluated with syndicated prescription data that track prescriptions written by specific physicians.

Second, there needs to be strong and sustained top management support for experimental learning. This is what Dwight Riskey had when he persuaded the top management of Frito-Lay to conduct a four-year-long, in-market test of TV advertising for their key brands.[7] It required a significant commitment from the firm but produced extremely useful results. The test gave one group of 15,000 households a normal media plan, while another matched group got no advertising at all. Among the findings were that only 27 percent of ads for the largest brands led to significant volume increases, but smaller brands showed much more favorable effects. These experimental findings were distilled into lessons and principles for managing advertising that were a sharp departure from the usual rules of thumb (such as "to achieve an X percent share you must spend more than X percent of all spending in the category"). For example, they have learned always to advertise when there is "news," and that ad spending on big brands in the absence of "news" is unlikely to drive sales volume increases. But these lessons are not chiseled in stone; the mind-set in Frito-Lay is constantly challenging entrenched beliefs and assumptions in the search for deeper insights into market behavior.

Finally, organizations need to tolerate what 3M managers call "well-intentioned" failures. Trial-and-error learning that relies on experimentation is quickly subverted if there is a fear-of-failure syndrome. Organizations that reward people for playing it safe and hold the risk takers solely accountable for their failures—even when they take calculated risks—soon discourage learning. Although failures should be avoided when possible, they do have a therapeutic role because they contain many instructive lessons. Yet, in most firms there are few incentives to study failures carefully. Audits of failed strategic initiatives that might sort out causes from their effects are seen as ways of assigning blame rather than a way to learn about new market opportunities. It takes concerted leadership to create a more open climate where learning from failures is possible.

SENSE MAKING

Before organizations can use the information they have collected, they must make sense of it by classifying, sorting and simplifying it into coherent patterns. The key to effective sense making is the development of mutually informed mental models throughout the organization. In our discussion of culture in Chapter 3, we examined how mental models are simplifying frameworks used to make sense of the world and keep the organization moving in a common direction. But when they are not fully understood, they can also blind it to market information and prevent managers from developing accurate insights into market realities.

Because of this role as filters, mental models have a significant impact on the process of making sense of the information that comes into the organization. They affect both the information managers seek and select during the inquiry stage, as well as the lessons they extract about appropriate actions.[8]

The Pitfalls and Power of Mental Models

Unexamined mental models can become traps. For example, the Multiplex Corporation, a large global manufacturer of industrial materials, was a pioneer in many of its markets. As it shaped its markets, it also developed mental models about how they operated. But these models needed to be reexamined as the markets matured. Early in the life cycle of these markets, when growth came by displacing other materials, the customers were relatively insensitive to premium prices. As competition intensified, large segments of the market were unwilling to pay a premium for the extra value Multiplex offered. This was a well-known and seemingly well-understood phenomenon, whose implications had painted Multiplex into a difficult corner.

The company continued to cling to its old mental model, to justify a strategy of focusing on high-end segments in which buyers were still willing to pay a premium for superior value and conceding the low-price markets to rivals. These "low-end" entrants were able to parlay increased volume into ever lower costs. Meanwhile, as the high end of the market continued to shrink, Multiplex faced sagging capacity utilization and rising unit costs, which placed the company at a further disadvantage in the growing commodity segments.

Because this strategic track was so unappealing, Multiplex management decided to challenge the premises they were following. Management identified three premises derived from their mental models of the operation of their markets. These premises dealt with the attractiveness of the low end of their markets, the process of market saturation, and the ways that customers exercised bargaining power.

Each of these mental models was well accepted in practice, widely communicated in planning documents and planning meetings—and potentially misleading. In combination they led Multiplex into several pitfalls, including making myopic decisions, triggering a self-fulfilling prophecy that accentuated the problem, and foreclosing the consideration of other strategic options:

• *Myopic Decisions:* Because they believed that profits were in the high end, and so the low-end market didn't count, Multiplex managers did not defend the low end against new competitors. It lost contact with these customers and rivals moved in. In industry after industry, from mainframes to motorcycles, the long-run threats are more likely to come from below than above, but their mental model kept Multiplex management from seeing this threat until the new entrants were too entrenched to dislodge. Collective myopia is especially prevalent within organizations that carefully segment their activities and keep functions separate and distinct. Even when these employees come together on teams, they tend to retain the functional blinders of their independent "thought worlds," and so have difficulty forging mutual mental models.

• *Self-fulfilling Prophecies:* Multiplex apparently had unwittingly contributed to two "self-fulfilling prophecies" because of flaws in its collective mental models. First, because it assumed market saturation was irreversible, it cut back on marketing and development rather than seeking to attract new customers, slowing growth and leading to further retrenchment. This pattern was reminiscent of the behavior of U.S. radio manufacturers in the late 1970s who concluded their market was saturated. By cutting back on new product development and marketing, they not only ensured the prophecy came true but created an opportunity for Japanese competitors to move in. Unencumbered with the mental models of domestic manufacturers, these new entrants proceeded to flood the market with a variety of new features, colors and styles. This lifted market growth over expectations by 3 percent per annum in the early 1980s—but this was too late for the U.S. manufacturers who had already begun their exit.

A second self-fulfilling prophecy was the view of Multiplex managers that interactions with customers were a zero-sum game. Managers assumed the use of their product by their customers created a fixed amount of economic value and powerful customers could use their leverage to take more of this value from the company. The downside of this mind-set was the encouragement of adversarial relationships with several of the firm's largest accounts, which, in turn, led to a zero-sum game. When managers recognized this self-defeating model, they began searching for more cooperative relationships such as joint technical programs and information-sharing activities to overcome the climate of distrust.

• *Foreclosed Options:* As with the example of U.S. radio manufacturers, mental models often foreclose options for the firm. An especially influential mental model within the Multiplex management team was the image of a "stuck in the middle" competitor—neither differentiated through superior customer value nor able to achieve the lowest delivered cost. Believing they had to choose between the two options, managers migrated out of low-cost segments to concentrate on the high end. By running all their decisions through this filter, they failed to see that it might be possible for them to use a "play the spread" strategy that has been employed successfully in other industries. This strategy combines superior customer value and the lowest manufacturing and distribution costs, using a modest price premium and low operating costs to produce gross margins sufficient to cover the extra overhead and marketing costs. But this option was fore-closed by the company's mental model.

Companies can avoid these pitfalls and improve their mental models only if they can actually see what models they are using. The most important step in understanding and changing mental models is to bring them out into the open.

Bringing Mental Models into the Open

By identifying its implicit mental models, Multiplex had taken an important step. The danger with mental models is not whether they are right or wrong, for all models are simplifications. The pitfalls arise when the models are tacit (i.e., functioning below the level of awareness) and therefore cannot be scrutinized and challenged. Many managers work on the basis of a tacit model that says product design is a low-level, cosmetic function to be done at the last minute. Because these managers remain unaware of this particular mental model, it remains unexamined and unchanged. Meanwhile, firms such as Braun excel by recognizing that good design not only appeals to the eye but is reliable and economical to manufacture and service. For firms without this enlightened interpretation, the gap between the tacit mental model and competitive reality leads to increasingly counterproductive actions. Identification of those models is the centerpiece of the learning process that was instituted at Shell Oil, as described in the boxed insert.

Assessing Advantage. One important dimension that shapes mental models is whether the company focuses on customers or competitors in assessing where and how they have gained a competitive advantage.[10] The competitor-centered General Electric Aircraft Engine Business Group strives to "beat Pratt & Whitney," meaning managers are concerned most about points of comparison of the two firms that reveal which has the lead in performance, service coverage, and so on. Conversely, a customer-oriented publisher of specialty magazines argued that it was not necessary to pay close attention to its myriad competitors, because what counted was the firm's ability to position their magazines to satisfy distinct life-style segments.

Either type of focus—on the customer or competitor—in isolation could eventually become a misleading mental model, narrowing the scan

USING SCENARIOS TO SHAKE LOOSE THE MODELS AT SHELL

Shell Oil views institutional learning as "the process whereby management teams change their shared mental models of their company, their markets, and their competitors." One way this institutional learning is triggered is through scenarios, which are developed by planners serving as the facilitators, catalysts and accelerators of the learning process.[9] The first step is to interview the management team and get the mental model of their strategies on paper. A good deal of learning happens when the inconsistencies and conflicts between team members are identified and resolved. Once this is done, the consequences for their strategy of various possibilities in the environment (a major change in the price of oil, for instance), can be studied. If these explicit strategies are modeled on the computer, then the dynamics are clearly revealed. Further learning takes place as the team considers how changes in their mental model can improve the outcome. Recently, a major carpet manufacturer used a variant of this process to get its management team to face up to three unpleasant realities: the power of their fiber suppliers was growing because of the visibility of their brand names with the consumers, the retailers were consolidating and wielding more power, and the manufacturer did not have a differentiated product. To avoid the inevitable squeeze, the company exited the carpet market.

of the market. A competitor-centered focus not only blocks the view of customer shifts but also of new competitors. When Echard Pfeiffer became CEO of Compaq Computers he recognized the almost exclusive focus on IBM as a major flaw. "You know 'IBM did this, and how can we outdo them, how do we make it better and faster?' It was our total focus. The addition of second-tier pricing wasn't welcome because it deviated from that focus. We didn't recognize who the new competition would be." But customer-oriented firms are equally vulnerable to myopia. By focusing so heavily on customer sources of information they may overlook shifting competitive forces until it is too late. The magazine publisher whose sole focus was on market positioning was vulnerable to a consolidation of competitors in adjacent segments of the market that was rapidly changing the economics of printing and distribution.

The market-driven organization achieves a balance between customer and competitor perspectives. It avoids the simplification inherent in representations that are overly biased toward either market player. It also constantly challenges its own mental models to identify weaknesses and assure they are aligned with the market.

IMPROVING MARKET SENSING

Usually, it takes an outside trigger to create widespread recognition of the need to improve the depth, quality and timeliness of the base of market knowledge and its availability when decisions have to be made. The usual triggers are large and unexplained performance gaps, unexpected moves by previously ignored competitors, belated recognition of market opportunities missed, or uneasiness with the viability of the strategy. But companies can develop greater sensing capabilities without waiting for a crisis.

How should businesses aspiring to become better educated about their markets proceed? Working to improve the sensing activities discussed above is an important step. But there are other ways to improve the sensing capability.

• *Assess Your Sensing Abilities*. Early in the improvement program, a self-assessment or, even better, a benchmark study of best practices is needed to identify learning disabilities and areas where changes are needed. The questions posed in "Assessing the Market Sensing Capability" in the Appendix of this book suggest, but don't limit, the breadth of an assessment. Unacceptable answers to the assessment questions become the basis for an improvement program. The most compelling motivation for such a program is to find a major deficiency compared to a competitor who represents "best practices." One consumer goods company with a long-standing commitment to understanding its customers, backed up with significant budgets, found to its dismay that it was two to four years behind its major Japanese competitors in its ability to identify emerging or latent needs. Needless to say, current practices were soon overhauled to close the gap.

• *Make Business and Marketing Plans True Learning Tools*. Another device for self-improvement is to shift the emphasis of the business and marketing plans from static descriptions of the current situation, with some extrapolations into the future, into true learning tools. In these plans there is often a central section summarizing what was learned about the market during the past year. Each of these lessons is then discussed in terms of its implications for the strategy of the business. This process will help create heightened sensitivity to surprises, emerging trends and new market requirements and bring them to the attention of others who might be able to use the information.

• *Map the Market-Learning Process.* Deeper insights into the ability of a business to learn about its markets comes from a mapping of the prevailing processes for sensing and sense making. These maps describe sequences of activities with clear beginning and ending points, and reveal where each of the activities is located. Although this process is rarely neat or easy, it is a tremendous learning experience. The mapping itself should be guided by the following questions: Where does the customer and competitor information enter the organization? How is the information provided? How is it distributed? Where is it stored? How is the stored information retrieved? What are the barriers to retrieval? When are specific studies commissioned? Who is responsible at each stage of the process? Is there consistent oversight or sharp disconnects? In particular does the marketing research function play a continuing role or are there handoffs to outside suppliers?

Another kind of mapping asks where and when market sensing is done in core business processes. One telecommunication equipment firm found it was surprisingly spasmodic when it reviewed the product development process for a major project that had failed. After carefully mapping a sequence of activities and decisions that stretched over four years, there was collective surprise upon realizing there had been only one formal market study. Worse, this study was done at an early stage in the development. Thereafter, the team had become enmeshed in the technical development, prototype testing, and regulatory and budget approval activities. As time passed and the product concept evolved, the conclusions of the study became outdated, but the development team made no visits to customers and did not test their assumptions about customer needs and trade-offs. Competitive activity was monitored, but only to check on their technical performance. Having lost touch with their market early in the project, it was no surprise the team did not anticipate emerging networking requirements of customers their project couldn't satisfy.

THE COLLECTIVE MEMORY

The capability for market sensing is part of a learning process. The organization collects information about the market to become more aware of opportunities to create value. The firm learns how to position itself to take advantage of those opportunities. But great "senses"—even with effective mental models that don't limit the view of the world—are not enough. The information that is gathered by the sensing process must be processed into knowledge that can be accessed when needed.

The approaches described above contribute to the superior ability of market-driven firms in sensing their markets. But where does all this information about markets generated by the sensing process and all the knowledge created through the sense-making process go? Unless there is a collective memory—a shared knowledge base—for the organization, all these insights will be lost.

To establish a continuous process of learning, the organization has to have a way to capture and retain the information and knowledge it has collected. The entire organization needs to be able to access this knowledge quickly and efficiently. Advances in information technology have made the process of designing and building these shared knowledge bases on a large scale much easier. Chapter 6 examines strategies for developing and managing this shared knowledge base.

Chapter Six

The Shared Knowledge Base

All the market sensing in the world will be for naught if people in the organization cannot access market knowledge when they need it. This was the problem faced by IBM before it used its own technology to unblock the flow of competitive information. At the peak of confusion, there were 49 departments in 27 organizations each studying the same competitors. Literally hundreds of people were analyzing the data, but they seldom knew what others were doing or shared their conclusions. The impediments were local databases and files, and locally restricted delivery vehicles and newsletters. The information and interpretations could have been widely useful, if they could have been found. Yet there were few incentives to surmount the systems barriers and integrate the knowledge. Excuses ranged from "It's too secret to put in a database" to "We don't have the time to be contacted by everyone in the corporation for the details . . ." and "My database is better and serves a different community."

A top-down intervention was needed to create a common worldwide competitor analysis system of players and searchers. The "players" compiled and entered the data into an integrated database containing full text or abstracts on more than 1.2 million items from internal sources, vendors and publishers. The "searchers" in marketing, development and research could access all this information through a network and database search engine that could easily extract data in response to specific inquiries. The payoff from this system investment was considerable. First, the analyses of competitors were improved, with the ability to identify and cross-validate patterns of behavior across different countries and functions. Second, the squeezing out of redundancy and duplicated effort meant more analyses could be undertaken with the same head count. This was important for an organization trying to keep track of five thousand competitors. Third, there were fewer surprises since news of anticipated competitors' moves was broadcast more widely, and field people could be alerted more readily.

Enhancing the Memory of the Firm

The knowledge base of a market-driven organization is arguably its most valuable asset. Some of the knowledge is the raw material the firm processes and sells—think especially of the work of consultants and employees in financial services or software firms. More knowledge is deeply embedded in the core processes. What distinguishes a market-driven firm is the depth and timeliness of market knowledge that enables it to anticipate market opportunities and respond faster than its rivals. When this knowledge is widely shared, it is a common reference point and assumption set that ensures the strategy is coherent rather than a disconnected set of activities.

Memory mechanisms are needed so that useful lessons are captured, conserved, and readily retrieved when needed. The most familiar memory repositories are institutional policies, procedures and rules. Firms are increasingly using information technology to create integrated databases with expert systems and decision calculus models embedded in them to enrich and maintain the collective memory. These technology fixes will only provide lasting aids to memory if supported by organizational processes that promote team learning and avoid the purging of memory through turnovers and transfers.

Few organizations match Honda's ability to learn, remember, and act with agility.[1] Their experience provides instructive guidelines for designing a market-driven memory:

- The key learning unit is the multifunctional team, which is embedded in a compressed organizational structure that observes few hierarchical distinctions. The absence of hierarchy and seniority makes it easier for ideas to be judged on their merit rather than on the basis of conventional wisdom. When teams are disbanded, their members are soon assigned to new programs, which speeds the percolation of knowledge through the organization.

- Team members are able to build careers with promotion prospects that are based on mastery of an area of expertise. These are not blinkered specialists because they have ample opportunities for brief rotations into other functions. Thus, as soon as a team is formed, it has a gateway to the collective knowledge of Honda through the team members' personal knowledge and networks of colleagues with similar expertise.

- Teams are guided by a deeply held belief that it is not possible to comprehend a market by relying solely on secondhand reports. Design teams are expected to be in the field regularly to gain shared insights.

- Failure is not stigmatized, which encourages teams to experiment. For example, the 90 percent or so of experimental research projects that Honda estimates fail the first time are analyzed for lessons on what to avoid and results are pooled for possible use in future projects.

Honda's ability to learn as an organization, and to remember this collective experience, depends on having this memory reside within individuals but remain at the service of cross-functional teams. The choice of what to learn is guided by a widely shared vision of Honda's competencies, markets and strategy. A shared vision has a very positive influence on the capacity to learn, because people are encouraged to expose their ways of thinking and seek new ways of thinking in order to reach the future implied by the vision.

When these processes for gathering and sharing knowledge are not in place, collective amnesia can result. Market knowledge is not fully captured in a usable form until the lessons and insights are transferred beyond those who gained the experience. These transfers are most likely to be thwarted by management turnover, which appears to be happening at an accelerated pace due to organizational downsizing, as well as misguided policies of rapid rotation and promotion that disrupt continuity. Similar problems occur when teams and task forces are disbanded too quickly, and no plans are made to place team members in positions where they can contribute to new teams. A more subtle problem of knowledge transfer with equally corrosive effects on memory is overreliance on consultants and outside research agencies. Outsourcing is an appealing way to control the head count and apply outside expertise for immediate problem-solving purposes. The knowledge gained at great cost, however, won't have much lasting value if the only trace is a shelf full of bound project reports.

Once knowledge has been captured in the organization, it won't necessarily be retained or accessible. Retention requires that the insights, policies, procedures and ongoing routines that demonstrate the lessons are regularly used and refreshed to keep them up to date. Information systems can solve some of the memory problems, for once the knowledge is codified within a system, it usually remains there in the form it was entered. But this doesn't mean it can be retrieved and put to work. Incompatible formats, databases that cannot be integrated, or software impediments may make it impossible to extract the necessary lessons in usable form.

Market-driven organizations can take two important steps to develop a shared knowledge base:

- Build systems for synergistic information distribution that are accessible throughout the organization to assure that relevant facts and insights are available when and where they are needed.
- Track strategic knowledge about market structure, response and value creation that contribute the perspectives needed to develop informed decisions.

SYNERGISTIC INFORMATION DISTRIBUTION

Most organizations don't know what they know. They may have good systems for storing and locating "hard" routine accounting and sales data, but otherwise have problems finding where a certain piece of data is known within the organization or assembling all the needed pieces in one place. Once the raw data has been organized so that useful information is revealed, the challenge is getting it to those who need it. The enemy of information distribution is the organizational chimneys or silos that bottle up information vertically within functions. This is especially true of competitor information: manufacturing may be aware of certain activity through common equipment suppliers, sales hears about initiatives from distributors and collects rumors from customers, while engineering may have hired recently from a competitor.

Recent developments in information technology are both enemies and aids to information access and distribution. On one hand, firms are being swamped by an avalanche of cheap but undigested data that their systems dispense so freely. At the same time, there are other advances that can help treat this indigestion while deepening market understanding and building relationships. *Data mining* techniques coax hidden meaning from data warehouses while *intranets* pass the information more freely around the organization. Firms may now be as confused as before, but at a higher level.

Coaxing Meaning from Databases

Information will remain out of touch if it is locked in the form of gigabytes of raw data that overwhelm one's capacity to identify useful patterns. The key to extracting meaning is a new generation of data-mining tools that use statistical models and artificial intelligence to identify what's worth noting and what can be ignored.

Consider MCI's use of data-mining techniques to comb through their database of 140 million households, each described on as many as 10,000 attributes such as life-style, income, location and past calling habits. For example, they would like to identify all those who have a high likelihood of switching to a rival, so they can either be encouraged to leave if they are unprofitable or enticed to stay with special rates and services. The problem is to know which variables are the best to monitor, and within what range of values. Is a declining monthly bill more significant than calls to MCI service lines? The technology can sift through all the possibilities to identify the most useful, and do it far faster than a human analyst.

Adroit miners of data such as MCI have mastered the four steps of the knowledge discovery process:[2]

1. *Data warehousing* is an enterprise-wide data depository that draws on firm-relevant internal systems such as transaction processing and costing.
2. *Discovery* uses descriptive statistics and visualization techniques to collapse the data into summary measures, build predictive models in which a number of variables are used to specify the value of a dependent variable (such as responding to an offer or remaining loyal) or to

cluster customers into more or less homogeneous groups. The purpose is to identify interesting relationships that hadn't been seen before.

3. *Confirmation* is the process of validating the models on a new set of data to see if the findings are the same. If not, it's back to the drawing board to try a new model.

4. *Scoring* is the application of a valid model to the whole database. For example, American Express developed a neural network model that mimics the processes of the human brain to find patterns in the billions of transactions in its database that tell how and where card members use their cards. The results are used to create "purchase propensity scores" for each card member. With these scores, American Express can send offers in billing statements from affiliated merchants to the card members that are most likely to respond.

Making Market Information Available: Unleashing the Intranet

The biggest ally in the battle to disseminate information broadly and put it to work quickly is the Intranet. Instead of separate functions working hard to pass around information in buckets, it is now feasible for separate functions to dip into the same information pool. Intranets apply standard Internet protocols—simple software-based rules for the transmission of data across networks—to allow different networks within the firm to speak to each other, often for the first time. This provides a new medium to exchange information and ideas, establish mutual goals and track progress. The simple "page and link" metaphor of the Internet, where one finds information by clicking on highlighted words or phrases on a Web page, provides a key to previously inaccessible data. Because the network is internal to the firm, an Intranet is more secure than the Internet.

Intranets are a simple concept with profound implications. Not surprisingly, computer companies were the first to see and seize on the possibilities. DEC, Dell and Intuit have each implemented sophisticated call centers that capture customer information (as varied as leads, profiles, interactions, complaints, purchase history and so forth) and make it accessible, on demand, from a single source via an Intranet. This enables information sharing among such groups as sales, customer order management and technical support.

The information content embedded in an Intranet is increasingly being made available to customers via "extranets" which link customer and supplier networks. Federal Express began giving their customers access to their internal package tracking system via the World Wide Web in 1995. Until recently, U.S. West could only give customers vague, uninformed estimates of how long it would take to deliver a new service, because customer service representatives couldn't access the internal databases where the information resided. Now it is readily available to both internal and external users.

One consequence of these new capabilities is that some companies are aligning their traditional marketing research functions much more closely with their information technology departments. Their intent is to overcome the problems of uncoordinated and incompatible systems and databases, while speeding the dissemination of the data captured by these systems. This enhanced market research function now has responsibility for system integration, and becomes a cross-functional facilitator and informed interpreter, rather than simply a data provider and analysis resource.

CONVERTING INFORMATION INTO STRATEGIC KNOWLEDGE

What knowledge should the organization focus on developing? Simply packing the shared knowledge base with undigested information is about as useful as reading an encyclopedia cover to cover. Information only becomes knowledge when it is converted into a solid basis for action. Managers want answers to questions that are not just interesting but illuminate pivotal strategic issues and clarify the direction to follow. Then market knowledge has high leverage during the strategy dialogue. The primary issues to be addressed are:

- *Market structure:* How are the competitive boundaries shifting and market segments evolving?
- *Market responses:* What are the drivers of customer value and retention and how will consumers, competitors and channels respond to these drivers?
- *Market economics:* Where are we making money, and what moves will improve our profitability? Where is value migrating in the market, and how will that impact us?

Making knowledge more explicit is crucial to understanding each of these issues. Usually the knowledge in these areas is tacit. It is not likely to be in a codified form in databases, information systems or documents. It is what we know, but can't readily explain. Because it is unstructured the answer varies with the context; it takes the form of wisdom and experience—not formal and explicit rules and procedures. When knowledge is mostly tacit it is much harder to verify that it is still valid, or ever was valid. What is knowledge and what is untested conventional wisdom or "facts" that started life as wishes and were repeated so often they became accepted as reality? To be tested, discussed and challenged, this tacit knowledge must be made explicit.[3] For example, managers at medical equipment supplier Medcom had tremendous differences of opinion about strategies for setting prices for a new product. The company used a knowledge gathering process to move from opinions to explicit knowledge about the market, as described in the boxed insert.[4]

Market-driven organizations recognize there is an inherent and irreducible uncertainty to tough strategic choices. They also know they can make better decisions if their market knowledge is more explicit, empirically grounded and widely available so it can be critically scrutinized. What are these best practice companies doing to become more knowledgeable?

Knowledge of Market Structure

To accurately assess their markets, companies need to understand the current market structure. Outdated and static views of the structure—based on standard industrial classification (SIC) schemes, industry convention or convenient measures such as customer size or demographics—can limit market knowledge. When asked why they rely on these measures, managers usually give the following excuses:

- "We've always done it this way"
- "That's the way we are organized"
- "That's the way our competitors do it"
- "That's the way the data are given to us (by the trade association or census bureau)"

To break free of these conventional approaches, companies need to be able to gather knowledge about the structure of their markets as they

HOW MEDCOM BRINGS KNOWLEDGE TO PRICING DECISIONS

Pricing decisions are strategically significant because of the leverage on profits (a 1 percent increase in price will increase profits by 11 percent in the average Standard & Poor's 500 firm with 9 percent operating income—so long as volume is maintained), and the influence on customer perceptions and competitor responses. All these factors were being weighed when Medcom began the pricing process for its new blood analyzer. A new technology platform meant the product could be adapted to serve several segments.

Sharp differences of opinion on the appropriate launch price soon emerged. The finance people argued for a price based on projected costs and customary mark-ups. They had little confidence in the hunches (as they saw them) of the marketing people. The product manager advocated an aggressive penetration price to forestall any moves by potential entrants and build share rapidly before their major rival could respond. The sales manager supported lower price levels because it would make the selling job easier—but didn't see the point of a very low initial price. The general manager who was naturally cautious about strategic moves wanted a higher price to begin with, so they could gauge the response to the unproven features and also leave room to reduce prices later.

It was soon evident that the firm lacked essential knowledge about the market. How important were price and product attributes to the different segments? How would the performance of the new equipment compare to competition on these attributes? How quickly could competitors respond—what development activities did they have underway? How would the different segments respond—what were their preferences, volumes, and likely willingness to purchase? Each member of the group could cite evidence for their position, but there was no shared knowledge to resolve the disputes.

To avoid a complete stalemate, studies were undertaken to address these issues. The results provided a common basis for discussion. Any disagreements or deviating opinions had to be substantiated. All this took time, but yielded a far more effective pricing structure that reflected market complexities and realities. The most important conclusion was to develop more variants with differentiated prices to respond to the segment differences in price responsiveness that were uncovered.

continue to shift under pressure from changes in technology, customer requirements and competitor moves.

Companies pay a high price when they are slow to recognize new segments or competitors. Intel was slow to recognize the appeal of "sub-$1,000" personal computers, and as late as 1997 was still denying that these "good enough" machines would ever become popular. In part this new category did not fit its strategy of pushing the PC market forward with ever faster and more powerful microprocessors. Concerns about the effect of low-cost microprocessors on its margins also colored the thinking of Intel's management. They were not prepared when Compaq successfully launched low-cost machines with cheaper and less powerful chips from AMD, and customers rushed to buy them because they adequately performed basic functions. Not only did they miss the market by a year, their smaller rivals gained a toehold, and a costly crash program with 600 of their top chip designers had to be mounted so they could get back in the game.

When Intel eventually acted, it chose a classic segmentation strategy. Different chips were aimed at specific markets such as "sub-$1,000" PCs, mid-tier "performance" PCs and powerful corporate servers. That meant the company could balance its profits from chips like the Celerons, which sold for as little as $86, with highly profitable workstation and server chips, which sold for $2,000 and served totally different markets.

While the overheated turbulence of the PC market is perhaps a special case, few industries are exempt from evolutionary forces. Retail banks, for example, are being attacked on many fronts: money-market mutual funds are displacing basic checking and savings accounts, non-banks are major issuers of credit cards, and manufacturing firms with financial subsidiaries like GE Capital are in pursuit of the lending and leasing market.

Developing New Knowledge of Market Structure

Following conventional guidelines is likely to lead to imitative strategies, and to obscure emerging opportunities. Strategically useful market knowledge has a more ambitious goal, which requires satisfying three conditions:[5]

- *Market boundaries are defined by competitors and customers.* Market-driven firms use potential customers and competitors to define the boundaries of the market rather than relying on preexisting definitions of the market. This definition will be jointly informed by customers' perceptions of "substitutes-in-use" and the assessment of present and prospective rivals who have the capability to serve the needs of the target competitors.

- *Segments are distinct.* The dissection of the market into segments should result in homogenous groups of customers, where the groups are:

  1. Sufficiently *distinctive* in consumer needs, purchase criteria and behavior, and cost and capital requirements, that meaningful differences in strategies to serve the groups can be justified,
  2. *Substantial* enough to justify the additional costs of strategies tailored to the segments,
  3. *Identifiable* so each segment group can be efficiently reached with a targeted sales and communications effort,
  4. *Durable* enough that the differences used to justify the distinct strategies will not evaporate before the profit potential is realized.

- *Market evolution is anticipated.* Finally, the segmentation scheme should be more like a movie that anticipates how the market will evolve in the future, and explains the migration of customers between segments, rather than a static snapshot of a present that is soon obsolete.

A dynamic view is especially needed in markets like data communications equipment where new segments keep emerging. Some customers have stayed with centralized approaches with purchasing controlled by a strong MIS department. In a distributed computing environment it is more likely that different user groups within the firm will bypass MIS and set up their own networks. To combat the chaos and inefficiency of incompatible approaches that can't talk to each other, many firms are either consolidating these networks or starting all over with a clean sheet of paper and designing a single integrated architecture. Each of these phases brings different needs and decision makers into play that vendors must anticipate.

Knowledge of Market Response

The decisions to launch a new product, change a pricing structure, invest in more salespeople, or cut an advertising budget have one thing in common. They are risky and often irreversible choices that depend on sound assumptions and beliefs about the shape of the relationship between the change to be made and the response of the market. If these judgments are wrong the strategic moves will be ineffective or counterproductive.

Knowledgeable judgments require deep insight into the consumer acquisition and usage experience. This was, of course, the theme of the chapter on market sensing. Beyond this, the capability should be directed toward getting answers to three strategic questions:

1. What are the drivers of customer satisfaction and value?
2. What are the relationships between the variables we manage and the response of the market?
3. What are the relationships between customer behavior and measures of performance such as customer loyalty, share and profitability?

A market-driven organization is better equipped to answer these questions with confidence and take forceful action. How can each of these questions be answered?

Drivers of Customer Value and Satisfaction

These drivers can be derived from a familiar three-step process. First, what are the attributes of the product or service that create value for customers? These attributes go well beyond the physical or manifest features, to encompass everything that augments the core product. In the lodging market, the key attributes are honoring reservations on time, good value for money, and the quality and amenities of the guest rooms. Often these attributes can be revealed by specifying the value equation for the customers; that is, how do they decide the perceived benefits exceed the identifiable total costs over the life cycle?

The second step digs deeper to find out which attributes are most important to customers, and how these importance weights differ by segment. This is an essential step for if you don't know the relative importance weights you won't know where to put your effort. As described in the boxed insert, Ford used this process to determine that fixing the car

---

DRIVING CUSTOMER SATISFACTION

Knowledge of customer satisfaction was crucial to Ford when it undertook a major program to improve the parts and service organization which supported its 5,000 dealers. Managers were fortunate to have a database with detailed information on 200,000 customers over a five-year period. This database had long been used to develop the features and prices for new vehicles, but never applied to understanding the role of the service component. They found that customer satisfaction was driven by three factors: vehicle reliability, durability and serviceability (accounting for 40 percent of the variability in satisfaction), the sales experience (30 percent) and service (the remaining 30 percent). But which part of the service experience mattered most? Where should the improvement effort be directed for greatest effect? Again the database revealed three drivers of service quality:

- Customer handling = 9% of total satisfaction
  - courtesy and integrity
  - timeliness
  - convenience
- Fix it right the first time (technical fix) = 15% of total satisfaction
- Parts availability/ready on time = 6% of total satisfaction

The surprise here was that having the repaired car ready on time was only half as important as getting it fixed right the first time.

Further investigation showed that the service organization played a broader role in vehicle satisfaction through its ability to communicate customer and dealer concerns to the product development group. Armed with this knowledge the division could see where it needed to direct its improvement program.

---

right the first time was more important to customers than having the job done on time.[6]

The final step is to learn how customers judge our performance on each driver using the toughest standard—the best of the target competitors. When 3M did a fifteen-country study of the drivers of customer satisfaction with their consumable medical products, managers expected product attributes would dominate. After all, the company was the global leader and had pioneered many of the products such as disposable face masks, gowns and so forth. Imagine their surprise when customers replied that what mattered most was sales support and availability. What really hurt was hearing the customers say that all the products were acceptable and no one offered noticeably superior performance. Of greater concern was the finding that local competitors in each country market were often viewed as offering superior service and better availability. This knowledge led to some long overdue changes in 3M's distribution systems and dealer policies.

Knowledge About Strategic Linkages

The managers of market-driven organizations know—with confidence— the relationship between the variables they influence and the responses of their customers. They can track their success from management decisions and investments in assets and capabilities through employee attitudes to customer satisfaction and retention and financial performance.

Most business models that provide an integrated picture of all the strategic linkages are variants of the so-called balanced score cards that are currently fashionable. However, in best-practice companies, the relationships between the hard financial numbers and softer data on employee attitudes and customer satisfaction are not just untested assumptions. This greatly improves the quality of strategic thinking, for when key linkages can be quantified and scrutinized the discussion is about how to act on what has been learned rather than uninformed disagreements and unresolvable debates.

The models of these relationships are purpose-built, so no two models can or should look alike. What works for a labor-intensive general merchandiser like Sears, with 820 stores and millions of customers, will look very different from the business model of a fast-food chain or a chip fabricator like Advanced Micro Devices. Yet all three models will reveal the critical relationships that link management behavior to financial results.

The experience of Sears reveals both what is possible and how these models can be used to run a company. What is unusual about their model is that it is solidly based on statistically verified leading indicators, rather than the lagging indicators of financial performance. The raw material for the model was a complete array of financial measures for all full-line stores, hundreds of thousands of data points from a 68-question survey of

FIGURE 6–1

Modeling the Strategic Linkages: Sears, Roebuck

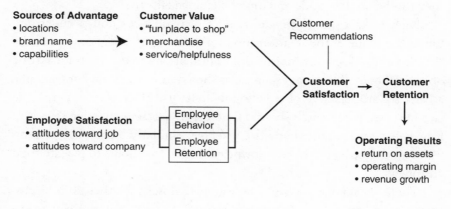

employee satisfaction given every two years, and millions of data points on customer satisfaction. These data were organized by the structure of Figure 6–1,[7] and used causal modeling to identify strong and weak relationships.

The results of the modeling effort were impressive; sometimes eye-opening and other times confirming management's beliefs about the real drivers of performance. For example, they learned that, "a 5 point improvement in employee attitudes will drive a 1.3 point improvement in customer satisfaction, which in turn will drive a 0.5 percent improvement in revenue growth."[8] Employee attitudes and satisfaction drove customer service and employee turnover. With turnover as high as 75 percent in some stores any steps to reduce it would simultaneously improve service, since employees with longer service are more knowledgeable, and cut the costs of recruiting and training new staff. Two dimensions of employee attitudes—toward the job and toward the company—had the greatest effect on loyalty. Their conclusion was that without a trained, literate, motivated and competent work force, with some decision-making responsibility, it was not possible to get satisfied customers no matter how good the merchandise offering.

Firms in service industries are finding that employee satisfaction has such a close relationship to customer satisfaction—and eventually customer retention—that it can almost stand as a proxy. Such proxy measures are valuable, for they provide a continuing report on management performance and because they have empirical validity they are accepted. Not only are they an essential ingredient in sound strategic thinking, but they can be used to guide and direct a change effort.

Each linkage in the model has its own nuances and peculiarities. Often the shape of the relationship is of greatest interest. Sometimes the "breakpoints" or discontinuities are of primary interest—both for setting objectives and allocating resources, as shown in Figure 6–2. For example, a bank set an objective of reducing its teller wait line at peak periods to two minutes, yet research showed that any investment to reduce the wait time below four minutes had little leverage. Similarly, a computer systems firm found they had to reduce downtime below four hours to placate their customers.[9]

These breakpoints have to be watched closely, for they shift as customer expectations evolve or competitors' improved performance sets new reference points.

Knowledge of Market Economics

If competition is a game then someone is keeping score. But when there are so many possible measures of performance to use for keeping score one is not always sure what game is being played. Firms routinely watch their market share, contribution margins, sales from new products, customer satisfaction (did we hit our target of a 90 percent rating of very or some-

FIGURE 6–2

Satisfaction Breakpoints

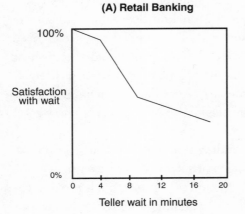

(A) Retail Banking

Satisfaction with wait

100% — 0%

0 4 8 12 16 20

Teller wait in minutes

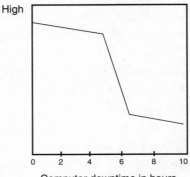

(B) Computer Systems

High

0 2 4 6 8 10

Computer downtime in hours

what satisfied?), customer service (are we better or worse at on-time deliveries?), while tallying product defects (are they rising or falling and where?), customer inquiries—and many other factors.

Some of these measures are "hard" and historical, while others are "soft" but good leading indicators. Some have high credence among top management, others are dismissed because of lack of reliability or validity. Different people or functions have their favorites, that have meaning to them. The resulting confusion makes it difficult to share knowledge meaningfully about market performance.

What sets market-driven firms apart is the priority they assign to a few common indicators that reveal where, how and when they are making money. They know that "what gets measured gets managed" and that their customer portfolio is an asset to be managed like any other asset. There is no surefire recipe to say what belongs in this part of the knowledge base—it all depends on what drives performance. Nonetheless, few firms will achieve superior long-run profitability without managing these indicators:

- value of the customer portfolio
- rate of migration of value
- return on marketing initiatives

Valuing the Customer Portfolio

Not all customers are equally valuable. Yet few firms know which of their customers are profitable and which are being subsidized. When they finally find out the results are eye-opening. For example, retail banks and other financial service firms have struggled for years to estimate customer profitability because of the limitations of their systems. If a customer had a current account they couldn't tell whether she also had a mortgage, credit card, savings account or mutual fund, or what it cost to serve her.

When one money-center bank finally overcame these barriers, it found that 10 percent of its retail banking customers were subsidizing the losses from 60 percent of the customers.[10] As shown in Figure 6–3, the bank segmented its customers by cost to serve (where a high-maintenance customer would make fifteen or more visits a month to a branch), and risk-adjusted revenue (where low revenue would be below $100 per month, largely because they carried a small balance).

These findings prompted the bank to rethink its strategy. Many com-

FIGURE 6–3

Profitability of Retail Bank Customers

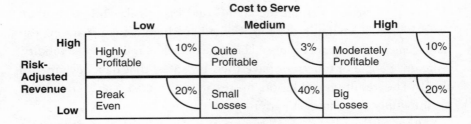

pelling questions had to be answered: Why are we promoting accounts with a minimum $300 balance? How can we add value and retain the top 10 percent of our accounts? Will the non-banks such as Merrill-Lynch continue to pick off these accounts? How can we make money from the rest of the accounts? What about more cross-selling?

Similar results are being found by many companies. In the cellular phone industry the "best" accounts may be ten times as profitable as the "worst." But if you don't know what your customers are worth it is hard to make sound decisions about how to serve them. Fortunately the search for answers about profitability is becoming easier.

First is the shift from measuring customer satisfaction to loyalty. The economics of customer retention are so persuasive that these measures have become a focal point of the knowledge base. Second, the tools of activity-based (ABC) accounting are steadily being refined. These approaches yield much sharper insights than the usual method of comparing the profitability of segments and accounts according to their relative contribution margins after direct costs and factory overheads have been assigned. One manufacturer used this yardstick to conclude that its small customers—who paid full price—were more profitable than the hard-bargaining large customers. Yet when full costs were properly assigned, it appeared that smaller accounts were actually unprofitable, because of the high costs of sales, ordering and engineering incurred on each of their small orders. This insight led to a round of price increases and a search for lower-cost distribution arrangements.

Finally, advances in information technology are helping firms surface the information they really need about the economics of their customer portfolio. At the leading edge of these advances is FedEx. For years, profits on package deliveries languished as prices were driven down by intense competition.[11] Between 1991 and 1995 average revenue dropped from a high of $17.33 to $14.62 per package. Only a doubling in volume kept profits from skidding. But in 1996 yields started to improve to $15.11.

The upturn in profits was aided by the newfound ability of the company to extract information about individual account profitability. It took a huge investment averaging between $2 and $2.5 billion per year to build the information infrastructure. This included installing computers at 100,000 customer sites and supplying proprietary software at another 650,000 sites, so all transactions could be completed digitally. Armed with the profit information FedEx sales people began dealing with unprofitable customers either by dropping them or winning price increases.

Tracking the Migration of Value

Measures of profitability are inevitably historic. But what about prospects for the future? Value migration provides a useful framework for keeping track of the market forces that will shape the answer. Value migrates when economic and shareholder value flows away from obsolete business models toward new competitive offerings. The U.S. steel industry saw its collective value seep away to low-cost foreign mills, aluminum and other materials and to minimills. The early stages of value migration are difficult to see, especially when the challenge comes from small players and nontraditional entities operating at the periphery of the market. It took a long time for the Big Three television networks to take seriously Turner Broadcasting, TCI and Blockbuster Video. Underlying all value migrations are an evolution in customer needs and new competitive alternatives for responding to these needs.

Good strategic thinking requires early measurable signs of value migration before the process begins to accelerate and it is too late to combat.[12] Useful early indicators include:

- declining share among "leading edge customers"—the ones that influence opinions
- deteriorating quality of share, reflecting higher turnover rates, reduced participation in growing segments, poorer profitability, and growing reliance on promotional discounts
- shrinking customers' share of their market (e.g., disk drives for mainframe computers)

- profits from new products below historic levels, because time-to-breakeven is longer while life cycles shorten

These factors all influence the acid test of value migration which is a declining ratio of market capitalization to revenues. This is the equity market's pronouncement of foreseeable trouble, and should mobilize the strategic thinking process to seek explanations and solutions.

Evaluating Returns on Marketing Initiatives

The usual procedures for evaluating investments are routinely ignored for marketing initiatives. Should we create a special sales force to open up a new market segment? launch a new advertising campaign? try a direct marketing campaign? or create a state-of-the-art web site? These decisions are treated as operating expenditures—as though the benefits were used up immediately.

The fallacy of a short-term, expense-oriented mind-set is that it leads to a "pay as you go" requirement that confuses cause and effect. Budgets for the sales force or advertising are set according to what can be afforded from next year's sales forecast, rather than making heavier investments that would spur future sales.

There are many indicators of an expense-driven mind-set. This thought process highlights the following questions:

- What is the sales forecast for next year?
- How many sales people can we afford at that sales level?
- Are our expenditures on advertising, sales, promotion and so forth (as a percent of sales) in line with our competitors?
- How can we cut these expenses?
- Are we gaining or losing share?

Certainly, these questions should be considered at some point: we need to know whether competitors are trying to outspend us, and marketing has been singularly unable to improve the productivity of its activities. The danger is giving primacy to these questions and falling back on arbitrary rules of thumb such as "we have to increase our spending in line with cost increases," or "20 percent of revenues should be spent on marketing."

Strategic insights come when marketing initiatives are seen as drivers of future revenue, and not the other way around. Building a customer base and brand equity is a long-run process of raising awareness, inducing trial and usage as a precursor to gaining customer loyalty, and then tightening the relationship as discussed in the following chapters. Why should marketing spending not be treated the same way as investments in quality improvement, systems for speeding the response to customer expectations or innovation that enhances performance? Otherwise, the integrity of the strategy is going to be compromised.

Accountants will resist efforts to capitalize marketing expenditures. They argue, with some justification, that much promotional advertising and sales activity is for short-term, defensive purposes. They are on weaker ground when they contend that the customer base can't be treated like the traditional plant and equipment assets which have an established market value, and can be traded. A further argument is that both the knowledge base and the customer base are intangible assets whose value will eventually show up as future profits, and don't need to be recognized on the balance sheet.

In the face of entrenched habits, the inertia of familiar procedures and the resistance of the accounting and finance community, change will only come when the mind-set shifts and credible evidence of the long-run value of marketing investments is presented. Such evidence is not easily attained, but as we saw in Chapter 5, the experimental procedures adopted by firms like Frito-Lay can be very influential. The replacement of the expense-driven mind-set with an investment mind-set[13] comes by giving primacy to the following questions:

- Are the returns on the current marketing investments satisfactory? What would happen if these investments were doubled? cut in half?
- Where can we most effectively invest to reduce customer acquisition costs and enhance the rate of retention?
- What is the quality of our customer base? Which customers should we drop or discourage because they have no lifetime value for us?

These are the questions that pervade the strategy dialogue in market-driven organizations. They replace the sterile negotiating game where marketing submits a high budget—knowing they will be given less than requested—and top management arbitrarily cuts the amount because they know the game that is being played. Instead of budgeting becoming a zero-sum gain with winners and losers, all functions participate in a transparent process that uses shared knowledge about market economics.

RETAINING KNOWLEDGE

Finally, companies need to hold onto their knowledge about how to learn so they can continually and consistently build their shared knowledge base. This helps improve the learning competency and avoid lapses in memory from management turnover and subcontracting.

Here is where managers need to ask hard questions about the role of the marketing research department: is it simply a purchasing agent for outside studies, or does it add value by contributing syntheses of market knowledge to the decision-making process? Just as important is the availability of staff teams and project groups with experienced members able to share and apply the collective learning. Market learning is of little use unless it is readily available to improve the quality of decisions.

Some firms are acknowledging that increasingly fluid organizational forms will disrupt their efforts to enhance internal continuity, and are turning to their subcontractors for help. Account people in advertising agencies and team leaders in consulting firms may be better informed about past market actions and are less likely to move around. To tap this source of knowledge firms have to be prepared to stay with a few outside sources and resist bringing in unproven entities in hopes of short-term savings on single projects. Market learning, wherever it is lodged, is the result of a long-run investment process.

Chapter Seven

Market Relating

Milliken & Company has garnered strong loyalty in the market for a mundane product by adroit market relating. Milliken sells shop towels to laundries, which then supply them to factories, garages and the like. Milliken's towels are indistinguishable from competitors, yet laundries willingly pay 10 to 15 percent more for them, and are strongly attached to the company. They are reciprocating with loyalty because of the great value they receive.

Milliken is not merely selling shop towels. It is creating relationships. Milliken gives the laundries special software to help them route their laundry trucks and handle their accounting. Milliken also trains their sales forces and undertakes marketing research to identify new prospects. No wonder the laundries feel obligated—in the good rather than the compulsory sense of the word. The benefits they receive are worth more than the price premium they pay. Higher profits and reduced competition are the rewards Milliken gets for continuing the program.

The market-driven organization has a superior capability in market relating. In contrast to the transaction mentality, it is focused on creating the kind of relationships with customers that were once the exclusive domain of small businesses. This chapter examines the distinctive orientation, knowledge and skills and integration of activities of a market-relating capability. It explores the spectrum of relationships between customers and firms. This will give us a sound basis for developing relationship-based strategies for consumer and business-to-business markets described in the next two chapters.

Costs of a Transaction Mentality

"As a merchant, you'd better have a friend in every town," says an old Middle Eastern proverb. Since ancient times, businesses have had close relationships with their customers. Before mass media, mass production, product standardization, and national or global opportunities, most firms stayed close to their markets. They knew their customers personally, understood what they wanted and earned their loyalty with personal attention. But such intimacy meant they had to stay small and local with high costs and limited assortments.

Then mass marketers, with lower costs, superior quality and wider assortments of mass-produced items, created efficiencies that could not be matched by smaller firms. For all their strengths however, these large organizations sacrificed traditional close personal relationships with customers. A transaction mentality took hold in which the sale was a conquest and encounters between salespeople and purchasing agents had an adversarial tone. These two negotiating parties—acting as agents for the rest of their organization—often obstructed the others' view into their organizations. Powerful sales forces also cut off market signals to the rest of the organization.

The remoteness of a transaction mentality had many negative consequences. More energy and marketing resources such as coupons and cents-off promotions were devoted to capturing the next sale rather than better satisfying existing customers. In business-to-business markets, a zero-sum mentality often prevailed in which the emphasis was on price bargaining with the outcome depending on who held the balance of power. Customers delighted in playing one supplier against another. The hard-bitten, unyielding purchasing agent was the hero.

This role was played with gusto by Jose Ignacio Lopez de Arriortria, the head of purchasing of General Motors in 1992–1993. He demanded and got major across-the-board price concessions that yielded huge savings for the company—in the short run. Later it became apparent the battered suppliers were only quoting to specifications and not investing in innovations they would share with GM. They rightly feared that any new designs or process improvements would simply be given to the lowest bidder in the next round of contract negotiations.

During the 1980s the costs of remoteness were becoming clearer.

Firms often had little knowledge of which customers were loyal—or why they were loyal. Nor could they tell which were profitable and worth retaining. There was a growing recognition of the limitations of large, impersonal surveys that yielded superficial insights without any sense of the purchase context. Japanese competitors, with a culture that emphasized deep, contextual insights and long-term trusting relationships, were demonstrating the value of deeper connections to the market.

Of course, market-driven firms have always resisted any tendency to dehumanize their customers and only deal with them through one-time transactions. Astute managers in both large and small firms have always recognized that the trust engendered by familiar brands and the continuing presence of knowledgeable salespeople were among their most valuable assets.

RELATING FOR ADVANTAGE

Today, market relationships have made a comeback. Nurturing these relationships has emerged as a top priority for most firms. Why the change in emphasis? Many managers have been persuaded by mounting evidence that keeping customers pays handsomely! For example, a study of one hundred companies in two dozen industries by Reichheld and Sasser found that firms could improve their average profitability per customer between 25 percent and 85 percent with each 5 percent increase in customer retention.[1]

Increased loyalty leads to greater profitability in two ways: First, it helps grow the customer base as the rate of defection slows. If the rate of new customer acquisitions stays steady but more customers are retained, the net effect is to grow the total number of customers. Second, loyal customers are more profitable. This second profit lever is due to the relationship of loyalty and the profit per customer.

There are many reasons why customers who have long been loyal (i.e., repurchase a high proportion of their needs from the same source) are much more profitable:

- *Lower costs to serve.* Loyal customers are easier and cheaper to service. Because they are familiar with the products and services they don't have as many questions, are less likely to make mistakes, and have adjusted their behavior to simplify their relations with the supplier.

- *Increased purchases*. They tend to buy more as time passes, either because they learn about other parts of the product line or they give a higher proportion of their spending to the favored source.
- *Less price sensitivity*. They tend to become less price sensitive and may pay a premium. As the relationship strengthens over time, they are less susceptible to competitors' appeals, and because they appreciate the value they are getting they are prepared to pay more.
- *Favorable word of mouth*. Finally, loyal buyers are more likely to pass on favorable recommendations to others who also tend to be higher quality prospects. This helps reduce the high costs of new customer acquisition. Much of the success of Intuit is attributed to the powerful word of mouth about its Quicken personal financial software.

Sustainable Advantages

Another reason for the rising interest in market relationships is that committed relationships are among the most durable of advantages because they are hard for competition to understand, copy, or displace. This is a persuasive argument when product-based advantages are short-lived and new competitors are posing challenges on all sides. Furthermore, with network technologies that enable addressability, interactivity, and demand chain coordination, firms now have both the motive and the means for moving closer to their customers.

BUILDING RELATIONSHIPS WITH THE MARKET

The hotel lodging industry illustrates both the size of the challenge and the potential payoff of a superior market-relating capability. Most hotels do a competent job of serving each guest, but seldom engender real loyalty. To be sure, there are some formidable barriers to overcome: the choice of hotel is often dictated by location and convenience considerations; most hotels in the same quality tier quickly copy each other and buy each other's properties so they become hard to distinguish; the choice of where to stay may be made by a third party such as a travel agent, or there may simply be no alternatives available.

Despite these challenges, Canadian Pacific Hotels, with 27 hotels in the quality tier across Canada, has been diligent in building loyalty. The company was already proficient with conventions, corporate meetings and group travel, but wanted to excel with business travelers. This is a notoriously demanding and diverse group to serve, but also very lucrative and much coveted by all other hotel chains. CP began by investing in deep learning about this segment to find what would most satisfy customers.[2] Frequent guest programs had little appeal, because they preferred airline mileage. They also appreciated beyond-the-call-of-duty efforts to rectify problems immediately. What they mostly wanted was recognition of their individual preferences and lots of flexibility on when to arrive and check out.

CP Hotels responded by committing to customers in its frequent-guest club that they would make extraordinary efforts always to satisfy their preferences for type of bed, location in hotel—high or low—and all the other amenities. Creating the organizational capabilities to deliver on this promise proved remarkably difficult. The company began by mapping each step of the "guest experience" from check-in and parking valet to check-out and setting a standard of performance for each activity. Then it looked to see what had to be done to deliver on the commitment to personalized service. What services should be offered? What processes were needed? What did the staff need to do or learn in order to make the process work flawlessly?

The biggest hurdle was the firm's historic bias toward handling large tour groups, so the skills, mind-sets, and processes at hand were not the ones needed to satisfy individual executives who didn't want to be asked about their needs every time they checked in. Even small enhancements such as free local calls or gift shop discounts required significant changes in information systems. The management structure was changed, so each hotel had a champion with broad, cross-functional authority to ensure the hotel lived up to its ambitious commitment. Lastly, they put further systems and incentives in place to make sure every property was in compliance and performance was meeting or exceeding the standards.

After implementing these changes, CP Hotels' share of Canadian business travel jumped by 16 percent although the total market was up just 3 percent and CP Hotels added no new properties. By all measures CP Hotels is winning greater loyalty from its target segment.

Three Elements of a Market Relating Capability

When CP Hotels set about to gain a competitive advantage through closer relations with business travelers, it deployed all three elements of a market-relating capability: First, it changed its *orientation* from processing group needs to catering to individual requirements. A new mind-set and supporting norms were needed. Second, CP Hotels invested in relation-specific *knowledge* and *skills*, which were embedded into its databases, routines and procedures. Third, the company realigned the organization around team-based *processes* that cut across functions. All these elements worked together to deliver superior customer value.

Although the three elements of a market-relating capability interact and reinforce one another, as shown in Figure 7–1, they can be dealt with separately for purposes of assessing the current capacity of the organization and guiding a change program. The further an organization moves along each vector in Figure 7-1, the closer it is to the capabilities needed for collaborative partnering with a few critical accounts. As discussed below, extensive market relating (at the outer edges of the triangle) may not be desirable or necessary in some markets, so CP Hotels was content to move only part of the way along each vector. What mattered most was

FIGURE 7–1

The Market-Relating Capability

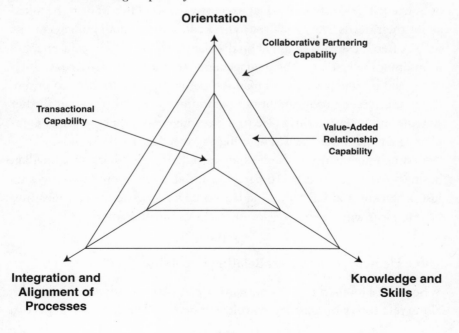

that the hotel firm moved farther along each vector than rivals, so it could be demonstrably better.

Orientation

A relationship orientation pervades all parts of the organization's mind-set, values, and norms and thus influences all interactions with the customer—before, during and after the sale. To appreciate how much it differs from a transaction mentality, compare how two competing makers of medical instruments handled similar customer repair problems.[3] In many respects the firms were alike with similar technology, performance and reliability—yet one was steadily gaining on the other. How did the winner prevail? First, it delivered a replacement instrument immediately with no questions asked. The procedure for exchanging defective instruments was designed to minimize hassle, and all communications were completely professional. A follow-up phone call was made to make sure the new instrument was functioning properly. This firm adopted the customer's point of view and took full responsibility to set things right.

In contrast, the second company seemed to view the delivery of the instrument as an end point; its focus was on selling the equipment and collecting the money. This mentality meant it handled the repair request very poorly. The person who took the customer's call was evidently unprepared to deal with the problem, so a lengthy hold was necessary. Eventually, the customer was told he would have to pay for the repair, and that a temporary replacement would cost an additional $15.

After some delay, the replacement arrived, but without instructions on what to do with the broken equipment or where it should be sent. A further call was needed to sort this out. After several weeks, the repaired instrument was returned, but with no instructions on what to do with the replacement. Finally, the customer received a letter demanding immediate payment, because someone had made a mistake by not sending the repaired instruments COD.

It is easy to decry the incompetency of the transaction-oriented firm in handling a straightforward request. While many parts of the organization were involved, no one took the customer's side, or considered the damage to the relationship. Indeed, the only person with a complete picture of what transpired was the customer. For the next purchase, which company do you think the customer will trust? There is no contest.

A relationship orientation is manifested in many ways. It is immediately evident in the mind-set of those who deal directly with the customer. Does the salesperson, gate agent, or customer service representative appreciate the lifetime value of the person being served? Does the check-out clerk in a grocery store attend only to the immediate transaction, or understand that she is serving someone who might be worth $50,000 or more in sales during the coming five years? Of course she will only adopt this point-of-view if senior management knows this, believes it, makes retention a priority, and behaves consistently with this belief.

A relationship orientation also opens the collective mind-set to new possibilities for relationship building. Many managers accept the value of relationship-building when there are a few valuable customers buying risky and expensive purchases, but dismiss it for products like soup or crackers. This is a myopic framing that misses the point that some customers are more valuable than others because they buy a lot of Heinz or Nabisco products across divisions, product lines, and time. If this is fully appreciated, the issue is how to identify these valuable customers and give them incentives to remain loyal. Of course the real opportunity in these markets is with retail and distributor relationships which have become a high priority for the leading firms. Because these firms had the orientation and leadership that made channel relationships a priority they were able to preempt their slower rivals.

Knowledge and Skills

For a relationship orientation to have leverage on performance, it must be guided by in-depth knowledge about the customer. Yet, most often what is known is tacit and dispersed through the organization and applied with antiquated decision rules from an earlier era when the salesperson owned the account. As a result most managers would be hard pressed to respond to such queries as: How secure are your relations with your key customers? What do we know about the key players in the customers' decision-making unit? How widely shared is the knowledge? How does the depth of relationship knowledge and skills compare to that of competitors—are they gaining or falling behind?

On reflection the answer is most likely to be that most of the knowledge is held by the sales representative, distributor or account manager who is neither willing nor able to share it widely. The transaction files that record purchase details are woefully unrevealing of the current state of commitment or the strength of the connective links. It was not long ago that most banks and insurance companies were unable to tell how many of their products were used by each customer: did they have a credit card and mortgage as well as a checking account? Even now most auto manufacturers are unable to obtain up-to-date files of their own new car buyers and have to obtain this data from outside data suppliers such as R.L. Polk.

Knowledge base. A knowledgeable firm has a detailed picture of the history of each relationship, the extent of their activity across all products and lines, their overall purchasing activity including competitors' products, and a profile of their requirements and potential. For example, Pioneer Hi-Bred, a major producer of seeds for corn, soybeans and the like, has created a farm information system that contains details about each farm and its crops, what seeds they have used in the past and important background on growing conditions that could influence subsequent decisions. At a minimum the firm should have enough data to be able to assess the likelihood of defection, the current profitability and long-run value of each account.

Knowledge sharing and learning. How does the organization learn from its experiences? Suppose an account team scores a real success with an innovative relationship-building strategy, or suppose it tries something and fails. What has the rest of the organization learned from the experiment? Studies of best practices in large firms find there is a surprising degree of "stickiness" to this knowledge—it simply doesn't get passed on, or when it is, isn't acted upon. There needs to be constant electronic communications, face-to-face forums for sharing and transferring people between teams plus targeted incentives before the impediments to learning can be overcome. Yet if the worst-performing account teams could just be brought up to average, the gains would be worth it.

Relative skills of account teams. This issue reminds us, first, that it takes skill to build an enduring relationship with a large, sophisticated customer, and second, that customers have lots of choices so they are constantly comparing the skills of the teams from competing vendors. Who do they most trust? Who best understands their business? Who seems to be able to solve problems, or even better, anticipates needs and offers imaginative solutions to problems the customers didn't know they had? Of course, the comparison doesn't stop with the people or person directly responsible for the customer. Every point of contact makes a contribution to the overall relationship, whether it be customer service or invoicing.

Continuity of experience. One way to secure relationships is to keep employees in place. Many firms are following the lead of Xerox to make employee satisfaction and retention a top priority in recognition of the damage that high turnover and poorly trained or disgruntled employees can cause to relationships. This is especially important when selling large, integrated systems, for it takes the average account manager up to five years to become fully conversant with a prospect's requirements, forge close personal relations with key members of the decision-making unit, and earn their trust. All this is thrown away if a new contact person or team is assigned every two years or so.

Integration and Alignment of Activities

Because many parts of the organization may have knowledge about the customer, integration and alignment are crucial to effective market relating. The third element of a market-relating capability is the alignment and integration of activities and processes that span boundaries between functions inside a firm or connect the firm to each of its customers. These activities may be integrated and aligned using interactive technologies (including electronic data interchange); coordinated sales teams, mass customization services and numerous other devices we will examine in the next two chapters. This integration can be both internal and external.

Internal integration. Many firms have been inspired by USAA to rethink their fundamental assumptions about what level of integration of internal activities is possible. This San Antonio–based financial service firm serves a military clientele with a full range of products from insurance to mutual funds, and inspires a level of loyalty that has been unattainable by its competitors.[4]

All the USAA processes are built on the platform of a computerized, integrated member database. Although the firm's clients are spread throughout the world and change locations frequently, it is a simple matter for any one of them to make a policy change. With a phone call, a member can insure a new car, add a driver, change an address, or provide coverage for a child who is going away to school. When the member's file is revised, all relevant departments are informed at the same time. In a single process, the transaction is completed and the new or revised policy is issued the next day. The updated information may also trigger a review of all coverages, leading to proposals for cost savings or new benefits. Nothing delights policyholders more than to learn they are getting a rebate they didn't expect. Since no competitor has this capability, there is no incentive for customers to even think of switching.

USAA knows its customers intimately and shares this knowledge widely within its firm. Sharing is facilitated by an electronic imaging system that enables managers to operate without paper. All correspondence is scanned onto an optical disc and added to the member's policy service file that contains a wealth of background information and details of all their policies and financial holdings. This file is accessible to all 2,500 service representatives, who can use the information to personalize and customize each service encounter. In this and a myriad of other ways USAA works steadily to build a close relationship with its customers.

External integration. The tightness of the connection between a supplier and a customer can range from a series of impersonal handoffs to a rich web of joint activities, social relations and systems links between partners. As the lines between customers and suppliers become more blurred, the stresses on organizational capabilities become greater. Few firms are able to coordinate and orchestrate all the linkages across several levels of two organizations for more than a few customers at a time. In Chapter 9, we look closely at how some firms are mastering this capability.

THE SPECTRUM OF RELATIONSHIPS

At one point there was such enthusiasm for relationships, it seemed that every firm was racing to create the closest possible connections with customers. Relationships were seen as the basis for a new paradigm.[5] However, this enthusiasm has been dampened by two harsh realities. One is that a strategy of investing or building close relationships is neither appropriate nor feasible for every market, customer or company. Some customers want nothing more than the timely exchange of the product or service with a minimum of hassle. And because close relations are resource intensive, not every customer is worth the effort. Second, market relationships create sustainable advantages precisely because they are so difficult to manage. Not every firm can or should try to master the market-relating capability. Companies are discovering there is a wide array of possibilities between arms-length transactions and intimate collaboration.

The Basis of Relationships

To understand this array of relationships, we first have to understand what makes them successful. Any meaningful market relationship begins with the expectation of *mutual benefits*. Buyers hope to realize cost savings, improve the efficiency of their decision making, reduce their risk by dealing with a trustworthy counterpart, get a solution that is tailored to their particular needs and budget, or realize social and other value-added benefits such as simplifying their choice process. The motivations of sellers are more transparent; they want to gain an advantage that can't easily be copied by competitors. Other reasons are to reduce the high costs of acquiring new customers, improve the predictability and efficiency of their operations, and reduce their risk exposure.

These expectations of mutual benefits are needed to initiate a relationship, but *reciprocity* is needed to keep it going.[6] A sense of obligation must be felt by both parties—but only in retrospect. Whereas self-interest may be the motive for entering into a relationship, reciprocity serves as a mechanism for crystallizing and sustaining the relationship. Thus buyers will become loyal because of the extra value they receive from the first in a series of transactions. Each successive positive experience leaves them with a greater sense of obligation.

How does one distinguish a real and meaningful relationship built on reciprocity from a series of unconnected transactions? The defining features are mutual benefits—the rationale for entering into a relationship—mutual commitments, trust and connective links, as shown in Figure 7–2. These four facets of a relationship work together to form a connective tissue which can be quite flimsy and short-lived, or strong and enduring.

FIGURE 7–2

Forming a Relationship

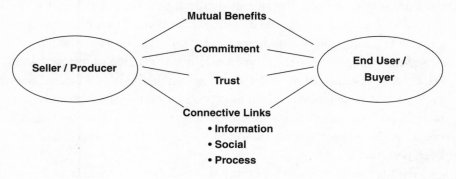

Mutual commitments

This reflects the extent of shared goals, incentives and even contractual commitments. The lowest level of commitment is found with loyalty-building programs such as frequent-shopper or frequent-flyer programs. The customers who are attracted to these programs are often the most interested in pricing incentives and vulnerable to a competitor with a better deal. These programs are often fairly easy to copy, and so American Airlines was matched by 23 airlines within three years of launching its AAdvantage Frequent Flyer program. At the other end of the commitment spectrum the seller and buyer become partners who work hard to ensure the continuance of the relationship. There is a clear understanding of where their goals converge or conflict, and incentives are aligned so that people are rewarded for behaving in ways that support the partnership. If contracts are used, they are seldom viewed as enforcement mechanisms, but instead serve as the basis for a negotiation process that clarifies expectations and identifies obstacles.

Trust

An essential cornerstone of any relationship worth the label is trust. This requires a belief that one relationship partner will act in the best interests of the other, and the expectation that the other party will fulfill their (implied) obligations. This is usually derived from their track record in delivering on their commitments, and the conduct of their personal relationships—their behaviors, attitudes and willingness to cooperate—which are a reflection of their market-relating capability.

Any suspicion on either side of the dyad that the other is not to be trusted will quickly sour the relationship. It has often been observed that trust takes a long time to build, but can be destroyed by a few thoughtless or self-serving actions. Trust is an especially critical glue in service-based relationships because of the complexity and intangibility of services.[7] Services such as automobile repair or food preparation that are performed out of sight of the consumer are difficult to evaluate before they are experienced, and some services remain hard to evaluate even after they have been performed.

Trust is valuable precisely because it is so difficult to earn. In business-to-business markets where an adversarial, transaction mentality has long prevailed, the complete mind-set has to be changed. Instead of negotiations on price and terms being conducted in an adversarial "zero-sum" basis, where one party wins at the other's expense, a spirit of "share to gain" must prevail. But gaining trust is an uphill battle in all markets, because of widespread skepticism and a pervasive sense that credibility and integrity are too often lacking.

Connective Links

The number of ways a buyer and a seller can be connected is limited only by the imagination. Possibilities range across the following dimensions:

- Information sharing may range from simply opening the lines of communication and sharing the rationale for decisions to complete electronic data interchange (EDI) or extranet connections that link the partners with a digital umbilical cord of order, status and payment information.
- Close links can be created through social networks at all levels of management if a collaborative partnership is desired. In service markets social links can capitalize on the reality that a service encounter is also a social encounter. Harley-Davidson has built strong social links with the Harley Owners Group (HOG), a club sponsored by dealers that has activities that bring like-minded people together.
- The strongest linkages are formed when the processes of two partners are integrated. This may entail coordinating the order fulfillment process, as well as joint staffing of process teams. Some firms have cus-

tomers and suppliers on their new product development teams to get early inputs, share information more fully and achieve smooth integration.

The four dimensions of mutual benefits, commitment, trust, and connective links are present in all relationships. The mix and level of intensity along each dimension vary widely. In the next section we look at the range of possibilities and then in the next chapter we turn to the question of how to manage these complex webs.

Relationship Continuum: Marriage or One-Night Stand

Central to every market relationship is an exchange process where value is given and received. Even in the most tenuous and short-lived "relationship" each side of the dyad gives something in return for a benefit or payoff of greater value.

These exchanges line up along a continuum with one end a single transaction and the other a long-run two-way collaboration. *Transactional exchanges* include the kind of anonymous encounters a visitor to a city has with the taxi or bus from the airport, as well as series of ongoing transactions in a business-to-business market where the customer and supplier focus only on the timely exchange of standard products at competitive prices. Both partners view the exchange as a zero-sum game where one side wins at the other's expense and so everything rides on the negotiation of terms and conditions. At the other end of the spectrum *collaborative exchanges* feature very close information, social and process linkages, and mutual commitments made in expectation of long-run benefits.[8]

Between these two extremes are *value-adding exchanges*, where the

FIGURE 7–3

The Relationship Spectrum

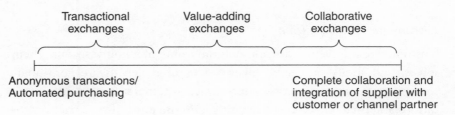

focus of the selling firm shifts from getting customers to keeping customers. The firm pursues this objective by developing a deep understanding of their needs and changing requirements, then tailoring its offering to
these needs as closely as possible and giving continuing incentives for the
customers to concentrate most of their purchases with them. Thus Hertz
takes reservations from preferred customers on a dedicated line, and pre-
sents them with the waiting rental car with the customer's name in lights.
And your dentist calls to remind you when you are due for a check-up.

Choosing How Far to Go

Firms have some latitude in choosing where to participate along the relationship spectrum. There are limits imposed by the character of the market, and some customers are more equal than others when it comes to
deciding how close a relationship will be formed (as will be discussed in
the following chapter). The choice of where to land on the spectrum of
relationships will dictate the type of communications, the tightness of the
linkages and the coordination mechanisms, which are summarized in
Table 7–1.

Standardized items like packaging materials or cleaning services grav-
itate toward the left side, with the extent of feasible relations being limited to long-term supply agreements and just-in-time inventory programs.
Long-term supply agreements are often negotiated efforts to lock up customers into a take-or-pay basis. The customer accedes in order to assure
security of supply or protection against price fluctuations. These are often
purely contractual arrangements with no emotional commitment to
keeping the relationship going.

Customized, high technology products such as semiconductor test
equipment are much more amenable to collaborative partnerships. The
feasible linkages range from co-design of manufacturing systems, supplier
participation in new product development teams and full responsibility
for installation, training, and ongoing service.

Disruptions to Relationships

Customer relationships do not naturally and inevitably sustain themselves, and should never be taken for granted. Rivals are continually
working to attract the best accounts away; customer requirements, expectations and preferences keep changing, and the possibility of friction-free

TABLE 7–1

The Relationship Spectrum

	Transactional Exchanges	Value-Adding Exchanges	Collaborative Exchanges
Distinguishing Theme	•Broadcast marketing	•Tailored interactions •Emphasis on retention	•2-way collaboration
Communications	•Targeting based on information about customers •Negotiations	•Targeting based on information from customers	•Joint problem-solving •Multilevel contacts •Extensive sharing of proprietary information
Linkages	•Persuasion •Arms-length competitive bidding	•Sales/service teams •Key account selling	•Information system integration •Process integration •Social networks •Joint planning
Coordination	•Deliveries •Contractural conditions	•Customer value proposition •Maximize lifetime value	•Mutual commitments •Shared incentives and goals •Trust

exploration of options in real time on the Web all conspire to raise the rate of customer defections. Some firms lose half or more of their customers every three years and the worst is still to come.

How can firms overcome the gravitational pull toward the transaction end of the exchange spectrum? The essence of the answer is to find new ways to add value to their relationships with their preferred accounts. Baxter International has been working to protect its health care products and services businesses from the pressure brought on the revenue of its hospital customers by health maintenance organizations, insurance carriers, and the government. To collaborate more closely with these hospitals Baxter has begun negotiating risk-sharing partnerships and taking over the management of their inventories.[9] For example, Baxter reaches an agreement with each hospital on a cost target for medical suppliers and shares the savings or absorbs the additional costs if expenses outrun the target. Hospitals that participate in the ValueLink program cede ownership and management of their inventories to Baxter, which arranges to deliver supplies to each department, often several times a day. They may even take over the routine tasks of cleaning and sterilizing equipment, freeing the hospital staff to care for patients.

The hospitals recognize that such a collaboration gives Baxter a motivation to innovate that far outweighs the short-term cost savings offered by arms-length competitive bidding or the bruising negotiations that characterized transactional exchanges. Instead of defining requirements and having qualified suppliers scramble to meet them at the lowest prices, it is better to explain their needs to one or two dedicated suppliers and let these firms suggest solutions of their own.

The Threat of Frictionless Markets

The Internet threatens to create an even stronger pull toward the transaction end of the spectrum, although it also offers opportunities for even stronger relationships. Some Internet observers predict a weakening of relationships because they are thought to bias the efficient clearing of transactions at the lowest possible price. They foresee a future where the Web enables automated purchasing, anonymous transactions and the virtual elimination of intermediaries (see boxed insert on GE purchasing network). In this scenario client server software and search routines come to the aid of the buyer, not the seller.[11]

How could purchasing be automated? In one system the employee uses a browser to request goods such as copying paper or services such as travel. Direct comparability of the offerings is achieved by having all qualified suppliers put their catalog into a specific electronic format. The system checks to see if the employee is eligible, compares prices and features and makes the choice. Vendors are forced to participate or they lose the account. Beyond this, some see an anonymous exchange for products such as insurance or standard electronic components where eligible buyers and sellers wouldn't even know the identity of the other party. A buyer participating in such an exchange could enter an offer without a price and wait for multiple sellers to bid. The choice decision is based on whatever comparative information is available—much like any tradi-

---

THE TRADING PROCESS NETWORK[10]

(http://www.tpn.geis.com)

General Electric developed this Web site to exploit the ability of the Internet to locate suppliers who can meet their needs at more competitive prices than in the past. It has software that lets GE purchasers specify where to send a request for bids and what information to include: the software manages the bids and after the bids are evaluated, orders go out in 24 hours. Because all the information is digital, sourcing is a matter of simply pointing and clicking to send out a bid package.

By mid-1997 GE was doing $1 billion worth of purchasing a year from 1,400 suppliers. Procurement is now so streamlined that the length of time it takes to find suppliers and award the business has been cut in half. Because requesting bids is so easy, many more suppliers are contacted. The resulting competition has lowered the cost of goods by 5 to 20 percent.

Because TPN uses standard Internet protocols, it is easily expanded to other firms. Eventually the suppliers serving the Trading Process Network will use the same network capability to negotiate with their suppliers; thus the community will continue to expand.

---

tional sealed bidding procedure. This is most unappealing to sellers who would lose their brand identity in the process and face shrinking margins.

Some markets will approach this frictionless ideal where transaction costs are minimal and profits depressed. But this is not inevitable. Sellers will have only themselves to blame by not meaningfully differentiating themselves. Intermediaries such as travel agents who mainly provide information are especially at risk of being bypassed when potential providers can list what they have to offer and potential buyers can easily learn where the cheapest fares can be found. To avoid this fate travel agents and other intermediaries will need to become trusted advisers who add value in other ways. They can simplify the choice process by creating attractive total packages and reducing the risk of picking the wrong alternative. In short, they can start to build relationships with selected clients and prosper by getting paid for their services.

SUMMARY: RETHINKING MARKET RELATIONSHIPS

All firms are being forced to rethink how they relate to their customers. Whether they succeed in developing a market-relating capability that is superior to their rivals depends on their willingness to change their mindsets and behaviors, acquire thorough knowledge about their most valuable customers, and integrate and align their key processes. They must master a whole panoply of management trends, such as business process management, partnering, employee empowerment and customer satisfaction management that have often been beyond management's reach.

Whether they will prevail depends on the resources they can draw upon, and the will and persistence to overcome a transaction mind-set. Some indication of the effort required can be gained from the questions posed in the assessment form in the Appendix of this book. These questions will help calibrate the current situation; in the next chapter we will look more deeply into the strategic choices that are available.

In practice there are two types of strategies for building and nurturing relationships. Each presumes the business has gained competitive parity in costs and performance, for relationships can't flourish in the presence of pronounced disadvantages. The customer-responsive strategies discussed in the next chapter are especially applicable to mass consumer markets and virtually all services. The strategies of collaborating with customers and bonding with channel partners that are addressed in Chapter 9 are especially designed for business-to-business markets. Each of these strategies contains elements and principles that can be profitably used with the other strategies. The choice of strategy depends on the nature of the exchange process, the capabilities and intentions of the competitors, and the depth of resources of the firm. A small brokerage firm can't invest as deeply and widely in systems, people and programs as a Merrill Lynch so it must be very selective in the types of customers it chooses to serve.

Chapter Eight

Competing for Customer Relationships

Market-driven organizations excel at retaining their most valuable customers. Their strategies emphasize adding customer value through service enhancements, incentives and tailored interactions that reflect differences in the prospective lifetime value of each customer. The intent is to offer compelling mutual benefits and tighten their connections to their customers so they won't defect to rivals.

The motivation to follow these customer-responsive strategies is especially strong in maturing mass markets where most competitive advantages have been lost or greatly diminished, and customers react to the sameness of the competing choices by becoming more price-sensitive and less loyal. The firms that are best at combating these forces of uniformity are alike in many ways:

- *Different Treatment:* There is a willingness to serve customers differently, with the best customers getting the best treatment. The airline industry has created multilevel frequent flyer programs, with dedicated reservation lines, priority upgrades, rapid check-in privileges and so on to recognize the best customers.
- *Information-Based:* Decisions are based on fine-grained information about their customers. Databases pull key data from internal operating systems (such as a retailer's transaction system) and merge it with

descriptive information from external sources. This enables database marketing and micro-marketing campaigns.

- *Customer-Centric:* A "have it your way" mind-set prevails. This can range from tailoring messages to micro-segments like the custom binding of *Parents* magazine according to the age of the children, to Nordstrom's ability to enable its clerks to range through the entire store to put together clothing ensembles for their customers.
- *Flexible:* Core processes are flexible and facilitate multiple modes of producing and delivering the product or service. Measures and incentives are aligned to retention as a priority.

Most firms can't measure up to these requirements because they are unable to overcome the conquest mentality that is part of the traditional emphasis on customer acquisition. This chapter examines how customer-responsive strategies work and provides a process for devising and implementing these strategies. It also explores the potential of the Internet to increase the interactivity of relationships and further cement the ties between companies and their customers.

CUSTOMER RESPONSIVE STRATEGIES

The evolution of the office superstore market illustrates both the motivations behind the responsive strategies and a workable process for developing them.[1] Early office superstores were modeled after grocery stores: low cost, high turnover, wide assortment, and self-service. Customers went often because these stores had the best prices for paper, fax machines, pens and other office supplies—but this didn't mean they were loyal.

Staples took the lead in pursuing a more customer-responsive strategy when it realized its expansion programs meant increasing confrontations with Office Depot and Office Max, who were well able to match their prices. To move ahead, Staples first invested in customer databases loaded with detailed information about buying habits. Customers provided this information each time they used a membership card, which gave them a discount on some items. From the database, Staples could learn who were the heavy buyers and whether their stores were properly located to serve these groups.

The second step was to retain the best customers by giving them incentives for their loyalty. Small business customers who spent at least $100 per month got a rebate. Special attention was paid to defectors who suddenly stopped buying. A salesperson would call them to learn what happened and see what Staples could do to entice them back. To build confidence and trust that Staples offered the best value, further steps were taken to make it easier to shop. All the stores were redesigned with better lighting and wider aisles, and with access to information that anticipated customers' questions. This in turn freed up sales associates from answering routine queries, so they could be used where most needed in selling computers, printers, fax machines and other electronic gear.

These steps paid off handsomely, but only because the capabilities were in place. This required a change in management's mind-set. Whereas management time had been spent on the pressing need to open more stores, now it needed to be redirected to thinking about better ways of serving the customers. It meant investments in training, communication and compensation plans that encouraged employees to stay. Each quarter featured a town meeting where senior management reported on performance and solicited ideas from employees. Training was guided by using outsiders to visit stores or place orders by phone to evaluate the quality of service and identify persistent shortcomings. These reports were also used to determine the bonuses received by each store manager.

Staples represents best practices in following a systematic process for devising customer-responsive strategies that keep customers coming back, buying more and staying loyal. Figure 8–1 outlines the steps in this process. These steps are far easier to implement within organizations with histories that incline them toward a relationship mind-set, or have the luxury of a clean start without the drag of history and past practice. Those that have matured and prospered in a transaction environment will subtly resist the transformation. Marketing may feel threatened as product managers lose autonomy to segment managers; advertising feels uncomfortable with micro-marketing campaigns targeted to hundreds of segments; the systems group argues that the legacy systems can't handle flexible approaches to data capture; and financial people are skeptical about efforts to estimate probable lifetime customer value.[2] In short, these strategies are difficult to implement, but when they work, they are the source of a powerful competitive advantage that is very difficult for rivals to imitate or leapfrog.

FIGURE 8–1

Devising a Relationship Strategy

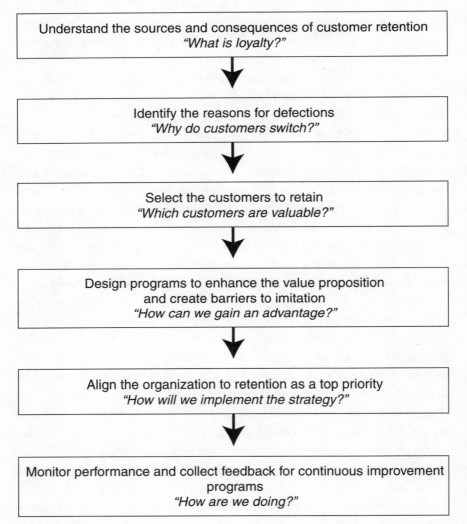

Understand the sources and consequences of customer retention
"What is loyalty?"

Identify the reasons for defections
"Why do customers switch?"

Select the customers to retain
"Which customers are valuable?"

Design programs to enhance the value proposition
and create barriers to imitation
"How can we gain an advantage?"

Align the organization to retention as a top priority
"How will we implement the strategy?"

Monitor performance and collect feedback for continuous improvement
programs
"How are we doing?"

What Is Loyalty?

The starting point for any customer-responsive strategy is a deep understanding of the nature of loyalty using the concepts developed in the previous chapter. The central message is that loyalty is more than a customer's long relationship with a particular company or frequent visits to a store. It is a feeling of affinity or attachment to a firm's products or services. Ideally, this is manifested when customers spend most or all of their budgets with the firm. In practice, this is very hard to measure because we seldom can track spending at other companies. Proxy measures such as length of the relationship, store visits or spending per visit are often not very meaningful. For example, one computer hardware company bragged about its ability to retain almost all the customers it had sold to, but received a shock when it found that almost half its customers actually had gone on to buy add-on capacity and services from other sources.

Loyal relationships are characterized by commitment. One capital equipment maker uses the following hierarchy to assess the commitment of its major accounts:

Lowest commitment

Willingness to defend the purchase of our products and recommend us to others

and

Intentions to repurchase

and

Willingness to wait for the company if competition launches a superior product

and

Resistance to adverse opinions by experts: Does the customer trust us more than other credible sources?

and

Increasing evidence of commitment and loyalty

Willingness to pay a price premium over competitors' products

Why Do Customers Switch?

The next step in the process of developing a customer-responsive strategy is to determine why some customers defect. With the high and growing rates of customer defections in most markets, companies usually have plenty of raw material to study. Because defectors have been captured by competitors, they also provide valuable clues about what rivals are doing.

A fair question is what exactly is a defector? Some are easy to spot: they drop you from their list of qualified suppliers, cancel your contract or close their account. Seldom is the separation so obvious; instead of a dramatic announcement, their purchases simply dwindle, or they buy a smaller share of their requirements.

Quality analysts have devised a number of useful procedures for exposing the root causes of defections. They recognize that a customer's decision to be loyal or to defect is the sum of many small, ongoing encounters with the firm. There is seldom an overriding reason for defection—instead, a series of disappointments or frustrations leads to a decision to seek better value elsewhere. One also has to be alert to the possibility that performance was acceptable, but a competitor was able to persuade the once-loyal customer that it could provide better service.

Integral to root-cause analysis is a process known as the *five whys*.[3] This requires an exhaustive clinical analysis of a selected sample of defectors who were once good customers and are worth understanding because they fit a profile of the kind of prospects to be encouraged. The general principle is that you usually have to ask why something happened at least five times to fully reveal all the reasons. It is useful to begin by learning whether the applications or usage situation of the defector has changed—and why—and then review the history of the purchase process to identify the decision to change. Any number of reasons will be discovered: there were concerns about reliability, complaints about service were mounting, requirements were changing, the fees are excessive and so forth. Each needs to be explored carefully to learn why it was a precipitating event or concern. This sets the stage for the most valuable part of the conversation, which asks what could be done to save the relationship.

Effective root cause analysis goes beyond carefully listening to customers. Customers can identify their concerns and frustrations, but may not be able to explain why they defected. For example, defectors from one bank to another will seldom identify branch employee turnover as the reason. Instead they will note that they always seem to be dealing with strange faces who are still learning their jobs, and don't understand their needs, or take far too long to process a simple transaction.

Despite the gold mine of information that defectors provide, managers are often reluctant to pursue this source. Sometimes it is a cultural bias that values successes and discourages introspection. More often it is simply that the reasons are painful to hear, or managers are not comfortable with the task. Another concern is uncertainty that the customer will actually give a straight answer rather than a "feel good" rationalization that conceals the real reason. These concerns and objections must be dealt with directly, and overcome with a combination of management determination that this is a priority and evidence of the strategic importance of the results.

Which Customers Are Valuable?

The next step is to determine which customers are valuable and so should be the focus of the loyalty initiative. When Staples first began forging value-added relationships, it wasn't particularly discriminating in its choice of customers. By 1995, it had a vast database of customers, some of whom bought as little as $100 per year. However, all customers were treated equally. This not only swamped its system, it diluted the company's ability to focus managers' energies on the best prospects—those who had demonstrated loyalty and had the greatest lifetime value.

To sharpen its focus, the company established a new tiered reward system for those customers with more than $1,000 annual volume, which gave them larger volume discounts and rebates that applied to the cumulative volume. The intent was to encourage these valued customers to allocate Staples a higher proportion of their purchases, and also to improve their ability to learn more about their purchasing patterns and requirements. To serve the largest 125 customers, with potential volume of $1 million or more per year, Staples went beyond value-added relationships to outright collaboration. A separate division, Staples National Advantage, was formed to manage the whole procurement process for these high yield accounts. This included helping them to consolidate all buying of office supplies on a national basis, switch to electronic ordering processes and introducing just-in-time delivery to reduce inventories. To do this they needed to promise the customers large benefits, in turn for complete access to the customers facilities to find areas for improvement.

Valuable customers are usually identified by their attractive lifetime value—based on some combination of high annual revenues, profitability and long-term potential. The difficulty with this heuristic is the forecast of their future behavior. Past loyalty is not a valid guide to the future if it is due to inertia or lack of suitable alternatives. It is doubly risky if it leads to defining "ideal" customers as the ones who can do the most for us, perhaps because they promise big volumes.

It is better to think of the ideal customers to pursue as those for whom we can do the most, because our capabilities mesh better with the customers requirements and circumstances. These are the ones that derive the most benefits from the relationship. A supplier of cost-reducing additives for paint, ceramics and other products fell into the "ideal customer" trap. Although the company's material was demonstrably cheaper to use and yielded a higher-quality end product, it required major changes in the manufacturing methods of the customers. To break into the market quickly the firm targeted the largest prospects because their volume would help them reach break-even quickly. After several years of fruitless efforts at switching these accounts, the company finally turned to smaller, fast-growing companies who were looking for a cost advantage and weren't already locked into big plants. These smaller companies valued the suppliers' capabilities in conducting tests because they couldn't afford the sophisticated equipment; whereas the large, established firms already had test facilities in place. When the firm redefined who were its ideal customers, success and long-term relationships were attained.

Customer selection also means discouraging or at least not actively pursuing some customers. This is especially difficult for firms that have traditionally had a transaction mentality where success is measured in volume and market-share terms. There are many indicators of a poor customer, including a history of switching, a lack of interest in broader solutions, a bargaining mentality that puts the priority on price concessions, or an unwillingness to be open about their needs. The choice of indicator should isolate those that are demanding, very costly to serve or don't fit the firm's capabilities. Ultimately the choice of customers to target for relationship building depends on the opportunity to gain an advantage. This is the next step in the process.

How Can We Gain an Advantage?

Why were the customer-responsive strategies of Canadian Pacific and Staples successful? Both programs created a durable competitive advantage, and the returns from increased loyalty exceeded the full costs. It is not easy to satisfy these conditions, but the odds of winning go up if the strategy can address all the elements of a fruitful relationship, and put plenty of barriers in the way of competition who want to copy.

FIGURE 8–2

The Virtuous Circle of Loyalty

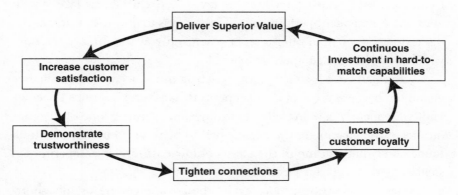

A Virtuous Cycle of Loyalty

A relationship advantage is reinforced by a virtuous cycle of loyalty, as illustrated in Figure 8–2. The company delivers superior customer value, thereby increasing customer satisfaction. Only when customers are fully satisfied with performance are they open to efforts to tighten their connections with the company. These closer connections lead to stronger feelings of loyalty and the relationship created by this loyalty allows the company to develop customer-specific information and capabilities that are hard to match.

Xerox activated this sequence to regain its leadership in the office copier market. By the mid-1980s its copiers had become costly and unreliable, and it was losing ground to Canon and other Japanese competitors. The turnaround required wholehearted commitment to total quality management, rigorous benchmarking against competitors and a customer satisfaction program that introduced new metrics and team-based field organizations so sales, service, and operations took collective responsibility for customer problems. Previously the salespeople dropped out of the picture once the machine was sold while regional service and operations people didn't communicate with each other.

These efforts paid dividends as customer satisfaction steadily rose and Xerox share losses were arrested. Only then was Xerox in a position to forge stronger relationships. The first step was to demonstrate both its confidence in its copiers and its trustworthiness by offering a strong guarantee. Xerox chose a "no questions asked" guarantee where if the customer decided to have the copier removed Xerox would replace it with another of equivalent performance. The key was to give the customer the discretion, rather than offer a replacement only at the firm's discretion, which was what the competitors offered.

Xerox gained 4.5 share points when it introduced its performance guarantee because none of the competitors had Xerox's service coverage and consequently couldn't offer anything equivalent. As one of the conditions of the guarantee, the copiers had to be serviced by Xerox, which immediately put a crimp in the efforts of low-cost service competitors to steal away this lucrative business.

When there is no virtuous cycle, the advantages are usually short-lived. This applies to many programs launched under the guise of relationship building, that involve "micro marketing" by tailoring communications to narrow segments, or product line extensions that aim to offer greater variety to fragmented markets. Too often these are only warmed-over traditional mass marketing efforts that overwhelm consumers with a proliferation of products, messages and appeals for personal information. Often they are badly conceived, as when a bank's "privileged" customers were sent solicitations with offers of special credit card rates that were available only to new customers. Much money has been wasted on short-term rewards through gifts or one-time rebates for loyal customers. These are nice to receive but don't do anything to strengthen the relationship.

The benefits of frequency programs that provide rewards to frequent patrons, flyers, or guests are more subtle.[4] The obvious drawback of these programs is that competitors are forced to match them to protect their share. At the beginning of 1995 there were no loyalty programs in the British grocery market. Once Tesco broke ranks all its competitors were forced to follow suit. No doubt Tesco benefited by being first, but the others apparently suffered an increase in their cost of doing business without gaining new customers. The focus on market share effects overlooks the beneficial effect of reward programs on market stability from reducing price sensitivity and customer churn. These programs provide accumulating benefits—free air travel, free hotel stays, or free products—that create customer switching costs. Better yet, they deflect customers' attention away from price, and encourage all competitors to avoid the downward price pressures that have such corrosive effects on profits. Thus, the true benefits of loyalty programs are seen in profit margin growth, not market share gains.

A strategy that successfully activates the virtuous cycle of loyalty to gain a relationship advantage meets the following conditions:

- Delivers superior customer value by personalizing the interaction
- Demonstrates trustworthiness
- Tightens the connection with customer

All of these elements were employed by Daewoo in its successful entry into the UK car market in 1995. (See boxed insert.)

Delivering Superior Value

The difference between repeat behavior and loyalty is that the former is for sale while the other is earned. This sums up why gifts and other one-time rewards have little lasting impact—they are not relevant to the brand's value proposition, and demonstrate neither more benefits or lower costs than the competition.

Relationships that add value for customers require some form of personalized interaction. They are built on the recognition that every relationship is different, that it is based on two-way communications, and that it should continue to build and change over time. Savvy hotels like the Ritz-Carlton put this to work by accumulating and remembering information about their guests' preferences and interests so they don't have to keep asking the same questions at every check-in. Successful life insurance salespeople have always understood the need to personalize relationships by staying in touch, anticipating the impact of family life-cycle events and demonstrating responsiveness.[6]

Value is often delivered through coaching that combines instruction with encouragement that helps a customer deal with a difficult task.[7] Among those daunting tasks is choosing flowers that will suit the recipient and are appropriate for the occasion and that won't perish quickly—without spending too much. One alternative is to find a local florist that can be trusted and rely on their guidance. But that means a special trip, there is no assurance they will have the right flowers available, and because of inefficiencies in flower distribution the flowers could be seven

HOW DAEWOO GAINED A RELATIONSHIP ADVANTAGE[5]

When Daewoo entered the UK car market in 1995, its brand name had minimal recognition, its cars were technically unimpressive and the country of origin (Korea) was unfashionable. The environment was not promising: There were over 40 brands competing for a share of a saturated market, and Ford, Vauxhall and Rover accounted for half of all new cars sold. The best dealers were tied into exclusive deals with established manufacturers. And many companies had a "Buy U.K." or "Buy Europe" policy for their fleet purchases, which accounted for half the total market.

Despite these hurdles, Daewoo was able to gain a 1 percent market share in its first year, and become the most successful launch of a new brand name in over 20 years. How did Daewoo achieve this? First, its market sensing found a large target segment that simply wanted a reliable, economical car, but was overwhelmingly hostile to car dealers. It learned that these buyers found showrooms intimidating and salespeople pushy, and believed they were treated even worse after the sale.

More important, the company acted on its research insights and decided to become "the most customer-focused car company." This led Daewoo to dispense with dealers altogether and sell direct. Not only did this save dealer commissions, but it meant the company was able to control all customer contacts. The other elements of the value proposition were all designed to demonstrate trustworthiness and build closer relationships with customers.

- *Absence of hassle.* The dealer network was designed to look like stores, product information was available on interactive terminals, salespeople were on a fixed salary and there was no bargaining on price.
- *Peace of mind.* The price included a three-year warranty, three years of free servicing, a 30-day money-back guarantee and three-year membership in the auto association.
- *Courtesy servicing.* Daewoo offered free pick up and return of the car, a free courtesy car, and direct contact with the mechanic who serviced the car.

to ten days old before they even reach the store. Calyx & Corolla devised a direct marketing approach that allowed growers to ship flower arrangements to the ultimate consumer by FedEx in as little as one day from the time they were cut. To keep customers coming back they added a number of services that made buying flowers simple, satisfying, and appealing. The key was to provide informative catalogs and understanding telephone service people who were trained to ask tactful questions that would help people get what they wanted without being judged.

Demonstrating Trustworthiness

Once the capabilities are in place to ensure the value proposition is clearly superior then a virtuous circle of relationship building can begin. Only when customers are completely satisfied will initiatives to demonstrate trust and tighten their connections to the firm be cost-effective. In fact if you can't deliver on the basic promise of reliable performance those efforts are likely to be counterproductive.

Frank and frequent *personalized* communications are effective means of demonstrating trustworthiness. This is especially important with high-involvement, long-term service commitments like auto or life insurance. Many customers are not trustful of their insurance companies because they hear from them only when a premium is due. That's when they find out the rates have been raised; usually with no explanation. When they need the service they bought—after an accident, say—the insurer seems bent on canceling the policy or making it more costly. Life insurance customers are even more removed. Because of high turnover among agents, they are likely to have lost their initial point of contact. To build trust and confidence some firms are carefully crafting individual mailings that explain the policy benefits, describe the current status, and make proposals for changing the coverage to make it more useful. They don't presume the customer has the interest or ability to wade through a confusing policy. When it comes time to renew or expand coverage the policyholder is much more inclined to stay with his present insurer.

As with Xerox, guarantees can be used to build trust by symbolizing a company's commitment to fair play with their customers.[8] They also maintain the pressure on the entire organization to continue to improve their performance to avoid the costs and conflicts created by frequent payouts and replacements. Guarantees can also put intolerable pressure on competitors if they can't match the terms.

Tightening the Connections

Once the relationship has a solid foundation in superior value and trustworthiness it is time to tighten the connection. The objective is to make it more attractive for the customer to remain loyal and more difficult to defect. Incentives to remain loyal run the gamut from frequency marketing programs, epitomized by the American Airlines frequent flyer program, to providing membership in clubs. For example, Nintendo, the Japanese video game company, has enrolled two million members in its Nintendo Club. For an annual fee they receive a magazine with "inside" tips on how to win, previews of new games, and so on, as well as access to a help line they can call with questions or problems. These incentives work when they enhance the core value proposition, but if they are simply a "me too" response to competitive moves they become an added cost burden. Their main function is to avoid market share losses because of a competitive disadvantage.

Another effective inducement is the reward scheme that offers points for each dollar spent, so each successive purchase becomes more valuable. This also introduces a disincentive to switch to a competitor because the opportunity cost is too high. Here the principle is to increase the buyer's switching costs.

The closest connections come when the solution to the customer's requirements is designed into the delivery system. The resulting web of financial, system, and even social connections is very difficult for the competitors to penetrate. Federal Express uses this approach to tie its customers ever closer. The company has placed automated shipping and invoicing systems in the offices of its highest-volume customers. This Powership system can assign the correct weight to each package, combine package weights by destination to obtain volume discounts, and print address labels. The customers get other benefits by being able to trace their packages and analyze their shipping expenses. The more experience customers have with this system the less likely they are to drop it in favor of someone else's approach.

Brands also help tighten the connections. Brands have great value to the firms that own them because they represent the history of past relationships and the promise of future relationships. Because of the deeply embedded quality of these relationships, firms have long recognized that their brand names may be their most valuable asset. Why are brand relationships so valuable? A strong brand name creates value in four ways:[9]

- High *awareness* reflects familiarity gained from past exposure. It is essential that a brand name be remembered at the time of purchase because buyers consider surprisingly few brands. Buyers of ink-jet printers consider Hewlett-Packard and only one or two others. If your brand is not in that set, it will have great difficulty getting distribution.
- A perception of high *quality* represents what customers know about the ability of a product or service to meet their needs. These perceptions of fitness for use are often based on past experience, and whether the product delivered the promised benefits.
- A meaningful *brand promise* captures all the positive associations consumers make with the brand—and any future exchange relationships should reliably fulfill. Nike promises performance shoes based on superior technology—"just do it" captures the feeling; Hallmark's cue is "when you care enough to send the very best"; and Lensmaster promises "lenses in an hour."
- Finally, strong *brand loyalty* is commanded by strong brands because of effective performance during past relationships. This is why the equity in a brand name is so valuable; there is a predictable stream of sales at a price premium over weaker brands, the strong relationship is virtually invulnerable to short-run attacks by competitors, and the brand can command preferential treatment by the trade. This is one of the most compelling arguments for investing in customer retention.

Brands play different roles in low-risk consumer product than they do in high-risk technology products. Because a purchase of a new brand of jeans or a trial of new cereal is almost risk free, brands facilitate and simplify the choice process when there are many alternatives to consider. With a high-risk product like a microprocessor, MRP system, or a communication network, the brand is a symbol of expected performance, quality, service, and support and gives the buyer reassurance and confidence. The brand carries with it the history and performance of the company, the technical leadership and past support, and embodies the strength of the relationship.

How Will We Implement the Strategy?

The completion—and beginning—of the virtuous cycle of relationship building requires enhancing and strengthening the underlying market-relating capability. The more successful the overall program the greater the risk of imitation. The best defense is to stay ahead by continuously learning and innovating, and then make it as difficult as possible for rivals to grasp the organizational recipe. The defense plan must address every element of the capability.

- *Engage the entire organization—both minds and hearts.* There must be broad acceptance that every interaction matters; what Jan Carlson of SAS airline called the "million moments of truth" that determine success. To capitalize on this belief all functions must be part of the program. The Hertz #1 Club Gold program would have been much less successful had operations not been fully involved in rebuilding the systems and facilities to save customers going to a counter and provide covered pick-up spots that identify customers by name.
- *Tighten organizational alignment.* A capability emerges from a complex interaction of many elements, and will only be as good as the weakest link. Every element must be scrutinized for improvement. For example, the commission system has the power to encourage salespeople to chase the next easy conquest, or alternatively to carefully screen prospects on the basis of their likelihood of defecting. Many firms no longer pay commissions on new accounts that stay less than 12 months.
- *Make learning a priority.* There are always ways to improve. The best-of-breed companies are never satisfied. Instead they use pilot tests and hot houses to try out new approaches and learn more about what their target customers really value. To exploit this learning it is necessary to keep key people on the team long enough for them to have real impact. Solid relationships require continuity, both inside and outside.
- *Refresh and maintain the databases and records.* As soon as a database is created it is obsolete. Just keeping up with the 20 percent of households that move every year is a daunting task, but if it is not done

conscientiously the program will soon falter. Companies that have strong relationships with their customers are in the best position to do this, because the customer has an incentive to stay in touch.

Despite diligence and vigilance, the basis of the customer-responsive strategy may be at risk if a new business model emerges or there is a technological discontinuity. Interactive commerce represents that kind of game-changing discontinuity. While it is too early to see clearly all the possibilities of network-based relationship strategies, few firms can afford to delay in finding out.

EXPLOITING INTERACTIVITY

Interacting and relating are almost synonymous. Without a dialogue that helps a firm learn about a customer, the communications and value proposition are based on descriptive information *about* the customer. This is the mass market, broadcast model of marketing that targets segments based on their presumed response profile. Contrast this with the interactive ideal in which a firm has the ability to address an individual and then remember the response of that individual. With each successive interaction the firm learns more and uses this information *from* the customer to personalize further communications in ways that take account of that unique response and the value proposition. This relationship gets smarter and smarter with each interaction and becomes closer. This in turn creates a hurdle for competitors to surmount, since they would have to repeat the learning process and the customer may be reluctant to reteach them.

This was always the ideal. As illustrated in Figure 8–3, most customer-responsive strategies fall short of this interactive ideal. At best they are able to address micro-segments extracted from huge databases and send personalized messages to carefully selected individuals. But these are still one-way messages and compete for attention with all the other messages flooding the market. A modicum of interactivity is achieved when an advertisement elicits a response such as returning a coupon or making a toll-free call. This response is then stored in a database and replied to with a personalized direct mailing. Higher levels of interactivity are achieved when incentives and programs are based on individual behavior, as in airline frequent flyer programs.

The rapid rise of the Internet has changed the rules of interactive

FIGURE 8–3

Striving for Interactivity

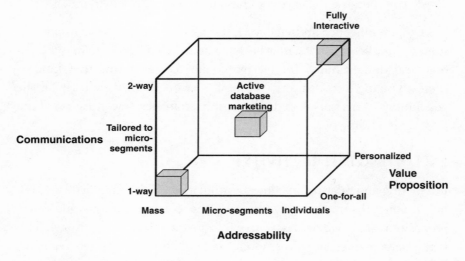

marketing. It permits complete addressability and two-way interaction. When a customer visits a Web site, many cycles of messages can be exchanged in a short time, and remembered on the next visit. With all this information *from* the customer the offering can be highly personalized if that is appropriate. This is a uniquely responsive interactive medium.[10]

Some observers predict, however, that this new channel will undermine interactivity as the frictionless market described in the previous chapter leads to a transaction-focused marketplace with customers using the Net to strengthen their hands. There would be little possibility for relationships in this world. Another scenario is that relationship building is facilitated by the Internet. It makes it easier to engage in personalized communications and permits efficient "mass customization" of products and services.

Mass Customization

This strategy employs a highly interactive dialogue with customers to help them articulate their needs, find the option that best fits these needs and then make their order.[11] It is the closest to the "sense-and-respond" strategy that has yet been achieved. Examples are Personal Pair, a Levi Strauss program in which jeans for women are made to their exact specifications; Custom Foot who can make shoes to order from a choice of 10,000 variations for women and 7,800 for men; and Andersen Windows, which lets customers design their own windows. Common to all applications is a daunting variety of alternatives that overwhelms and frustrates customers who have to choose.

The "mass" appellation recognizes that the products are made one at a time by a flexible manufacturing system that can anticipate a wide variety of options. Costs are competitive because the products are designed to be assembled or made at high speed from standard modules, and inventories are kept to a minimum. Motorola uses such a system to produce pagers in a wide variety of colors, sizes, shapes and tones, but no product is made until an order is received.

This offers a powerful tool for forging close relationships with customers. First, the company learns and remembers about the customer while gathering extensive—and sometimes personal information about customer needs and preferences. Armed with this information the firm can look out for the customer's individual special interests. Meanwhile the customer has invested time and trouble to teach the firm about his own shoe specifications, size of jeans, and so on, which makes it much easier to order the next time. When there is an affinity between a mass customization strategy and the Internet the results are eye-catching.

Dell Computer found this when they put their direct response method of selling personal computers in the Internet. Prospective buyers could design exactly the PC they wanted, get a price and delivery quotation, and place an order all at the same time. Dell's build-to-order model already gave them a big cost edge over indirect marketers like HP and Compaq whose product usually sat on dealer shelves for 50 days, whereas Dell could turn its inventory in 15 days. By ordering over the Net customers saved time, could directly access in-depth information in real time, and later have a wealth of service information available at a keystroke. Granted Dell is selling a product that is well suited to the Internet environment, but that doesn't diminish the enthusiastic response of customers who were buying $3,000,000 worth of computers a week over the Net only 90 days after the service was offered. The company also benefited: only half as many phone calls per customer were needed to make a sale, 85 percent of the customers who bought from the Internet store were new to Dell, and the average system selling price was higher over the Net than over the phone.[12] Best of all the company could initiate an ongoing dialogue with informational updates, solutions to recurring problems and so forth, that help to build loyalty.

Which Markets Will Benefit Most?

For companies that can write and exploit the new rules of relationship management, the prospects of the Internet are exhilarating. For most firms, the Internet raises troubling questions. If it takes off, it will be too profitable to ignore, and they properly suspect that their rivals will use this disruptive change in the rules to find a way to attack their markets. Both incumbents and newcomers need to have a point of view on the following questions.

- Is our market a likely candidate for interactive media and marketing approaches? Which markets are most attractive?
- How will relationships be altered? What will happen to brand values—will they mean as much?
- Who will likely gain an advantage?

The situation is still too fluid for definitive conclusions so the best posture is to participate actively and continually experiment with different approaches to keep refining the answers. While keeping options open during the learning process is important, this does not mean passively delaying until the picture clears. The stakes are too high and the momentum behind the Internet is too great.

The first reaction to the Internet was to view it as a supplement to established ways of relating to customers—a new medium or a way to lower the cost of traditional sales processes. Many companies put their catalogs on-line because of the savings in mailing and production costs. Auto dealers promoted themselves through Auto-by-Tel as an economical way of generating leads. Another easy step was to use the Web to provide customers with additional information. At Vanguard's Web site visitors interested in mutual funds have easy access to detailed product information, profiles of fund managers and guides to retirement planning that otherwise would be difficult to find. Firms like FedEx and UPS saw the possibilities in automating routine customer service functions like tracking parcels. The pull of the past could be seen in the ways things were described; we had electronic malls, digital cash, and advertising was sold using the old metric of cost per thousand messages.

As experience revealed broader possibilities, the focus of Internet applications shifted from *information provision* to *relationship enhancement*.[13] Direct marketers like L.L. Bean saw it as an additional avenue for highly personalized marketing. They could provide deeper information including lessons on topics like orienteering, collect information on their customers' interests, and provide discussion forums with Bean experts which would help build detailed customer profiles. Indeed the Web facilitates the first step in relationship building by creating databases that can be used to identify attractive, self-selected users or prospects and then tailoring communications and new offers.

The breakaway from the ways of the past came when imaginative start-ups such as E-trade and Virtual Vineyards or entrants from other sectors such as Intuit saw how the Internet could be used to *restructure the value chain*. These innovative firms created "virtual" enterprises that existed only on the Internet. One of the best known is Amazon.com, which began as an on-line bookstore offering more than three million titles. Customers can find the book they want by searching the database, and when they order Amazon will automatically suggest related titles of interest. As Amazon learns more about customers' interests they send recommendations as new books arrive. Customers can share their views on books and create a community that is tied to Amazon. This formula is being extended beyond books to include music, videos, watches, games, toys and even software and apparel. The intent is to make Amazon the Net's premier shopping destination.

Specialty markets are often ripe for restructuring by a virtual organization. This is what a new, closed (or private) network called Title Link is doing to streamline the cumbersome process of issuing property titles. Its objective is to electronically connect all the parties in the transaction—agencies, banks, insurance companies, lawyers, and title companies—to cut the cost and time of doing business. This will be a great relief to buyers and sellers who find the paper-based system can take up to three months.

Identifying Opportunities

Prospects for the Internet are best in categories such as books, software, travel, and financial services that are information intensive, where transactions can be made on-line, and the target market is already active in the Internet. Other categories such as computers, automobiles, appliances, and almost anything sold through a catalog are attractive because of the potential for personalized offerings and relationship building.

Do New Entrants Have an Advantage?

The history of disruptive technologies seldom favors the incumbent. The Internet is not likely to be an exception to this rule. At one time the ability to digitally connect with customers was limited to electronic data interchange (EDI). This favored large companies because it required proprietary networks, complex and application-specific software, and large-scale system integration. The advent of the Internet has put the power of the network within reach of anyone with a PC and modem. Not only does this put small firms on the same footing as their large competitors, but it eliminates a major barrier to entry. Newcomers are swarming onto the net to exploit these opportunities for new services and closer connections to their customers. This may mean a cash register that does double duty by collecting customer names and buying preferences, or Web sites for exchanging know-how. Indeed small firms have an advantage because they can target and build relationships in smaller niches than large firms can afford to serve. Meanwhile the incumbents are often constrained from acting as quickly because the business model is unfamiliar, doesn't fit their culture and capabilities, and threatens to cannibalize their existing profit stream.

While the Internet usually gives the newcomer a head start this doesn't mean an incumbent can't eventually prevail. But the established firms will have to jettison old habits, be willing to invest heavily to understand the consequences of a migration from a physical to a digital value chain, and use their capabilities and brand name attack aggressively. Barnes & Noble has tried to do this to catch up to Amazon.com.

Amazon.com took full advantage of the low barriers to entry to become the first on-line bookseller. Their start-up costs were kept low by using distribution partners to handle the time and capital-consuming aspects of stocking a million titles and shipping orders. Barnes & Noble should have been able to match these advantages. As the nation's largest bookseller, it got the best prices, so it was able to launch its Web site with a 30 percent discount on all hardcover books. Its site had the same interactive features as Amazon's such as chat rooms, reader feedback and book reviews that encourage greater loyalty.

Despite Barnes & Noble's experience as a retailer, well-known brand name and heavy spending to launch its Web site, the company's sales have lagged far behind Amazon's. Some of Barnes & Noble's problems are those of any incumbent: it was late to enter, slow to recognize the possibilities and its store-trained executives took longer to learn a new set of rules. What Barnes & Noble couldn't match was Amazon's ability to personalize the customer's experience by analyzing their purchases and suggesting other books that people with similar purchase patterns had bought. To solidify relationships with its customers, Amazon offers an array of new services such as Gift Click, which lets customers choose a gift and simply enter the recipient's e-mail address to send the gift. Why didn't Barnes & Noble see the same potential for relationship building in the new technology? Perhaps it is because of its traditional transactional mind-set, which makes it very difficult for Barnes & Noble to develop the same depth of market-relating capability.[14]

SUMMARY

In an era in which management fads emerge and quickly fade from view, the value of building customer loyalty is one business precept that won't go out of fashion. Instead, issues of managing market relationships are moving steadily to the center of the strategy dialogue. Not only are the economics of customer retention providing a compelling rationale, but the relationships themselves are seen as among the most valuable and durable of all assets. Meanwhile, rapid advances in information technology are making it more feasible to rapidly learn about individual customer requirements, customize offerings, and tighten system linkages. Of course, many firms are also realizing they need to curry favor with their customers to avoid being caught in the gravitational pull toward profitless transactions in a frictionless market.

At the same time that these changes are occurring in relationships with customers in consumer markets, a parallel shift in relationships between companies and suppliers is occurring in business-to-business markets. Companies and their suppliers are moving from arms-length, adversarial relationships to collaborative relationships. This collaborative partnering is the focus of the next chapter.

Chapter Nine

Collaborative Partnering

While mass marketers have been pursuing the beneficial economics of customer retention, business-to-business marketers are working to reduce the high costs of adversarial relations with their customers. These are not the obvious out-of-pocket costs—instead they are obscured from view as lost opportunities to reduce joint costs and improve collective performance. If only short-run contracts are given, to make it easy to switch to a new supplier with lower prices, and orders are allocated to multiple suppliers to keep them in line, there is little incentive for information sharing and joint activities that eliminate redundancy or improve methods.

The market-driven organization creates collaborative partnerships with channel partners to reduce costs and increase its connections to the market. These close bonds give it sharper insights and more opportunities to create value for its immediate customers and end users. In contrast to manufacturers in the past that had little understanding of retailers and almost no way of gaining insights into the actual purchases of end customers, these close collaborations in the demand chain give manufacturers a direct connection to customers.

Sheer Perversity

For sheer perversity it would be hard to match the demand chain that once linked grocery product manufacturers and supermarket retailers. In the old *push* system, manufacturers made informed guesses masquerading as forecasts, from which production and distribution were scheduled and promotions were planned to create demand. But the objective of each party was to shift as much of its cost to the other as possible. This led to dysfunctional practices such as forward buying to take advantage of manufacturers' promotional offers, resulting in excessive warehousing expenses and costly spikes in production levels. Traditionally contacts between parties were limited to lower-level sales representatives calling on buyers who emphasized prices, quantities and deals.

Recent changes in these relationships between manufacturers and many retailers have transformed supermarket retailing from a marketing minefield to a model of cooperation. In recognition of the payoff from collaboration, many manufacturers have converted to a *pull* approach, which takes purchase information directly from the point-of-sale systems of retailers and schedules production and delivery from actual product movement information. No more guesswork here. Only when an item is removed from a shelf is another made to replace it. This smooths out production, reduces out-of-stocks, and saves both parties by reducing inventories. A typical before-after contrast is shown in Figure 9–1. Of course, this requires very close coordination with harmonized systems, shared logistics and product movement information, and joint planning for promotions and product changes.

Demand chains that link suppliers with downstream producers also benefit from the coordination of overlapping or duplicated activities. An industrial chocolate firm found large system savings by agreeing to deliver bulk chocolate to confectionery makers in liquid form in tank cars rather than in ten-pound molded bars. Not only did the firm save on the cost of molding and packaging but the customer was able to eliminate costly handling and remelting.

What distinguishes business-to-business markets is that end customers, wholesaler-distributors or retailers play as big a role in shaping the relationship as the supplier. They move from being adversaries to being partners. Although there are many similarities between the process of collaborating with customers and bonding with channel partners, the differences are large enough to treat them separately.

PARTNERING WITH CUSTOMERS

In healthy collaborations, the traditional demarcations between suppliers and customers become blurred and sometimes eliminated. Both parties

FIGURE 9–1

Coordinating Demand Chains

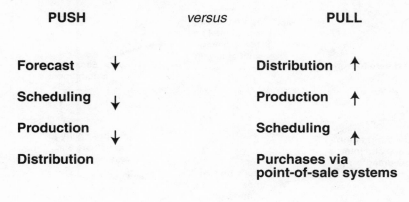

PUSH	*versus*	PULL
Forecast ↓		Distribution ↑
Scheduling ↓		Production ↑
Production ↓		Scheduling ↑
Distribution		Purchases via point-of-sale systems

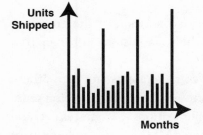

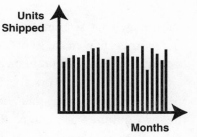

are committed to working closely together to achieve a shared objective and find the best solutions to commonly defined problems. With the escalation of mutual commitment comes a greater sense of mutual obligation. Neither partner wants to be blamed for losing the benefits that brought them together. As time passes, the two partners become so tightly integrated that the costs of separation are unthinkable. So when the inevitable conflict or disagreement arises, the instinct is to seek solutions rather than switch partners.

Most collaborative partnerships ripen slowly, as illustrated in Figure 9–2. They start with small efforts that build up credibility and mutual understanding. Perhaps they work together on the development of a new product, service or process. The supplier may offer an exclusive or a new

FIGURE 9-2

The Evolution of a Partnership

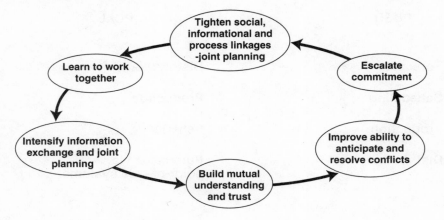

technology that strengthens the competitive position of the customer. The partners may make joint sales calls to help the customer open up new accounts or deal with problem areas.[1]

As they learn to work together, they come to appreciate each other's special abilities, constraints and "hot buttons." There is a growing sense the two cultures are compatible, communications become easier and more open and there is more shared history. All this helps to build trust that one partner will keep the interests of the other in mind. There is less second guessing, following up and worrying.

As mutual commitments continue to escalate, there is greater inter-dependence. A natural next step is a coordinated program to reduce the customer's cost of doing business. The partners can now contemplate making large and irreversible investments in joint materials requirement planning (MRP) systems, electronic data interchange (EDI) systems to link order entry and production planning or even just-in-time (JIT) inventory programs. With a clearer understanding of each other's priorities, style, rhythms and strategies, communications become streamlined, conflict resolution is routinized and the structural links become tighter. This is a continuing process.

Some of the most advanced—and mutually advantageous—partnerships are integral parts of just-in-time (JIT) manufacturing systems. A leading practitioner of the art is Johnson Controls, the world's largest maker of automotive seating "systems." These include not only the seats in ready-to-install form, but all the straps, bolts and contouring devices. Johnson has an especially close partnership with Chrysler, the first of the Big Three automakers to realize it could not afford the costs and inflexibility of a vertically integrated manufacturing system. Logically Chrysler turned to Johnson Controls to provide the seats for the sporty Neon subcompact it launched in 1994. This privileged supplier was given responsibility for product planning and styling, design engineering, source control, assembly and delivery.

Since this was already a well-oiled working relationship, it was easy for Johnson engineers to work alongside Chrysler's engineering and style teams to jointly arrive at form, fit and function requirements. As lead supplier of 80 percent of the Neon's seating systems, Johnson Controls integrated the system development with Chrysler's other outside suppliers. It also raised the stakes by building a new manufacturing plant next door to Chrysler's assembly plant, giving it the ability to deliver a seating system ready for installation within two hours of Chrysler's order.[2]

Committing to Close Collaboration

The benefits of single sourcing from a partner are sizable, especially when a just-in-time manufacturing process is used. In the ideal JIT system, a supplier only ships the component or material when it is needed. Since the parts are supposed to be of perfect quality, the customer can run this process without interruption or inventory buildup. This means big cost savings. There are other benefits as well:

1. Having suppliers participate in design and development taps a much broader base of knowledge. Also the supplier is motivated to invest in the best available technology without fear that the customer will share it with competitors.
2. When there are many suppliers for each item, it is difficult to find, let alone solve, quality problems. Engineering changes are hard to coordinate when the supplier base is fragmented. With one supplier, there is clear accountability.
3. A single supplier can realize scale economies and have enough volume to justify a special-purpose facility. With the security of a multiyear commitment it is also more motivated to make these investments.

To make a close collaboration work, both parties have to give up some of their freedom and run the risk of being held hostage by the other. By contrast, in transactional exchanges, the buyer has the comfort of having other suppliers whose competitive offerings provide an easy point of reference for assessing supplier performance. In moving from transactional to collaborative exchange that market discipline is replaced with joint agreements and contracts, guided by internal communications and reliant on mutual trust.[3] This can be very stressful for managers brought up in the adversarial school of unyielding negotiating stances and playing suppliers off against each other. How can they be sure they are "getting the best deal" and are being treated fairly when they have no other suppliers for comparison? At some point they may be tempted to look around, see if lower prices are available and even consider renegotiating the arrangements and inviting another vendor to share in the requirements. Faced with this possible defection the supplier may start looking around for more trustworthy customers. It doesn't take long before hard-earned trust evaporates and the carefully nurtured relationship starts to break down and even dissolve.

The Capability for Collaborating

Despite the well-publicized benefits of collaboration, few firms relish the prospect of tying their fortunes so closely to a partner. Initially parties are likely to be dubious about the other's motives and until the relationship has solidified, there will be nagging concerns about trustworthiness. When a customer is approached by a supplier who seeks a closer bond—and inferentially a privileged position—some of the management team will welcome the overture. Others may wonder if the supplier simply wants to keep them from actively shopping around for the best deal. Suppliers also hesitate to get into bed with their customers. Are they trying to strengthen their bargaining power by increasing the level of dependency? Once committed, will there be pressure for better terms?

With this much skepticism to overcome—never mind the inertia from staying with comfortable and familiar, albeit flawed practices—there has to be a compelling strategic logic. This is usually supplied by the customer, when it recognizes that the success of a quality program or time-based strategy hinges on supplier participation. In the 1980s many firms were just trying to catch up to their Japanese rivals who had already mastered the management of highly linked webs of suppliers. There were many pilgrims to Toyota City to admire the Kanban system firsthand, returning either fired by enthusiasm or overwhelmed by the magnitude of the task they faced in emulating this system.

For suppliers, the urge of their customers to partner was a very sharp, double-edged sword. On the downside it meant many fewer suppliers were needed, so attrition rates of 80 and 90 percent of the supplier base were not uncommon. During the 1980s Xerox went from 5,000 to 300 suppliers (although many of the smaller suppliers became suppliers to other suppliers). On the upside, the survivors like Johnson Controls who mastered the needed capabilities gained an unassailable advantage. Anyone who tried to displace them from their privileged position would have to retrace the same long trust-building path. Attackers seldom get a chance unless the incumbent gets complacent or the customer's requirements shift because of a new generation of technologies or a new management team that wants to throw out what the old team had done. Even when attackers do get an opening they won't succeed unless they can build an equivalent capability by changing their mind-set, acquiring a whole new array of skills, and then successfully integrating and aligning their processes.

Picking Partners

Because the stakes are so high, and the long-run resource commitments so large, the most capable collaborators have very refined skills in picking the ideal candidate for partnering. They think of their customer list as a portfolio: some customers only warrant an arms-length transactional approach while other relationships may be in the process of being upgraded and tightened. Only a few warrant wholehearted commitment.

Who is the ideal candidate? This is a bit of a trick question. It is not necessarily the one that can do the most for you, but rather is the one for whom you can do the most. These are the customers that value the benefits, or whose strategies and resources lend themselves to partnerships. Chrysler has always been a better partner than General Motors despite being smaller. After its brush with bankruptcy Chrysler realized it couldn't afford to be fully vertically integrated and that outsourcing tasks to suppliers would allow it to concentrate on styling and assembly where it could gain advantage. Typically large companies that are self-sufficient or make cost reduction the centerpiece of their strategy are less attracted to the value-added activities of their suppliers. Other attributes of attractive candidates for partnering are:[4]

- *Cultural compatibility.* Good partners share a common philosophy of doing business—ideally a "total cost" orientation which enables them to appreciate the additional value provided. There is also compatibility in attitudes including willingness to be open and share sensitive operating information.
- *Learning and stretching opportunities.* These candidates are constantly striving to improve their position and willing to experiment and learn. Because they demand a lot from their suppliers they are not the easiest to deal with, but the suppliers who keep up with or exceed their requirements have developed valuable skills they can apply elsewhere. These are the firms first to see the promise of the extranet, team-based management and other innovations, and create learning opportunities.
- *Share to gain.* These customers understand that to motivate their suppliers, and reduce the perceived risk of a close partnership, they have to be prepared to share in the value that is created. Some consulting firms are negotiating long-run arrangements for massive change-management initiatives where the compensation depends on the client reaching certain milestones. If the cost savings target isn't reached, or the service quality didn't reach an agreed standard, then the consultant gets only partly paid. This is highly motivating to say the least, and encourages the consultant to become part of the management team to carry the project through to completion.
- *Track record.* The final criterion is how they have behaved with other suppliers. Watch for those that are impatient for quick results, who keep their suppliers on constant notice that they will look elsewhere for a better deal or seem unable to trust their suppliers and keep tight control over the relationship

Finally, before suppliers seek or agree to a collaborative partnership, they should be confident of the outcome. When a maker of corrugated boxes tried to collaborate with one of its largest customers, it hired a consultant to give a two-day seminar at the customer's office to help them refine their quality practices.[5] Their hope was that the customer would appreciate their superior quality and reward them with more business. At the end of the seminar the consultant recommended they establish a "quality circle." This group decided to study packaging costs and breakage levels. They found to their collective surprise they were spending far more on corrugated boxes than peer firms, without discernible benefits. In a further blow to the beleaguered supplier, the customer concluded that box "rejects" would suffice, so it switched suppliers. Good intentions were definitely not rewarded.

Shaping the Mind-Set

Some cultures are much better suited than others to the demands of flexible responses, win-win negotiations, joint problem solving and open communications that partnering requires. Companies that have long had a sale-as-conquest mentality, with the emphasis on persuasion, zero-sum bargaining and grudging compromise, are not likely to collaborate with much enthusiasm. If they do enter, their skeptical mind-set will see the inevitable problems as excuses to withdraw rather than opportunities to grab.

The problems are not usually with the front-line customer contact people who are the champions for the effort. It is their superiors who grew up in the old culture and agree to pursue a partnering approach because of customer or competitor moves that present the greatest difficulties. As soon as the extent of irreversible commitments and investments becomes clear, they start to hesitate or look for ironclad assurances from the prospective partner. Their behaviors and attitudes are in turn transmitted to other parts of the organization who may not appreciate why partnering pays and resent the unrealistic commitments that in their eyes should not have been made. Of course, the customer is often the first to see the internal dissension.

Acquiring Knowledge and Skills

Capable collaborators stand out in their knowledge of the customer (and the customer's customers) and their ability to share what they have learned throughout their organization. This knowledge can run very deep—right down to the strategies, aspirations, frustrations, and concerns, the personalities of key people and the strengths and weaknesses of their systems and procedures. Capable collaborators are also very skillful at putting this knowledge to work, and monitoring the health of the relationship for signs of dissatisfaction and stress and taking action quickly to resolve any problems. They are also sensitive to the customer's need for reassurance and frequent demonstrations of satisfactory performance. However most of the knowledge and skills component of their capability is devoted to the smooth coordination of joint activities.

Integrating and Aligning Processes

As relationships become more collaborative the social, process and system linkages become ever tighter. They may include most or all of the following:

- Multilevel and multifunction contacts, where senior officers talk to each other, and systems and operating people work and even socialize with their counterparts.
- Joint planning sessions where the two partners share proprietary information about capabilities, forecasts and schedules, and deal with outstanding issues and conflicts. During these sessions, opportunities for joint cost savings by relocating activities are discussed. The supplier might propose taking over some onerous assembly operations from the customer.
- Tightly linked production planning and scheduling, to the point that the supplier's order fulfillment process is tied directly into the customer's ordering and replenishment system.
- Personnel exchanges and assignments of experts to each other's teams. This is particularly helpful in new product or process development where customers and suppliers become active members of each other's teams. Then requirements can be anticipated and early feedback received.
- Joint sales calls and shared promotion programs can be used to help the customer open up new accounts.

The challenge is to coordinate and orchestrate these linkages, and keep all the players involved and informed. This is best done in a team-based organizational structure of the hybrid variety—combining horizontal and vertical structures—which will be discussed in more detail in Chapter 10. The team leader is often the key accounts manager who is assigned from the sales group to live with the customer on a full-time basis. It is this person's responsibility to keep everyone involved in the ongoing task of strengthening the relationship and fighting the tendency to complacency.

Just because a customer is committed to a relationship doesn't mean it can be taken for granted.

Increasingly the relationship team includes a full-time information systems specialist. Manufacturing firms of all sorts have encouraged or demanded that their supplier partners invest in technology systems to support electronic data interchange (EDI) to slash the costs of processing orders and reduce logistical mishaps. At one time the large up-front costs of these proprietary systems obliged manufactures to limit their suppliers just as it obliged suppliers to concentrate on a few customers. One could easily conclude computers and collaboration went hand in hand.

Firms are now turning to extranets based on the Worldwide Web to do many of the same things they used to do with their proprietary systems. On one hand, the use of the Internet to establish secure and low-cost standing information links between companies has expanded the range of possible relationships and opened up opportunities for smaller companies to partner. However, it is unlikely that this greater accessibility will erode the advantages of tight relationships. Collaboration requires trust, coordination, and sharing of privileged information knowing that it will not be leaked to a competitor or used to strike a new bargain. An extranet will not erode the basis of the loyalty that earlier technology imposed because technology is only a facilitator and not a reason for a relationship.

CHANNEL BONDING

Few mental models are more misleading than the simplistic notion that channels are passive conduits for reaching markets. When suppliers were powerful and could pull their products through fragmented distributors and retailers, this myopic view didn't cause much damage. With channels in unprecedented flux and old power structures overturned, suppliers have been scrambling to build new capabilities to bond more closely to their newly discovered channel "partners." What has precipitated this more enlightened view?

• *Power is moving downstream.* Most retail and wholesale distribution lines of trade are coalescing around a few big players. Think of Wal-Mart, Toys "Я" Us, Home Depot, and Staples—each dominating all but a few of their suppliers. The sales of the top six grocery retailers exceed those of all European food manufacturers other than Unilever and Nestlé. These powerhouses can unilaterally impose standards for packaging, delivery, and systems integration, and the suppliers have no choice other than to acquiesce—or is surrender the better word? Powerful retailers can also insist that manufacturers sell directly to them, so the distributor is bypassed or disintermediated. These distributors are in double jeopardy because the growth of these large "category killers" also squeezes the small and medium-sized retailers they traditionally served.

• *The roles of channel intermediaries keep changing.* In business-to-business markets without the retail level, it is the distributors who are flexing their muscles as a few large players handle an ever-larger share of total volume. In drug wholesaling, the top three firms handle 73 percent of the volume. This is a mixed blessing for suppliers. They appreciate the efficiency gains, yet they are apprehensive about the inclination of these wholesalers to see themselves as agents of their customers rather than wholesalers of suppliers' products. As a result, wholesalers are performing many new functions that were not in their original purview: subassembly of components, consulting services, or supplying private label products that compete with their suppliers' offerings. In some cases they are entering into integrated supply agreements in which customers outsource their entire purchasing and procurement function to the wholesaler. The wholesaler is then in a position to decide that they don't have to carry all ten brands in a mature category, since they are virtually interchangeable, and may offer only three or four brands to improve internal efficiency.

• *Collaboration is needed to realize benefits from technology.* The possibilities for cost savings from the use of bar coding, scanning at the point of sale and elsewhere, EDI and database management can only be realized if suppliers and retailers work together. Of course, a necessary condition is standards for product identification and data interchange to overcome the welter of incompatible systems and protocols that grew up over time. But this technology can only be put to full use if the whole system is reengineered. Simply automating existing inefficient internal processes is both complex and wasteful. The point of initiatives such as Efficient Consumer Response (ECR) is to bring both suppliers and intermediaries together to redesign the linked processes. Then they can eliminate redundancies, such as order entry by both supplier and retailer, or reassign tasks for maximum system-wide efficiency such as moving the job of ticketing merchandise to the supplier so it is "floor ready" when it is delivered.[6]

Collaboration Versus Coercion

In principle the forging of close channel bonds has a lot in common with collaborative partnering in business-to-business markets. Certainly there is plenty of incentive for collaborations to reduce total system costs, shorten replenishment cycles and reduce inventories. So why wouldn't the parties come willingly together to realize these gains?

The main problem is the division of the benefits. The experience of a small midwestern maker of inexpensive housewares in dealing with Kmart, Wal-Mart, and Target, three giant retail chains, is sobering and instructive.[7] According to the company president, "We were encouraged—or pushed—into electronic data interchange." With this system, orders could be put directly into his system which cut errors and clerical costs. Each item and pallet was barcoded, saving the retailers on handling time. Initially those customers divided the savings of the system equally. Later, he noted, "they decided the savings were so great I should pay both halves."

The retailer's benefits from this collaboration are abundantly clear: inventory carrying costs are lower, there are fewer out-of-stocks and there is less need to rely on fallible forecasts of fast-moving items. The benefits to the manufacturer are less obvious. In the short run they gain increased sales volume from participating. If they have a strong brand name, they may be able to keep these gains. But here the second problem arises. Because retailers and wholesalers have to provide the assortment their buyers want, they can't and won't provide exclusivity. Eventually all eligible suppliers will be integrated into retail order and replenishment systems and prospects for advantage are gone. This raises a further difficulty. When a retailer or wholesaler has close partnerships with the main competitors in a category, how can confidentiality be maintained? One approach is for the manufacturer to have separate teams for major accounts as Procter & Gamble does with Wal-Mart and Kmart.

The final impediment to open sharing and collaboration is the legacy of long years of adversarial relations, and well-grounded skepticism about the motives of the other party. The reasons are rooted in differences in objectives and strategies. Manufacturers want to move high volumes at high prices while retailers want the lowest price. Manufacturers would like to capture the wholesaler's margin by going direct to the end buyer or retailer, and retailers also want to buy directly.

In short, it is hard to build trust in these complex channel systems, and even harder to sustain an advantage. Yet some market-driven firms will rise to the challenge and build a superior capability for bonding with their customers.

Capable Channel Collaborators

What are the characteristics of capable channel collaborators? The priority still has to be to reshape the organizational mind-set, demonstrate sustained commitment, and acquire the deep knowledge and skills needed to instill trust in the partner. While this will confer some advantages on a supplier, it may not suffice in complex channel settings where systems integration is table stakes and retailers and distributors are polygamous by necessity—they have to have multiple partners. However, there is usually one supplier that is more equal than others. Wal-Mart, for example, appoints one supplier to manage all aspects of a category; P&G has that responsibility for detergents but was not picked for hair care. What superior capabilities did these firms have that justified picking them over their rivals? In general, the distinguishing factors include:

• *Demonstrable and sustained commitment.* There are many ways to signal top-to-bottom commitment to making the partnership work. Surely one of the most dramatic and effective is to assign a dedicated team of specialists to the account, and then locate them on the partner's premises. When the team lives with an account they see things from a different perspective, and when properly motivated they will see more opportunities to add value through cutting costs or improving performance.

• *Continuous market learning.* All capable collaborators invest in learning about their immediate customers—but channel collaboration requires the same depth of insight into the needs of the end user, the customer's customer. General Electric discovered that its distributors for electrical supplies had a highly segmented end-user base, and had particular difficulty meeting the needs of contractors for quotation responsiveness in small jobs. Unlike big jobs with long complex quotation processes, the small jobs were won or lost depending on the contractor's ability to quote quickly. In recognition, General Electric developed a PC-based quotation system for its distributors that did not require inputs from the manufacturer. Because GE is recognized as having a faster quote it has a much higher share of the small job segment.

• *Attention to personal chemistry.* Although this is good practice for any would-be collaborator, it has been refined in the channels setting. In some leading firms customer contact people are given personality tests and assigned to accounts with the best "match." Sherwin-Williams, the paint company, even lets Sears, Roebuck participate in the selection of the people who will handle its account.

• *Careful alignment of incentives.* A long-standing source of difficulty between suppliers and retailers has been the misaligned incentives that rewarded retail buyers for high gross margins and salespeople for achieving sales volume targets. To unravel the problem the partners must first agree on shared objectives and then monitor their collective performance against these objectives (days of inventory, vendor shipment accuracy, in-stock levels, order lead times, and so forth). To provide the right incentives the partners need to devise joint compensation systems that reward the whole team on a collective basis, not just the individual contributors.

Effective collaboration requires as much attention to building the internal capabilities as will be devoted to forging the links with the channel member.

SUMMARY: THE ADVANTAGES OF COLLABORATIVE PARTNERING

It has been argued that there is no such thing as a sustainable advantage. This is undoubtedly true in some abstract sense, but in practice, trusting, mutually valuable collaborative partnerships come closer than almost any other source of advantage to satisfying the general conditions of real sustainability.

1. They are *durable* and not vulnerable to obsolescence or rapid depreciation because of the pace of technological change, shifts in customer requirements or the depletion of nonrenewable assets. Successful relation-

ships and partnerships achieve durability through mutual commitments, demonstrations of mutual trust and shared understanding. The two partners are drawn together by open sharing of information, the development of linkages between many people at different levels in the two organizations and the realistic expectations of mutual benefits. Why would a customer take a chance on a newcomer wanting its business when its present partner has a proven ability to adapt to its changing needs?

2. There are *barriers to imitation* because the competition has difficulty understanding how the advantage was achieved and even if they broke the code they still couldn't duplicate it.[8] Collaborative relationships with customers are especially difficult to emulate because it takes a lot of tacit knowledge and complex coordination to manage them effectively. Think of the tight collaboration between, say, Chrysler and a preferred supplier of components such as Magna Industries. Rivals can readily see what has been accomplished, but they can't overcome the barrier of "causal ambiguity" to understand how the results are achieved. This is not surprising, for the essentials skills and supporting knowledge are embedded so deeply into the people, the culture and the linking processes that they cannot be directly observed.

3. There is a *first mover advantage* that can be protected. Even when customers patronize several suppliers—as is the practice of major retailers such as Target and Wal-Mart—they usually pick one with which to form a stronger partnership. Often this is the supplier that is most adept at identifying and managing relationship opportunities. Indeed because they are known to be a good firm to partner with they are likely to be sought out in the first place. The first mover can sustain the relationship because it has formed the closest links, is better informed about the customer's future needs, and can be more responsive.

For all these reasons, closer ties to channel partners create advantages for the market-driven organization. They help companies to better understand, attract and retain valuable customers—both the immediate customers in the channel and end customers. As difficult as they are to manage, these relationships give companies unprecedented insights into understanding their markets and a mechanism for creating enduring ties with customers.

PART III

ALIGNING
THE ORGANIZATION
TO THE MARKET

From the preceding chapters, we have a clear picture of how market-driven companies outperform their rivals. But how do companies that are not closely aligned with their current or anticipated market successfully transform their culture, configuration and capabilities to become more market-driven?

Many solutions have been proposed to deal with the symptoms of misalignment. Too remote from consumers? Organize around segments. Costs too high? Restructure and de-layer. Decision making too clumsy and slow? Deploy teams around core processes. Incentives are ineffective? Tie compensation more closely to customer satisfaction and retention.

Each of these fixes is only a partial attack on the broader question of how to design an organization that can continually anticipate and adapt to changing customer requirements. The ideal is to have the customer drive the organization—not for it to be the other way around. While the ideal may never be reached, organizations can move closer to it by realigning their structures and strategy, and by following a systematic process for change.

As discussed in Chapter 10, companies that want to increase their market orientation often have to change their organizational structures. Market-driven organizations are supported by hybrid structures that combine the best features of horizontal processes and vertical, functional forms. With the aid of recent developments in information technology, they are better equipped to create interactive processes and organizational structures.

As discussed in Chapter 11, firms that want to align themselves more closely with the market also have to change their strategic thinking and their process for developing strategy. In contrast to the budget-cycle planning processes that often lead to an internal focus, market-driven organizations take the market as the starting point in developing strategy. The planning process of the market-driven firm is adaptive and focused on current, real-time issues drawn from market experience. They use approaches such as scenario planning and including customers in the planning process to ensure a close attention to the market. Strategy development then is concentrated on generating and evaluating strategic options to address market issues. This infuses a market perspective into all the company's strategic deliberations.

Finally, in Chapter 12, we formulate a systematic process for guiding the change from an internal focus toward a market orientation. We illustrate this process through the turnaround stories of three companies and the processes they used to transform themselves.

As with any strategy or organizational restructuring, the devil is in the details. Implementation of an effective change process is one of the most challenging issues in establishing a market-driven organization. It is often a current or potential crisis that forces companies to recognize the need to become market-driven. They usually face serious challenges from their established culture, capabilities, structure and strategy that make it difficult to establish a stronger market orientation. Consider the challenges facing the following firms:

- *With a diverse product line that was increasingly confusing for its customers, Owens Corning needed to transform itself from a product-focused manufacturer to a customer-driven firm.*
- *With declining profits and market share, Sears needed to make a quick change from a traditional department store to a market-driven organization.*
- *With its tunnel across the English Channel completed, Eurotunnel needed to switch tracks from a construction-focused firm to a market-focused organization that could now convince customers to use its new route to and from the continent.*

The transformation of these three companies highlights six conditions that characterize most successful market-driven change processes. These are: leadership commitment, understanding the need for change, shaping the vision, mobilizing commitment at all levels, aligning structure, systems and incentives, and the ability to sustain the change. Each of these conditions contributes to a successful change process.

The following chapters indicate the challenges involved in developing a market-driven organization. The stories of firms that have successfully made this transition show the tremendous opportunities for companies that can stay the course to become more market-driven.

Chapter Ten

Reshaping the Organization

Creating a market-driven organizational structure is more challenging than it might at first appear. In 1994, Digital Equipment Corp. set out to radically restructure itself to become closer to its market. It redesigned the organization to create autonomous minicompanies organized by customer type, the better to anticipate and serve customer needs. The intention was to get closer to customers and convince them to buy complete systems.

But several problems derailed the plan. First, each of the new businesses combined low-margin products and high-margin services, undermining sales of each. Second, most of the executives came from DEC's engineering department and knew little of the industries they were serving. Seriously, there was a major shift in the computer industry, in which the rise of standard hardware and software let customers build their own systems from various vendors.

The moral is that even the best-intentioned moves to align the organizational structure to the market can misfire. In DEC's case, its restructuring eroded critical capabilities, which were lodged in technology process and development capabilities. The company was eventually forced to organize itself around specific product lines, such as workstations, servers, and software.

TRADE-OFFS AND THE SEARCH FOR OPTIMAL DESIGN

Continuous organizational flux is the norm in most firms. If you aren't in the middle of a redesign, you are brooding on the deficiencies of the most recent effort and casting about for a better approach. As frustrating, time-consuming and seemingly unproductive as the constant rearranging seems, it is inherent in the design problem. There is no perfect design for all seasons. First, any design is the unsatisfying result of many trade-offs and compromises, as demonstrated in the case of DEC's reorganization. Adding to one side of the balance can detract from the other. Second, markets are also in flux, so what worked tolerably well yesterday won't work so well tomorrow. Third, our concepts of effective and feasible designs are being challenged by the changing economics and availability of information, and the compelling track record of team-based organizations.

The ideal of a market-driven organization is to have all functional activities integrated and aligned in the delivery of superior customer value. The difficulty is that functional differences are deeply rooted in incentives, backgrounds and interests, time scales and task priorities. Any effort to improve alignment requires balancing numerous contending forces. These present dilemmas require management to do several contradictory things at once. It's like driving a car. You want to get to your destination quickly and also safely. You must watch the road ahead and also look behind and around you. Some of the classic dilemmas are:

Maintain flexibility with small units	versus	Achieve economies of scale
Align with market and geographies	versus	Develop and leverage distinctive capabilities
Make it new and innovative	versus	Be predictable and constant
Develop deep functional expertise	versus	Subordinate functions to process teams
Facilitate coordination and information sharing	versus	Eliminate overhead and unproductive activities

These trade-offs are inherent in the choice among four possible templates for designing the backbone of an organization: The first and most prevalent is the *product* theme, which often dictates how divisions are created. Here commonality of product features or production process takes precedence. Within consumer package goods firms, the divisions are product-

THE CONTINUOUS CHALLENGE OF COMPLEXITY
General Electric Engineering Plastics Division[2]

When GE Plastics successfully launched its Lexan polycarbonate as a replacement for glass, a simple product-based organization structure was appropriate. During the 1960s the emphasis was on converting customers from other materials, and this structure provided a sense of ownership, team responsibility, and accountability.

The structure continued to work into the 1970s, even as GE Plastics introduced Noryl. This was another engineering plastic that suited applications such as auto dashboards and personal computers. As the product line expanded, so did the number of competitors. During the 1980s, growth slowed to single digits. Customers were more experienced with engineered plastics and more open to switching to lower-priced alternatives. The buying decision put increasing emphasis on price, manufacturability, and service. In the meantime, Noryl and Lexan were aiming at the same applications and competing more directly. By 1985, the autonomous product divisions were more a hindrance than a help. Customers were confused as Noryl and Lexan attacked each other, each claiming it was best for the other's applications. The costs of duplicate services—purchasing, service, finance, MIS—were mounting. Vested interests were solidly entrenched and resistant to change.

The solution was to divide GE Plastics into three geographies (America, Europe and Pacific). Within each geography, marketing, sales, manufacturing, and technology were common functions for all products. Profit-and-loss responsibility

based and individual product or brand managers are responsible for charting the course of their products. They produce a coordinating logic for the functional activities of logistics, manufacturing, sales and so on. The second is the *geographic* template, which is used by some large, money-center banks. The third option is to have the organization mirror the *segmentation of the market*. This is conceptually appealing but seldom found in a pure form. Instead, market managers may coexist with functional managers in a matrix structure, or parts of the organization may be focused on segments such as the high net worth segment in retail banking. The fourth is to design around *channels*, such as a retailer with separate store and catalog groups.

Each organizational template imposes painful trade-offs. It is difficult resided with the geography head. Marketing and product management became worldwide functions, with product managers the critical link for coordination within GE Plastics.

This solution resolved the problem of customer confusion, and enabled the business to get closer to customers. This new function of Market Development Rep (MDR) served the final customer, such as Ford, to provide integrated solutions. Many of the responsibilities of the product division general managers were assigned to product managers, including strategy, resource allocation, and pricing.

Although the new structure was clearly more market-driven, and moved the organization away from an intense focus on products, other problems emerged. The structure was more complex, with many more "indirect" reporting relationships, and the role of the global marketing management function was murky. Meanwhile more accounts wanted global solutions, leading to a need for global account managers who could maintain consistency. All these pressures for change led to further adjustments to the structure—and the job will never end.

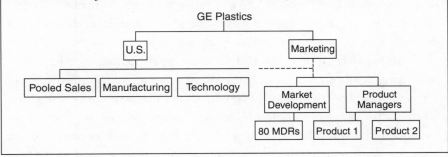

in a product-based structure to tailor the offering to the needs of specific geographies or end-consumer segments. A geographic approach makes it difficult to share knowledge across regions and may increase costs through the duplication of activities. An end-user-segment approach, such as DEC tried to adopt, raises the risk of fragmentation and erodes deep product knowledge.

Organizational dilemmas and trade-offs have always been with us, but they have become sharper and less avoidable with the recognition that core competencies or capabilities are at the source of the most durable and valuable competitive advantages. These capabilities transcend the traditional boundaries and functions of an organization, and are enhanced by learning processes that span the entire organization.[1] Sony's miniaturization capability or Wal-Mart's mastery of supply chain replenishment span the organization and its markets. Meanwhile, to achieve focus and gain intimate understanding of disparate markets, it is desirable to have businesses organized to target distinct markets.

There is no absolute or permanent solution to these challenges. Creating and re-creating the organization is an ongoing process, as described in the case of GE Plastics (see box). Each shift to a new organizational form brings some unwanted side effect and each shift in the market creates new challenges to be addressed by the next organizational form.

Layers of Complexity

As markets become more complex, the trade-offs built into the design challenge become more constraining, and the organization finds it harder to respond to all the demands placed on it. New structures, functions and activities have to be grafted on to meet these new demands. Each add-on serves a purpose but the cumulative effect is an increasingly unwieldy and complicated structure, which places intolerable demands on the ability of management to coordinate and integrate activities.

The experience of Procter & Gamble with the organization of its marketing demonstrates how organizations accumulate complexity. Procter & Gamble has traditionally been organized around product categories, often with complete functional organizations. As the product range expanded, the company began to add other brands, each needing a *brand manager*. Within detergents alone, there are nine brands, each with a full-time associate and assistant brand managers working for the brand manager. Because each of these brands is competing within the same category, their work needs to be coordinated by a *category manager,* otherwise brand managers would spend their time unprofitably trying to steal sales from other P&G brands.

The sales function also became more complex as the channels evolved. The most important to Procter & Gamble are the large supermarkets, warehouse clubs and mass merchandise chains. Relations with each of these retail chains is managed by a *national account manager* who is supported by a *customer service team* of specialists in logistics, finance and so forth.

These channels help P&G reach the home, but there are other big markets such as laundries and hospitals with *market segment managers* that develop special programs. These sales roles are evolving under pressure from the largest accounts like Wal-Mart who don't want to have a different team for each P&G product; they want a single point of contact to coordinate sales activities across the entire firm.

A similar structure is generally used within each of the major country markets, with local variations as needed. In a large country such as the United States, there are many regional differences in tastes, requirements and competitive realities. Consumer goods companies are increasingly adding *market area managers* to create programs that recognize these differences: What works in the Southwest won't work as well in the Northeast and vice versa.

The P&G marketing organization is a metaphor for any organization that breeds complexity in response to new demands. Each additional job function adds a bit more bureaucracy, slows down decisions because more people have to be consulted, and causes critical market knowledge to be dispersed to more points. Certainly each of these jobs adds value or it wouldn't have been justified in the first place, but the cumulative effect is to increase costs and reduce responsiveness. Sooner or later the situation becomes intolerable and a search for a new organizational template begins.

Cutting the Gordian Knot: The Promise of Information Technology

Will increasing market complexity continue to outrun the capacity of multiproduct, multimarket organizations to cope? Is the answer to simply keep grafting more components, activities, coordinators and integrating functions to an increasingly cumbersome structure? Cautiously, the answer is "no" because information technology is releasing us from the stifling premises of hierarchies. It can help cut through the raveled Gordian knot of these layered organizational structures.

Information technology allows us to challenge fundamental assumptions underlying traditional hierarchies.[3] These are based on a belief in *unity of command*, where there is only one reporting relationship. The *span of control* for any manager should then be no more than five to seven reporting relationships, to avoid going beyond the limit of direct communications. Another deep-seated belief about hierarchies is that *authority should be commensurate with responsibility.* Ambiguity about roles and responsibilities should be minimized with *clear job descriptions.* People who have lived within hierarchies for years are so comfortable with these principles they seldom rouse themselves to challenge them, despite all the frustrations of living with the consequences.

On closer scrutiny, these beliefs are predicated on the assumption that information flows cannot be rich and broad simultaneously. In fact, there are trade-offs. *Reach* is determined by the number of people who share the same information at the same time. *Richness* embraces the amount of information that can be communicated at one time, plus the extent of tailoring of the information that is sent or received, and the likelihood of dialogue or interaction. The hierarchy is constructed to live within the constraints of the trade-offs pictured in Figure 10–1.[4]

Within a hierarchy there is frequent interaction and intense dialogue among a few people standing in a vertical hierarchical relationship. With traditional communication channels the reach is restricted by time available, so greater reach means adding more layers to the hierarchy. This inevitably leads to information being divided up more finely as it proceeds down the hierarchy, and introduces serious asymmetries or imbalances in the amount of information at various levels. Because information is valuable and senior managers have a wider span for their knowledge base than their subordinates, they have greater power.

FIGURE 10–1

Changing Economics of Organizational Information

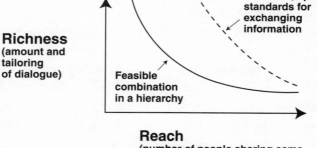

192

However, this structure interferes with the flow of information from the market. Information moves sluggishly up the hierarchy from the sensors that are in direct contact with the market. Top management will not be well-informed—just better informed than anyone else.

Information technology changes the trade-off between reach and richness. What would it be like if everyone could access the same data sources and communicate with everybody else with essentially zero cost and negligible friction and impediments? The emergence of the Internet, extranets and intranets provides opportunities for broad and deep information flows throughout the organization and with external stakeholders. This creates the opportunity to move away from rigid hierarchies to create new organizational forms.

It doesn't mean that organizations are moving completely away from vertical structures, however. They are creating organizational hybrids, combining horizontal business processes and vertical specialist functions. Among the most important organizational innovations to enable closer market alignment are the emergence of hybrid structures that are flexible and team-based.

THE EMERGENCE OF HYBRID ORGANIZATIONS

With this new technology, companies have more choices in transforming their structures to make them more market driven. They can select from a continuum of vertical and horizontal structures as shown in Figure 10–2. The extreme ends of the spectrum—totally horizontal or totally vertical—are problematic, which is why many companies are combining the best elements of both into hybrid forms. But to understand this hybrid organization, we first have to examine the strengths and weaknesses of the purely vertical and horizontal forms.

Vertical Organizations

The traditional vertical hierarchy is not quite a dinosaur. It can be a good approach for small firms with focused strategies and straightforward value propositions where the customers' needs are well known to all functions. "Line of sight" information sharing and strong leadership are sufficient to ensure alignment of functions with the market. Hierarchies also suffice

FIGURE 10–2

Organization Design Continuum

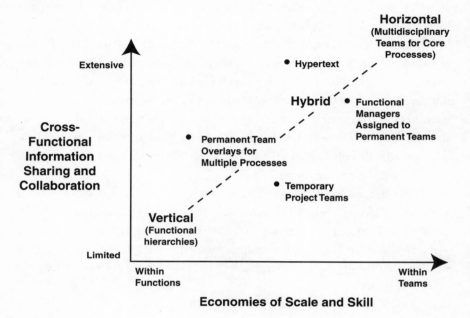

when it is necessary to optimize costly, capital intensive, and inflexible factories or systems. Because jobs are carefully divided into well-defined specialty activities, there is deep functional expertise.

The Achilles heel of vertical hierarchies is coordination. It takes a lot of middle managers to collect front-line information and feedback, and broadcast and clarify top management intentions and priorities. These managers accrue power because they control information flows and allocate resources. Because these managers occupy and identify with a functional home, they are prone to optimize their own parochial activities but not talk to each other in a systematic way. This results in a lack of product integrity, slow response times and high costs. These problems are accentuated by mounting market complexity and the threat of competitors who adopt sense and respond strategies. Sooner or later the tension between the forces of inertia that lock firms into their comfortable but ineffective structure and the mounting forces of change compels consideration of other structures.

Horizontal Organizations

The horizontal organization is built around natural work flows and core processes. The vertical silos of the functional hierarchies are now linked directly rather than through high-level handoffs or the intervention of coordinators and integrators such as product managers. Instead, integration comes through a shared concept of how to meet customer needs better than competition.

The backbone of the organization is the core processes that were described in Chapter 4. Each process such as supply chain management or new product development is the responsibility of a multidisciplinary team. Teams are accountable for external objectives such as customers' satisfaction with the outcome of the process, or performance related to competitive benchmarks such as order processing time. Information is readily shared with all team members through internal networks (usually intranets) that eliminate the filtering and interpretation once done by intermediaries.

A distinguishing feature of the horizontal or process-oriented organization is the creation of new managerial roles.[5] Gone are the familiar titles of department manager, section leader, director or supervisor. In their places we find three different roles within a business unit:

- *Process owners* ensure that the process they are responsible for is well designed, oversee the day-to-day activities of the team, and have ultimate responsibility for the team assigned to the process. These people work hard to get the highest yield from their assets and resources, and are given abundant and immediate feedback on how well they are doing. They are motivated by stretch goals and a sense of internal competition to continually improve productivity.
- *Coaches* are charged with maintaining skills and developing specialized talent in each area of necessary expertise. They are the gateways by which new practices, procedures and technical capabilities are introduced through educational and expertise-sharing opportunities.
- *Leaders* set the strategic direction and provide an integrating logic so the core processes can work together effectively. They exercise leadership through direct monitoring, the creation of operating principles that shape the assumptions of the rest of the organization and the allocation of resources. However, their choices and decisions are not

---

ASTRA MERCK: AN ANTIDOTE TO HIERARCHY[6]

Astra Merck has enthusiastically adopted a horizontal organization to build a billion-dollar ethical drug development and distribution firm with a solution selling capability. The company was conceived out of an unusual set of circumstances. It was created as a stand-alone joint venture in 1992 to combine the heart and gastrointestinal drugs developed by AB Astra, a Swedish firm, with the U.S. sales capabilities of Merck and Co. It also was seen as an opportunity to create a new and different model of a pharmaceutical company.

This greenfield approach was seen as the best way to deal with a major disruption in the market. Traditionally, drugs were sold to individual doctors through the detailing and sampling activities of large field sales forces. By 1993, the trend to managed care with centralized buying was well underway, seriously threatening these traditional relationships. Managed care buyers were more price sensitive and interested in a drug's cost-effectiveness, and restricted the access of the doctors in their network to only the drugs that satisfied these criteria. Meanwhile pharmaceutical firms were trying to reign in the very high costs of their traditional sales forces—which might exceed 25 to 30 percent of sales.

When the new management team was given a clean sheet of paper, they dismissed most of the conventional hierarchical wisdom about how to organize. Instead they started from the outside in with multidisciplinary teams as the basic building blocks. The structure of these teams was guided by a business architecture that linked 15 business processes. A key element is the business unit team, which is responsible for one of 31 regions of the United States, and carries a wide array of functions in addition to sales. Each unit has *medical information scientists,* who have the depth of knowledge to build peer relationships with the medical profession, plus *customer support people* who provide information and *business managers* who concentrate on large accounts. These business units are

---

unilateral and top-down; instead all of the main players have an active role in the ongoing strategy dialogue.

Horizontal structures have several other distinguishing features, according to proponents. First, there are fewer layers, because there are fewer supervisory responsibilities in self-managed teams, and only a lean

designed to be highly autonomous and expert in their markets with the capability of rapidly pulling together creative solutions for individual customers.

To support this decentralized structure Astra Merck invested heavily in company-wide systems—such as those that access product information. Further integration, to ensure responsiveness to customer needs, was achieved with "pharmaceutical solutions" management teams in each therapeutic area—such as gastrointestinal—that included development, licensing, marketing, sales, and product sourcing people. Additional staff were assigned to licensing, business development, and sourcing processes.

The horizontal model proved a resounding success on all performance measures. By late 1998, sales had reached $4 billion per year, powered by a 60 percent growth of a ten-year-old gastrointestinal drug, Prilosec. Between 1997 and 1998, customer satisfaction ratings led the industry because of a demonstrated ability to provide solutions.

How much was this due to the innovative organization? Skeptics attribute success to the acceptance of Prilosec, and predict that performance will subside when the drug loses patent protection and becomes a generic. This is true, but misses the point: Astra Merck had as good a drug as the competition, but it was also better equipped to exploit it rapidly and achieve superior results during the protected period.

Rapid growth did eventually lead to more layers. As the sales force expanded from 500 to 2,400 in 67 geographic areas, it became impractical to have full teams with business managers in each area. The solution was to create ten customer centers—each with IT, human resource people and business managers—to which the 67 customer units reported. As the solutions management teams became large and ungainly, the company created a hierarchy of teams directed by a value-chain management team, which sharpened accountability for decisions.

top management is needed to provide direction. Second, there is an emphasis on developing competitively superior capabilities—the complex bundles of skills and accumulated knowledge that enable superior coordination of the activities in the process. Finally, the organization is capable of being continually reconfigured as conditions change, rather than remaining static and rigid.

Horizontal forms that actually work do not exist in a pure form. Success stories about applications of horizontal design principles usually describe a partial attack on a few core processes. However, Astra Merck (now Astra Zeneca) has come as close as any to building a complete organization on these principles. The greenfield creation of this ethical drug development and marketing firm is described in the box. By the time the organization was fully in place in 1994, there were only three levels between the CEO and front-line customer contact people. This was in sharp contrast to the seven or more levels in a traditional pharmaceutical firm.

Hybrid Organizations

Most firms are not willing or able to shift to a purely horizontal form as Astra Merck did, and few are given a blank slate for designing a new organization. Instead, they are creating hybrid organizations that combine elements of vertical organizations with elements of horizontal structures. A recent survey of 73 companies found that none was operating with a true horizontal structure, but only 32 percent had retained a traditional functional design.[7] Of the others, 38 percent were laying process structures over their functional groups, usually by deploying functional specialists in project teams for specific projects of limited duration, and 30 percent were trying process structures with functional overlays.

Consumer packaged goods firms such as Unilever, Kraft and General Mills have been experimenting with hybrid designs since the early 1990s. For a generalized example, see Figure 10–3. Each firm is under pressure from low inflation, competition from generic and private labels, new retail formats, more powerful retailers that want to reduce costs through supply chain integration, and escalating promotion costs that sap profits. The traditional structures with brand or product managers responsible for coordination could not handle the increased stress.

Firms that create hybrid structures recognize that they need to foster vertical skills and disciplines such as the engineering skill to design ergonomically sound products, the financial skills and experience to create the financial services that differentiate GE Capital from its competitors, or the mastery of information technology that enables the seamless integration of a business and its customers. And despite the ambitious claims of the process engineers, there will always be internal handoffs, whether from research to product development or from the center to the field organization.

Hybrid structures combine horizontal business processes with integrating and specialist functions. Integrating functions such as marketing, strategy development and human resource management provide the mechanisms for coordinating and allocating resources to the core processes. Specialist functions such as R&D and marketing research are needed to provide technical expertise and replenish the horizontal processes with new ideas—either through new insights from outside the firm or the transfer of learning across teams. As a result, most firms start with "centers of excellence" based on traditional departments and disciplines, then modify the vertical function so it is more meaningful. Thus, sales might become customer interaction and engineering could be technical design. The coach—who was once a functional manager—continues to play a central role.

FIGURE 10–3

Hybrid Organizations for Consumer Packaged Goods

Category Management Teams. Responsible for leveraging deep understanding of the market and the equity of the brand name to formulate and communicate the value proposition to the consumer. Composed of representatives from marketing, finance, sales, operations and R&D.

Customer Management Teams. Responsible for maximizing total performance with the major retail and trade customers, by building solid relationships and integrating operations for mutual cost savings. Includes field sales, marketing, promotions, logistics and sales.

Supply Chain Management teams. Charged with the sourcing, production and delivery for major product categories; representatives come from manufacturing, purchasing, distribution and quality.

Product Development Teams. Find and develop product concepts that deliver compelling value propositions to target customers. Includes R&D, marketing and manufacturing.

Although there are many variants of the hybrid solutions to these problems, the main features of successful applications are the following:[8]

• *Permanent teams overlaid on the existing functional structure.* Three or four primary types of teams can be found—corresponding to the core processes of managing categories, customers, supply chains, and (sometimes) product development. Category management teams may look after line extensions and packaging innovations while new platforms or even breakthrough products will be assigned to a full-time new product development team. More details about these teams can be seen in Figure 10–3. The more complex the organization, the more teams are spawned. In 1996, Kraft had 35 category teams, 30 supply chain teams, and 175 customer teams. The popularity of category teams is a recognition that firms can no longer afford competition between their brands, and that for the other processes to work (and leverage common resources) there has to be coordination across brands.

• *Real teams—not temporary task forces.* They actually run the day-to-day operations. Members spend all their time on team activities, although they have a reporting connection to a functional group. They are integrated into the team via meetings, e-mail, and access to shared databases. To keep teams focused, they are evaluated on how well the category or retail account is performing against team objectives. All teams have access to specialized resources that are housed in the functions. This helps spread learning across teams. Thus, an interactive promotion specialist can serve a number of different category teams with expertise no single team could afford on its own.

• *Integration across processes.* One of the painful lessons of reengineering is that optimizing one or two carefully chosen processes won't likely optimize the whole. Without mechanisms for integration, new walls will be created, but these will be between processes rather than the usual silos between brands and functions. To overcome this tendency to fragmentation, there must be a common strategic logic. Some firms have strategic integration teams for the purpose of charting the overall direction: Who are the target consumers? What values are they seeking? What capabilities will we nurture and how will they be used to gain advantage? How will demands for private labeling be met? How much investment in new products? and so on.

Other integrating devices include interlocked teams that share objectives and have joint members who serve on several teams. They can communicate the thinking of a category team devising a new package to the supply management team so no time is lost in putting it into production.

Hypertext Organizations

With the continued development of information technology that facilitates information sharing, companies are creating new organizational forms to increase their connection to the market. The hybrid design is moving toward a hypertext form,[9] shown in Figure 10–4. This organization is analogous to the interconnected layers of a computer hypertext program that enables one to drill below a text for greater detail and amplification.

On top is a process or project team layer where multiple teams manage horizontal processes or engage in knowledge-creating activities such as new product development or charting a new interactive strategy. The team members are assigned from diverse functions or practice areas for the duration of the project, or in the case of core processes they would have a continuing commitment with the option of returning to a functional home.

In the middle is the functionally structured business system layer that develops the expertise necessary to support the business strategy and provides a talent pool for the functional teams. This layer also creates opportunities for networking and sharing functional expertise so learning is readily available to all teams. Where particular skills are needed by many teams, such as the design and sourcing of marketing research studies, the specialist with this knowledge may be permanently housed on this layer. These business systems are linked to each other and the business processes by information technology, rather than by a tradition.

The foundation is the "knowledge base" layer where cumulative organizational knowledge resides. This layer does not exist as a distinct organizational form, for it is composed of both the tacit knowledge contained in the corporate vision and culture, and the explicit knowledge contained within the information systems. Members of the hypertext organization can readily shift from the context of one layer to another layer as circumstances change. However, someone belongs or reports to only one structure at a time—in contrast to the matrix structure where it is possible to belong to two units at the same time.

FIGURE 10–4

Hypertext Organizations

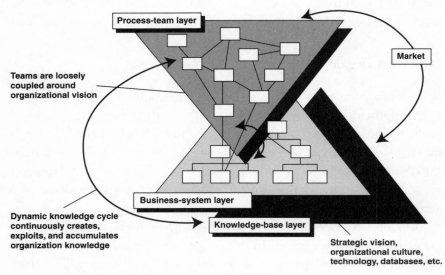

Process-team layer

Market

Teams are loosely coupled around organizational vision

Business-system layer

Dynamic knowledge cycle continuously creates, exploits, and accumulates organization knowledge

Knowledge-base layer

Strategic vision, organizational culture, technology, databases, etc.

Source: Nonaka and Takeuchi (1995).

Organizing for Interactivity

Organizations are being transformed because advances in information technology and growing understanding of the power of teams enables greater dispersion of information and decision making. These more fluid arrangements are ideally suited to the requirements of interactive strategies such as mass customization and collaborative learning. As Figure 10–5 shows, structure both follows and enables strategies of increasing dialogue and collaboration.

The essence of interactive strategies is the use of information *from* the customer rather than *about* the customer. While this is entirely natural for firms with a few sophisticated and well-informed customers, it is a radical departure for those in financial and travel services, apparel, publishing or standard industrial product firms that have traditionally used broadcast marketing.

Traditional Strategies

The least interactive configuration, shown in the lower left of Figure 10–5, is the traditional broadcast marketing strategy, using mass media and intermediaries to reach large market segments. This approach is well aligned with the traditional functional organization. As the strategy is augmented with interactive elements or becomes completely interactive, an organizational transformation is needed.

Augmented Strategies

Some companies augment a broadcast marketing strategy with slightly more interactive approaches. For example, many organizations have augmented their traditional media by putting their existing materials on a Web site. More substantial departures involve continuity and retention activities, such as frequent flyer programs or micro-marketing, which employs store-by-store or zip-code-by-zip-code distinctions between marketing programs. These augmentations can be implemented by grafting the following components onto a traditional or hybrid organization:

- Customer segment managers who have responsibility for designing tailored communications or micro-marketing programs.
- Technology support groups that provide an in-house capability to develop Web sites, support a continuity program, or experiment with

FIGURE 10–5

Aligning Strategy with Structure

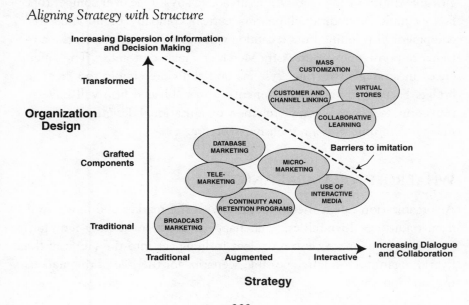

203

interactive media. These could be housed in the marketing services or information systems group.

- Outsourcing of specialist skills in areas such as usage tracking, or creative programming of interfaces.
- Ad hoc multifunctional teams (with guidance from a senior steering group) for more ambitious programs such as database marketing where tailored messages or catalogs are sent to individuals based on their profiles of interest and activities.

Fully Interactive Strategies

A simple augmentation does not take full advantage of the opportunity to repeatedly address customers as individuals in light of what has been learned from their previous responses. To exploit this capability, a transformed organizational design is required. Fully interactive strategies, shown at the upper right of Figure 10–5, include mass customization, virtual stores and collaborative learning to fit services to needs.

Because strategy and structure are interlinked, one of the advantages for market-driven firms that pursue interactive strategies is that it may be difficult for competitors to follow. As illustrated in Figure 10–5, these interactive strategies are very difficult for companies with traditional structures and strategies to emulate. Barriers to imitation of these strategies give transformed organizations an added advantage over competitors. For example, a traditional pharmaceutical company or an industrial equipment firm selling from a catalog will not be able to match the customer responsiveness of an Astra Merck or a mass customizer. The differences in strategy, structure, systems and skills are simply too great to bridge. Faced with such impediments, an established firm will have to transform itself with a completely new organizational design or set up an independent unit with a responsive structure.

WHAT ROLE FOR MARKETING?

As organizations align their structures with the market and move away from traditional hierarchies, what happens to the marketing function? Does it become more central or does it disappear into the fabric of the hybrid organization? Three possible scenarios for the role of the marketing function are:

• *Functional Fiefdom*. Here the marketing function has historically been separate and aloof. It is likely to be the lead function because the industry is customer-driven, and its power is enhanced by controlling access to market information. Its lead role will persist as long as the organization retains a traditional functional or product management structure, or external trends don't cause the balance of power in the organization to shift. However, in markets where the prices and products can be customized at the point of contact with the customer, new approaches will be required so that marketing programs can be launched independently by those closest to the market. In addition, in packaged goods firms the pressure to respond faster and better to the demands of retailers will enhance the power of the sales and logistics functions.

• *Subordinate Function*. This outcome is most likely for firms in capacity-driven or knowledge-focused industries where the organization structure has evolved into a hybrid form. Marketing people are likely to occupy a subordinate role in sales support activities or as participants in core process teams. This outcome is especially likely when the culture is very engineering or technology driven, and marketing's role is simply to implement tactical merchandising programs.[10] Many of the specialist marketing activities are likely to be outsourced.

• *Central Guidance Function*. It is increasingly apparent that market leadership will be attained only when a strong marketing orientation pervades both the culture and the organization structure. This central guidance function means that marketing, as a functional unit or integrated into the top management team in the business planning function, takes responsibility for:

> • *Articulation*, by defining and renewing the value proposition and positioning in the market, and specifying the mechanisms for taking the product or service to the market
> • *Navigation*, through effective market sensing and sharing of market information, opportunity identification and performance measurement
> • *Orchestration*, by providing the essential "glue" for a coherent, market-driven whole

It was once fashionable to say that "marketing is too important to be left to the marketing people" or "marketing is everyone's job." This line of argument has been attributed to David Packard—perhaps in a fit of frustration with the engineering-dominated culture of Hewlett-Packard in the mid-1980s. What he should have said is that the delivery of superior customer value is everyone's responsibility.[11] If marketing is everyone's responsibility, then it is nobody's responsibility—and bad things can happen. Listen to Carl Gustin, the chief marketing officer of Kodak,[12] on why his position was formed in 1995:

> Over time at Kodak we lost our central focus on marketing. Every business unit—and nearly every individual—adopted different marketing theories and practices. Some were strong, some were weak, but the combination was inconsistent.
>
> And we made a common blunder. Earnest but inexperienced people engaging in marketing tend to resort to promotion: discounts, rebates, coupons, etc. They neglect comprehensive planning strategies. They fail to differentiate their product to command a premium. Worse yet, they risk devaluing the brand—they try to do everything with price.
>
> We knew this wasn't working. We needed to re-establish a strong central marketing competence. We didn't centralize fully, but we formed a single point of accountability and expertise. My job as CMO is to make sure we have great marketing people in each business unit. They must understand the power of our brand, and keep its integrity, its symbolic force, its credibility intact.

What should be the responsibility of the marketing function? In determining whether marketing serves in a lead or subordinate role, managers should consider the following factors:[13]

1. *The current status of marketing in the organization.* Useful indications are the influence of marketers in the strategy dialogue, the reliance of decision makers on market intelligence, as well as size of budget and head count. The functional background of the top management team and their direct experience with marketing activities offer additional clues.
2. *The character of the industry.* Is it capacity-driven, consumer-driven, or knowledge-driven?
3. *The prevailing culture.* The role of marketing will be strong in an organization that puts the customer's interest first, and defines each job in terms of its contribution to the delivery of superior customer value. In

a strong sales, technology, or internally oriented culture these interests will be subordinated, and marketing's role will be weaker.

4. *The pace of organizational changes.* This, in turn, depends on the prevailing satisfaction or frustration with the existing structures, and the ability of the organizations to overcome the barriers to change.

Many organizations will decide that marketing has multiple roles. Just as they choose to create hybrid structures rather than fully functional or fully horizontal organization, they will see marketing activities through two lenses. As a specialist activity it provides the expertise in market sensing, customer linking, and channel binding to keep the organization continuously apprised of opportunities and threats in the market. As a general management responsibility—through the leadership of its CEO and CMO—it defines and articulates the value strategy, provides aids for navigation through market turbulence and provides the rationale for coordinating the core processes. When these responsibilities are effectively carried out all other functions, processes, and activities will be better aligned to the market.

ACHIEVING CLOSER ALIGNMENT TO THE MARKET

The ideal of an organization that can continuously adapt to changing market opportunities, competitive challenges and customer requirements is closer to being realized. Information technology and new approaches to organization design, along with sharp challenges to the restrictions of the traditional functional design, have led to an unprecedented era of organizational innovation. Now it is the customer that drives the organization—not the other way around.

Underlying this fundamental reorientation are four premises that have been developed in this chapter:

1. Firms will increasingly evolve toward a hybrid or hypertext form of organization—combining the best features of horizontal process and vertical functional forms—in order to get closer to their customers.

2. There will be a great deal of variety in hybrid designs that are adopted, depending on the alignment of the value strategy and the core capabilities that are exercised in the processes. This will dictate

the relative importance of staff groups, function specialists and process teams.

3. Advances in data networks will permit firms to better link internal teams, make decisions faster and devise more interactive strategies that use information *from* the customer rather than *about* the customer.

4. As strategies become more interactive, leading to increasing dialogue and collaboration with customers and channels, there must be greater dispersion of information and decision making throughout the organization. As we proceed through the book, culminating in an action agenda in the last chapter, it will become clearer what is involved in aligning all aspects of the organization to the market. At this point, a useful supporting step is to assess the current organizational design using the questions in Part V of the Appendix.

As part of the overall configuration of the firm, structure plays a powerful role in creating a market-driven organization. The wrong structure can doom all other market-driven initiatives in the organization to failure. Is your current structure interfering with your ability to align the organization with the market? How could it be changed to make the firm more market-driven? If a radical move would be attacked by the "white blood cells" of the organization as a foreign intruder, are there grafted components or augmented strategies that might be more palatable and lead toward more substantial changes in the future?

Chapter Eleven

Setting the Direction

The choice of strategy plays a powerful role in aligning the organization to the market. Any firm seeking to transform itself into a more market-driven organization must ask whether it has the right approach to setting its strategic direction. Are the firm's strategic thinking and strategy-creation process driven by internal concerns or are they externally focused? Do they begin with corporate planning cycles or begin with the market? Is the strategy reactive, or does it anticipate new ways of delivering superior customer value?

The impact of an outward-looking strategy is apparent in market after market. One or two market-driven catalysts keep altering the basic structure of their industry in directions that benefit them or devise new ways to win in their markets. Think of Intuit in personal financial software, USAA in insurance, Canon in digital imaging, Nucor in steel or Con Agra in grocery products. These companies are closely attuned to the market, are skilled at anticipating opportunities and moving their organizations to seize them before competitors. They employ a strategic thinking process that is externally focused and real-time, issues oriented, in contrast to the inflexible, budget-cycle-oriented planning procedures of many of their rivals.

Why, for example, has GE Capital dominated the financial services sector in innovation and profitability performance for the past decade? This is a firm that is driven to add value to assets—not just to finance them. It brings a market-driven mind-set to its equipment leasing, insurance, real estate and asset management businesses that views money as a raw material to be converted into a service.

GE Capital's approach is the antithesis of the risk-averse, careful style of most banks. This is how it became the world's largest provider and servicer of private-label credit cards for retailers such as Federated Stores and Home Depot. This market had stagnated as consumers switched to universal cards such as Visa, MasterCard, or American Express, rather than carrying different cards for different stores. GE Capital revived these cards by forming partnerships with retailers and providing them with value-added services such as targeted marketing campaigns, tailored credit programs, segmented risk levels for card holders, billing and collection teams with expertise in credit scoring and instant credit for new customers. These initiatives were supported with electronic linkages, team approaches to customer service, and a stream of innovations the competition couldn't readily match.

Similarly, consider how strategies aligned with the market provided advantages to the following companies:

- Arrow Electronics foresaw that the new economics of information plus changing customer requirements would trigger an industry consolidation, and became an aggressive amalgamator.[1]
- Hewlett-Packard was four years ahead of IBM and DEC in putting in place low-cost distribution and global account management to serve systems markets.
- Andersen Windows pioneered the use of mass-customization methods to assemble windows that are uniquely tailored to the demands of individual customers, and now dominates the industry.[2]

These firms were able to envision how they could direct the evolution of their markets in ways that would be advantageous to them and build an organization-wide emotional commitment to the chosen strategy.

The rivals of these market-driven firms either watched what is happening and then reacted, or wondered what happened. When markets were stable or slowly evolving in predictable ways, their reactive approach was tenable. This put a premium on maintaining programs and activities that seem to be working and dropping those that aren't working. The implicit assumption was that the organization could react faster than the market is changing. This was always a shaky assumption but is increasingly dangerous when change occurs on Silicon Valley time—

where seven years of events and disruptions occur within one calendar year—or a catalytic competitor is devising nonlinear strategies to transform the industry.

The ability to think and act strategically is not uniformly distributed throughout most industries. If it were, there wouldn't be so many cases where different competitors, armed with similar information and seemingly endowed with comparable resources and market positions, followed such different paths. What is it that sets the successful companies apart from unsuccessful firms?

Many Explanations and One Enabler

The field of strategy offers many conjectures as to why the leaders are able to outperform the laggards.[3] Is it because of their core competencies? knowledge management? coalition building? value disciplines? structural advantages? resource commitments? or superior execution? Each of these concepts has been advanced by its advocates as the key to strategy, and impressive examples of their contributions are offered in support. But are they always valid? For example, as we saw in Chapter 7, the customer retention framework is extremely useful in many service contexts, but where else does it apply? Similarly, does a market leader always make a choice between the value disciplines of operational excellence—"the best price" play—versus performance superiority and the "best product," or customer intimacy which provides the "best overall solution"?[4] In some markets, the structure and opportunities force everyone to play the same game and there is no choice to be made.

We are not going to enter that debate. Instead, our proposition is that a market-driven organization is better equipped to find and implement a compelling strategy—regardless of its origins or guiding concept. Being market-driven is an *enabler* of superior strategies. The key enabling factors are the resources we have already discussed, in the form of culture, market sensing, and market-relating capabilities, and organization design, to which we now will add the aiming mechanism which is the strategic thinking capability.

MARKET DRIVEN STRATEGIC THINKING

Market-driven firms think differently about strategy. They have an externally oriented process for developing strategic direction, in contrast to the internally focused process used in most organizations. The strategy begins with an understanding of the market and works back to the organization, rather than moving from the organization to the market. This externally oriented strategy is supported by a shared knowledge base (discussed in Chapter 7) and by a culture that is willing at all levels constantly to challenge mind-sets and assumptions (discussed in Chapter 3).

In particular, market-driven organizations have two important characteristics:

- *They use an adaptive planning process.* In contrast to the budget-cycle strategic planning used by internally focused organizations, the market-driven organization uses an adaptive planning process focused on real-time issues. This tends to keep the organization keyed to the evolving issues in the market and helps prevent it from slipping into short-term, cost-conscious strategic planning.
- *They anticipate the market.* The market-driven organization combines a clear-headed understanding of its capabilities and limitations with a broadly informed point of view about the future of its markets. It brings a strong market-sensing capability into a wide-ranging dialogue that includes rebels and dissatisfied customers and uses scenario thinking to understand a range of possible futures in the environment. These firms see more possibilities and see them earlier than their rivals.

The payoff from a superior strategic thinking capability comes when strategic choices are better informed, risks look more manageable and the employees are motivated to stretch their efforts. By focusing attention on a desired leadership position and continually searching for new sources of advantage, the actions and aspirations of the organization are given meaning.

Adaptive, Real-Time Issues Planning

Traditional planning processes are often the biggest obstacle to market-driven strategic thinking. Despite incessant complaints from line managers that their planning systems stifle insights, creativity and dialogue, companies persist in using excessively routinized procedures that are burdensome, time-consuming and geared to preparing for the annual budget ritual. These planning processes were installed when environmental change was slow or negligible. They provided a useful mechanism for reducing uncertainty, coordinating activities and allocating resources. Their fatal flaw was that they were too internally focused—they lacked robust mechanisms for challenging accepted assumptions about the market, or surfacing new strategies—and emphasized maintaining control by the center:

> The plans thus produced were formally adversarial—briefs in a kind of litigation for control between a corporation and its business units, or among business units. Their style was to advocate, not inquire; their output was a single right answer, not options; their data were used for proof in argument, not for implementation in the real world.[5]

By contrast, market-driven organizations don't confuse strategic thinking with control-oriented strategic planning. Instead, they use a process of adaptive planning that unhooks strategic thinking from the rigidities of the budget cycle. The company engages in real-time issues planning, resolving strategic issues on a schedule that is dictated by the pace of events, not by the annual calendar. The assumptions underlying strategic thinking are systematically and rigorously challenged by senior management, and the entire organization focuses on reflecting on and learning from its experience.

Market-driven firms deploy an adaptive process for devising and improving their strategies. This is a team-based activity that draws on multifunctional capabilities to exploit the shared knowledge and resources, and is guided by an integrating theme that emphasizes the delivery of superior customer value. It is a key ingredient of a motivating vision that realistically challenges the management team.

The trigger for a scan of issues and sorting for potential impact may be the arrival of a new general manager or CEO, a serious downturn in performance, or a restructuring of the industry under pressure of deregulation, technological change, or new customer demands. In periods of turbulence, the identification and sorting of issues may have to be done once or twice a year. When the environment is stable and the strategy is on course, there may be no need to do this more often than every three years.

When issues resolution activities are distinct from the formalities of budgeting, the quality of strategic thinking improves. Conversely, when the planning process is obviously a precursor to the preparation of an annual budget, management attention is narrowed to short-run implementation concerns, rather than possibilities for strategic moves that play out over a longer time frame. Insightful strategic thinking is then made a prisoner of short-run pressures. We shouldn't encourage more myopia by designing systems that encourage bad habits.

Real-Time Issues

Issues are the most valuable currency in a market-driven strategy dialogue, and an important impetus to deep strategic thinking. They help the management team distill the plethora of market opportunities, problems and uncertainties into manageable chunks. In this form, they become focal points for decision making, and specify the needs for information collection and interpretation. Once all the issues have been properly framed, the full array can be compared in terms of their relative immediacy and impact. Then priorities can be set so only those few problems and challenges with a significant impact on future performance will be addressed. The focusing of scarce management time and energy on high payoff issues is probably the most compelling reason for adopting an issues orientation. No wonder management teams trying to spread their limited time across many issues—and seeing little from their dispersed efforts beyond frustration and unremitting fire fighting—are quick to embrace a tool that better harnesses their collective energy.

As a rule, no more than five to seven issues should be considered by the full management team. Trying to handle too many more will dilute time and energy, so priorities are essential. This means arriving at a consensus within the team on the immediacy and impact of each issue—and ranking them by importance. This can be a tense exercise if the members of the management team don't share the same vision, have divergent views about the customer value proposition, or disagree on critical assumptions. In practice, teams with shared knowledge about market structures, responses and economics usually converge on a common set of issues once the divergent assumptions are surfaced and examined.

Identifying and Framing Issues

A strategic issue is a condition or pressure on the business, created by internal or external developments, that involves:

1. *possible outcomes* that will have a high impact on future performance
2. *controversy*, in that reasonable people can take and defend different positions on how to deal with the issue
3. *strategic consequences*, since the resolution may mean implementing a change in strategy.

Issues with these characteristics should be posed as questions, to make it obvious that a response is needed. It is hard to overstate the importance of formulating the issue questions correctly, to facilitate the discovery of a solution. Suppose, for example, a business is persistently unable to satisfy its delivery promises. If we frame the question as: "What should be done to reduce late deliveries?" many answers will suggest themselves: work overtime, promise realistic schedules, build buffer stocks, and so on. But these are not solutions, they are remedies to symptoms. None of these responses will tackle the underlying strategic issue.

Digging deeper might reveal that the critical issue should be framed in the following way: "Should the business expand production capacity?" Different questions might be suggested by probing into other reasons for the late delivery problem. Whatever emerges should be in the form of a question ideally answerable with either a yes or no answer. If analysis suggests the answer is no, there isn't enough capacity, then a number of solution options can be explored. Big issues, such as, "How can we deal with the migration of value to our channels?" need to be broken down to more manageable issues, under this broad issue umbrella.

Generating and Evaluating Strategic Alternatives

To think strategically is to make choices, but to choose one must have alternatives from which to select; therefore managers must generate alternatives—several distinct approaches for dealing with each issue.[6] Seldom will "more of the same" be an acceptable alternative, but, without adventurous thinking about new possibilities, such a pedestrian outcome is likely.

It is essential to separate the creative act of generating alternatives from their detailed evaluation. If critical questions and comments aren't held until all the possibilities have been identified, the atmosphere of the meeting soon resembles a "day in court." This will quickly suppress adventurous thinking and novel solutions. What is needed is a supportive and open setting for stretch thinking that encourages half-baked ideas with potential for elaboration. The flow of ideas may lead down blind alleys, but also may trigger new possibilities that combine the best features of several different options.

Invariably when issues resolution is treated as a creative activity, the process leads management out of the trap of narrow, unquestioning variations on current themes. There are many procedures available to achieve this end. A manufacturing division used a creative strategy session to address its top ten issues. The participants were first loosened up with creativity exercises, and then put into five groups and given three hours to exchange ideas. The groups were told to concentrate on the quantity, not quality, of ideas; to defer judgment; not to argue; and to focus on "what's" not "why's." Over 150 ideas/solutions/options were generated. Next, the participants were reshuffled into five new groups. Their task was to rank all the earlier ideas by their attractiveness. Then the leaders of the new groups were asked to report their conclusions. Eventually, five strategic programs emerged.

When all members of a planning team participate in the full discussion of all the options for dealing with an issue, and understand the reasons why one was selected (or why their proposal was rejected) they are much more committed to implementing the options. But besides these process advantages, it is essential for team members to identify meaningful strategic options before they can enter into the dialogue with corporate management on the trade-offs in resources and objectives for the business.

Anticipating the Market

In addition to focusing on issues rather than the mechanics of budgeting, market-driven organizations also look more intensely to the market during their planning process. They bring in dissident voices to challenge the insights from their market sensing activities. They use scenario thinking to identify key changes and encourage both reflection and anticipation about the market in the planning process. As Winston Churchill once said, "It is difficult to look further than you can see." Each of these approaches requires a sense of urgency and concerted leadership to sustain the challenge to the strategy and the search for a new path.

Broaden the Conversation

Snow begins melting around the edges. By bringing new voices from the periphery of the organization into its planning process, the company can identify some of the first signs of emerging changes that could move the organization in new directions. The planning process needs to seek out these divergent voices of dissent inside and outside the organization.

For example, many senior managers find it difficult to take the Internet seriously; they don't see their friends using it, nor do they have the time or inclination to become facile. This is a form of myopia that makes them vulnerable to new entrants or more farsighted competitors. The problem is compounded when the senior management team shares a common background, having grown up in the industry and risen through the ranks together. To encourage diversity of viewpoints and overcome homogeneity in the strategy dialogue new and usually younger outsiders must be added to the management team.

In addition to expanding the dialogue inside the firm, market-driven companies also bring in outside voices of dissent. One of the most valuable ways to get a management team to confront market realities is to introduce a vocal and dissatisfied customer or distributor into the strategy dialogue. Nalco Chemical often brings in large prospects for its specialty chemicals who are either loyal to a competitor or who have recently defected. The conversation can be painful when the customer details shortcomings and frustrations, and energizing when the dialogue turns to what could be done to overcome the problems. Contrary to the usual objection to this approach, these outsiders pull no punches and don't hold back in their criticisms. In their view, the benefit of participation is that they might develop a supplier that is better attuned to their needs.

Use Scenario Planning to Think the Unthinkable

All managers are awash in speculations, predictions and unverified data about the future of their market. But these data do not carry their own interpretation. As we saw in Chapter 6, meaning must be provided by selecting and using the data. The danger is that potentially significant peripheral events and low-power signals will be overlooked because the data are filtered through the prevailing mental model. Conventional planning approaches are more a hindrance than an aid to insightful interpretation. There is a tendency to squeeze all forecasts of complex indeterminate futures into "best case–expected case–worst case" outcomes—and then only pay attention to the expected outcome.

There are no cut-and-dried procedures for expanding the managerial mind to think about nascent threats, market discontinuities and complex interactions among events. The future is not certain; instead it is necessary to confront a range of possible factors. Suppose Japan's structural problems remain unreformed or there is a sharp financial crisis followed by an impressive turnaround; that Internet telephony enriches the telecommunication firms or introduces ruinous competition. What then? One way to find answers is scenario thinking, a flexible process for developing descriptive narratives of plausible alternative projections of the future.[7]

The aim of scenario thinking is not to make forecasts but to provide an expansive interpretive framework into which subsequent events can be placed. Scenarios combine estimates of what might happen if the driving forces in the market continue, with assumptions about what could happen. The rationale is that if managers have already contemplated a range of possible outcomes, they should be quicker to react when one of them emerges. But scenario thinking isn't just about reacting. It should also lead to contemplating actions that increase the likelihood of a preferred outcome. This is a methodology with wide applicability:

- In 1995, 3M used scenarios to think about the distribution of its office products in Europe. Would very powerful pan-European distributors appear on the U.S. model? Or would European patterns remain diverse? What effect would the Intranet have on these markets?
- Knight-Ridder was mired in conflicting conjectures about the impact of the Internet on its newspaper empire. While it was obvious that classified advertising would be hurt, the company had trouble devising robust strategies for coping until it adopted scenario thinking.
- When Hewlett-Packard first used scenarios to think about the future of computing, executives found that wireless data transmission was a common feature of every scenario they envisioned. Yet they had only one development project focused on this technology, and no strategies for introducing it. HP quickly adjusted its priorities to force the pace of introduction of this technology.

Scenario thinking helps create a sense of urgency by posing surrogate crises that push managers beyond their comfort zones. To have this impact, however, the scenarios need to be plausible—that is, possible, credible, and relevant. The procedures for devising these scenarios and engaging managers are now well known. A common approach to scenario construction begins with the driving forces that will shape and propel the market. Different combinations of important and uncertain driving forces can be tried to see which ones yield scenarios with clear rationales or logics. For example, a wholesaler-distributor could create four different story plots based on the degree of possible consolidation among its customers and the level of value-added services needed by these customers. (See Figure 11–1 for an illustration.)[8] Each scenario plot describes an end state that needs to be tested for plausibility. Could it happen? Are there inconsistencies? Why might it happen? Are the future worlds sufficiently different to be strategically important?

Though all scenarios must be plausible, the most valuable may be those that don't seem likely to unfold. It is important to keep the management team's collective mind open to all possibilities. One way to do

FIGURE 11-1

Scenarios for the Possible Structure of a Fragmented Wholesale-Distribution Sector

Many Services

Status Quo
- Traditional two-step distribution channel
- Little consolidation in wholesale distribution
- Best case scenario

Strategic Renewal
- Emergence of large, national customers
- Innovative wholesaler-distributors lead channel change
- Substantial consolidation due to growth-by-acquisition strategies of a few wholesaler-distributors

Level of value-added services needed by a customer

Limited ← Degree of consolidation among wholesale distribution customers → **Substantial**

Profitless Persistence
- Competition based on price
- Increased pressure on margins
- Moderate consolidation in wholesale distribution

Disintermediation
- Emergence of large, national customers
- Innovative customers bypass wholesaler-distributors
- Substantial consolidation due to both bankruptcies and acquisitions

Few Services

this is to avoid assigning probabilities or picking one as "most likely." Serious strategic thinking occurs when the team explores the strategic challenges and requisite capabilities of each scenario plot. Is our current strategy sufficiently robust to survive in each plausible end state? What could be done to hedge the current strategy to be effective across a variety of futures? This kind of thinking is also a useful way to devise contingency plans: we're not sure this event is going to happen, but we'll monitor it closely and here is what we'll do to make it less likely to happen and how we'll respond if it does. In this way scenarios become an integral part of the strategy development process.

Challenging the Strategy

Gary Hamel argues that strategy is always "lucky foresight. . . . Strategy is always the product of a complex and unexpected interplay between ideas, information, personalities and desire."[9] This has major implications for the planning process. It means it is not enough to identify the pressing issues and the plausible alternatives for dealing with them. Much deeper reflection is required to challenge and replace cherished assumptions and envision new ways of extending the organization's capabilities to deliver superior customer value. It means recognizing and sidestepping constraining preconceptions. It means asking tough questions and not settling for obvious answers.

Why don't most organizations reflect more deeply on their future but act surprised when their strategy is undermined by unspoken or unwarranted assumptions? One reason is that the day-to-day pressures of running the business leave little energy for thinking about distant problems or opportunities. Another impediment is complacency: profits are up, the share price is strong, and replacement technologies or new competitors are barely visible at the periphery of the market. Most insidious is an internal orientation which is often nourished by complacency:

- Why were the Big Three auto makers in Detroit fixated for so long on sport utility vehicles and big trucks? For much of the 1990s they converted car factories to truck factories to capitalize on the boom in sales. Aren't they giving people what they want? The real question is whether they were anticipating what buyers would want—especially those aging baby boomers whose children were leaving home and might prefer something with a less jolting ride. The Big Three were very slow to conceive and develop car-truck hybrids to help retain these buyers as they migrated from truck-like sport utility vehicles.

- Why did McDonald's persist with a strategy of saturating the U.S. market and antagonizing the franchisees of their ubiquitous outlets? In the face of a seemingly finite population of fast-food eaters McDonald's has become its own worst competition.[10] With an expansion strategy of filling in all the niches and corners of the market, the company has spread revenues and profits more thinly among their franchisees, and antagonized many.

Market-driven organizations use a rigorous process of strategy review to challenge their planning assumptions and beliefs about the market. The quality of these reviews of strategy by senior management ranges from a carefully staged exercise that endorses a pre-sold plan to a rigorous challenge to the foundations of the strategy. To add value a rigorous strategy review must go beyond challenging the financial forecasts, capital appropriation requests and budget submissions. If the emphasis is on whether the numbers are achievable, the focus inevitably turns inward and becomes very short-term.

A value-adding strategy review is not a one-shot interrogation, but a continuing dialogue. In best practice companies the first round of discussions may be entirely about the strategic fundamentals of the business: What are the trends in the market? What are competitors doing? Where are the growth opportunities? What are the biggest constraints? The objective is to encourage deep strategic thinking.

During subsequent meetings attention turns to financial metrics and requirements. The message is that people will be held accountable for their commitments, and not allowed to routinely miss their forecasts. This means creating plans that recognize that some of the underlying assumptions are likely to be wrong, and creating options when that happens. Here is where the tough questions are asked: If we're going to grow 7 percent for the next three years, where are we going to grow? Which products? What about prices? Which competitors will give up share? How will these competitors respond?

Top management adds further value to the ongoing review process by forcing the business teams to think more broadly about global issues. In early 1998, General Electric management became concerned about the possibility of deflation in their global markets, and challenged every business to get ready—even if it didn't come to pass. Their belief was that even if deflation didn't happen, the discipline would make the businesses more competitive. Many initiatives were begun, including study of precursors like aircraft engines that had suffered price declines in flat markets. Several corporate themes were identified and every business was asked to build them into their strategies. One was to "own markets, not assets" since assets would lose value. Another was to lengthen purchase commitments and shorten sales commitments. High priority was given to increasing inventory turns and to reducing assets. The payoff was a more thoughtful and well-prepared organization.

Reflecting and Learning

This emphasis on challenging from the top leads to an organization that reflects and learns from its experience. One of the more illuminating debates in the strategy field is whether strategies are *deliberate*, as the result of a cerebral and top-down process of matching opportunities with capabilities, or whether they *emerge* from piecemeal, visceral responses to events and opportunities. Is strategy just "good luck rationalized in hindsight," as the creativity guru Edward de Bono has suggested? The answer is that both processes must be working if the firm is to successfully adapt. No top-down strategy can be so farsighted that it contemplates all eventualities. At best, it can provide a motivating sense of direction. But bottom-up strategies that emerge from a series of incremental moves are no guarantee of success, especially in turbulent environments.

Robust strategy processes combine the benefits of deliberation with the need for flexibility and learning. Strategies evolve as initiatives are conceived and then succeed or fail, in a process of trial-and-error learning. To foster this process it is essential to have many experiments underway across the organization. Try new programs in a few branches or regions and see what happens. For example, Met Life opened a retail insurance outlet in Florida. The original intention was to pilot a new channel, to better reach the wealthy retirees market. Although sales were disappointing, other unforeseen benefits were realized. In the course of answering queries about products, sounding out the shoppers about their needs, frustrations and objections, and observing the decision process, they found an invaluable window into the market. They had, in effect, reinvented the "antennae shops" that Japanese electronics have used so effectively to learn about their markets.

Learning and reflection don't occur spontaneously. Procedures and processes are needed to provide encouragement. One useful device is to require the annual plan for each product or function to include a "lessons learned" section, which also describes the actions that will be taken as a result of these lessons. In short, market-driven strategic thinking flourishes in a learning organization.

THE CAPABILITY FOR THINKING STRATEGICALLY

Market-driven organizations disdain the notion that strategies are good luck rationalized in hindsight. They are prepared to recognize and capitalize on any good fortune, but are unwilling simply to react to events and forces in their served markets. Instead, they are deeply immersed in the realities of their markets, and continually stretching to find new ways to gain further advantages and grow. All functions and attributes are aligned around a clear-cut value proposition that does not try to be all things to all people. In short, they have a superior capability for thinking strategically.

Two underlying factors account for most of the distinctiveness in the strategic thinking process of market-driven firms. The first is depth of market understanding that starts with the market-sensing capability. This knowledge is widely shared to ensure consistency of understanding and action by the management team and ensures integration of widely dispersed operating groups. Everyone knows where and how the business makes money. The assessment of the strategic thinking capability found in section IV of the Appendix will help you determine how close you are to best practices. Market-driven organizations also eschew top-down inflexible planning procedures that are barely concealed preludes to the setting of the annual budget. Instead they use adaptive processes that marry top-down guidance and resource allocation with bottom-up market knowledge. The defining features are real-time, issues-oriented planning and probing strategy reviews that require widespread participation. This encourages strategic thinking, builds organization-wide commitment, and provides a keen and flexible sense of direction.

Chapter Twelve

Guiding the Change

Even with a clear design for a more market-focused structure and a more interactive strategy, transforming an organization is a risky proposition. By one estimate, only 30 percent of all change programs implemented by a sample of Fortune 100 companies since 1980 produced an improvement in bottom-line results that exceeded the company's cost of capital.[1]

The path to becoming more market-driven is at least as perilous. Because of the complex and interlinked elements that contribute to a market orientation, achieving successful change in all these dimensions can be very challenging. Creating a deeper market focus often runs counter to entrenched beliefs of the culture and long-standing structures, strategies, capabilities and processes.

Change threatens people, provoking resistance. Organizations that have been successful in the past have a particularly hard time. "An unhealthy arrogance begins to evolve ... [and] arrogant managers can over-evaluate their current performance and competitive position, listen poorly, and learn slowly. . . . The combination of cultures that resist change and managers who have not been taught to [lead] change is lethal."[2]

Yet as challenging as change initiatives are to complete successfully, standing still is perhaps even more risky. The pace of change is accelerating, competition is intensifying, customers are more demanding, and emerging technologies are undermining traditional business models. The status quo has become unsustainable.

How can organizations avoid the pitfalls of the change process? This chapter outlines six conditions that increase the odds of success in translating the concepts of the market-driven organization into reality. We examine how three firms—Owens Corning, Sears, Roebuck and Eurotunnel—successfully used this process to transform their organizations.

Conditions for Successful Change

This chapter draws upon cumulative knowledge of successful change initiatives to provide a road map to guide a market-driven change process. In contrast with most other discussions of change, our focus is not on the leaders of the organization but on the conditions that will enable their people to produce good results. While there is tremendous diversity among successful leaders in personality, style, abilities, and interests,[3] most successful market-driven change initiatives were designed to meet six conditions:[4]

1. *Demonstrate leadership commitment.* There is a leader who owns and champions the change, who is investing time and resources and has created a sense of urgency.
2. *Understand the need for change.* Key implementers know what it means to be market-driven, know what changes need to be made, and see how the change initiative will benefit them and the business.
3. *Mobilize commitment at all levels.* Those responsible for the change program have experience and credibility, and know how to mobilize a coalition of supporters and overcome resistance.
4. *Shape the vision.* All employees know what they are trying to accomplish. They understand how superior value will be created and see what they have to do differently.
5. *Align structures, systems and incentives.* There is a credible plan for coordinating structures, systems and incentives. Key implementers have the resources they need for doing their work.
6. *Sustain the change.* Those responsible for the change program know how to get started and ensure an early win. They have a plan for keeping attention focused on the change, and benchmarks for measuring progress.

THREE STORIES OF TRANSFORMATION

Owens Corning transformed itself from a product-focused manufacturer to a company organized around the needs of customers. Sears, Roebuck, facing losses of profits and market share, transformed itself from an outdated retailer into a sharp, market-focused organization by targeting women and mobilizing employees. Eurotunnel shifted gears from a project-focused organization that built the tunnel under the English Channel to a market-focused organization that could attract enough traffic to make it a viable business. Although each organization arrived at the need to become market-driven by different paths, they used these six conditions to create a change architecture. And each of these organizations took risks for which they were well rewarded.

Owens Corning[5]

When Glen Hiner left GE in 1991 to head this venerable maker of fiberglass insulation, glass composites, and roofing materials, the company was mired in debt, besieged by asbestos litigation and suffering from a bunker mentality. Because the priority was to generate cash to reduce debt, few investments were possible and sales were stagnant.

The company's mind-set was dominated by product thinking. This was sensible given the realities of the business: (1) building products served home-building and remodeling markets that were both seasonal and cyclical; (2) the process for making fiberglass was only cost effective when it ran continuously at very high speed—so inventories built up very quickly; and (3) shipping bulky insulation and heavy roofing material was very costly, so distribution was a burden, not a source of advantage.

While the company was focused on its materials, customers were mostly thinking about their projects. Home improvers were having problems with unreliable contractors, scant information, and unforeseen problems. The materials were secondary and, anyway, the customers couldn't distinguish among brands. Builders and contractors, frustrated when the materials they needed didn't arrive on time, were also thinking in project terms. Meanwhile the greatest needs of retailers like Home Depot were sophisticated logistics and help with training their sales people.

Owens Corning recognized that it needed to offer one-stop shopping and solutions to problems posed by projects. This was a compelling value proposition but well beyond Owens Corning's capabilities. There were big gaps in its product line, and the balkanized sales and service organization couldn't offer a simple way to buy the complete portfolio of products. Retailers had to deal with separate sales forces for each product, plus four different distribution centers, four sets of invoices, and so on. To make the strategy work, the company would have to overcome serious information bottlenecks and rethink how information flowed through it and to and from its customers.

Some of these problems were solved with acquisitions of complementary products, others required a new enterprise-wide information system. Major changes were needed in each of the elements of the market orientation. For example, cross-functional collaboration did not come easily, so a wholesale re-organization led to combining sales, service and fulfillment into one horizontal process.

Sears, Roebuck[6]

Sears, Roebuck is a classic case of what happens when a firm loses touch with its markets. Until 1986 Sears was the dominant retailer in the United States with a strategy fully in harmony with the changing requirements of suburban homeowners. By 1992, it was struggling to absorb a loss of $3.9 billion and to overcome a declining market share, some of the worst customer satisfaction ratings in the retail industry and bloated selling and administrative costs of 30 percent of sales. Many observers wondered if Sears would survive.

Despite Sears's problems, its standing with consumers remained strong. Consistently it was picked as a good, honest place to shop, and 75 percent of Americans visited a Sears store at least once a year. This goodwill was steadily being dissipated by a ponderous and noncompetitive culture, antiquated systems, and excessive in-fighting. Customers were being siphoned off by trendy specialty retailers such as The Limited, category killers such as Home Depot, or discounters such as Wal-Mart and Target.

Arthur Martinez, who came from Saks Fifth Avenue and was the first outsider to head the retail group, led the turnaround. Within 100 days of his arrival, he and his team began a turnaround plan that led to the closing of 113 unprofitable stores, the termination of the 100-year-old Sears catalog, the divestment of the financial-services business—Allstate Insurance, Coldwell Banker real estate, the Discover credit card and the Dean Witter brokerage—and the sale of the 110-story Sears Tower that was their symbol in Chicago.

The quick fix worked, but the real challenge was to turn a short-term survival program into a long-term transformation that fully engaged its employees who were dispirited and anxious for improved performance. They needed to be motivated to support a new merchandising focus. Although the prevailing assumption was that Sears was a man's store, most buying decisions were made by women. Martinez refocused on "the softer side of Sears" and introduced new private-label lines of apparel and cosmetics. Another part of the growth strategy was a move to off-mall specialty stores, including Sears hardware stores and Homelife furniture stores. He summed up the challenge by saying, "A turnaround is a financial recovery. A transformation is much more. It's all about changing the structure and the approach to the business, and reeducating our people to feel comfortable outside a command-and-control environment. It involves getting them used to risk taking and innovation. And getting the very best out of our people."

Eurotunnel

Eurotunnel began life with the single objective of building a tunnel under the English Channel. When construction was completed it had to transform itself from a project organization to become an operating company with its own rolling stock for transporting lorries and cars through the tunnel. While it did not operate the Eurostar passenger train or freight trains between London, Brussels and Paris, it charged these trains for usage.

A change in culture wouldn't suffice—it needed a complete reversal. The entire organization had to go from spending whatever it took to get the tunnel finished to controlling costs and earning money. The company had to become efficient in attracting, serving and retaining customers and competing against the established ferries and airline services. To add to the challenge, Eurotunnel was designed as a binational company with joint English and French management.

There was one overriding problem creating a sense of urgency. Huge and unacceptable losses were projected if big cuts weren't made to the bloated cost structure. However, the focus of the change process was on growing revenues as this was judged to be a more energizing goal and would help overcome the early suspicions that it was a cost-cutting exercise.

The first step was to organize around customers and processes and jettison the old functional structure. Separate teams and strategies were devised for the truck, rail and tourist travel segments. Coordination was critical since the key to making money was to optimize the use of a large, shared asset. The overall change effort was guided by a team with strong support at the top. This team in turn created a complex change architecture that involved over 1,000 people in 85 different cross-functional teams. Priorities for teams dealing with everything from timetable planning to introducing a club-class service were guided by customer inputs. Each team was given broad authority but was held accountable for a set of benefits.

Just as demonstrable progress was being seen, and a £100 million net revenue benefit achieved, a tragic fire in November 1996 closed the tunnel and caused £200 million of damage. Fortunately a resilient organization was in place that was able to get the tunnel open and recapture the lost share of market.

DESIGNING THE CHANGE PROCESS

What do the experiences of Owens Corning, Sears, Roebuck and Eurotunnel have in common? Each had to change: they had to get closer to their markets and do a better job of satisfying and retaining customers or face dire consequences. Each of their change programs was carefully tailored to fit their heritage, market strategy and the personality of their leadership. But they all followed some well-known design principles that helped them avoid most of the serious obstacles to becoming market-driven.

Guidelines for Managing Change

Successful change programs in a variety of settings follow some general principles. These can be applied to market-driven changes:

- *Change requires a sense of urgency.* This is most likely to be achieved with a real or manufactured crisis that exposes flaws in the firm's approach to customers. A crisis can be manufactured by painting a scenario that would put the firm out of business in ten years, or get-

229

ting teams to adopt the role of a predatory competitor probing the weak points in the strategy. Of course, the threat of crisis must be credible or skepticism will be aroused.

- *Deeds count for more than words*. Only sustained consistency of actions with statements by the leaders over long periods of time will bring lasting change.
- *Understanding comes from experience*. It is difficult to direct the path of change solely from the top down. Instead, make it possible for the organization to run many bottom-up experiments to address problems and performance shortfalls. This will generate options to examine, experiences to learn from, and quick wins to celebrate.[7]
- *Cultural change follows from behavioral change*. Although culture is always a major impediment to change, there is no evidence that efforts to try to change it first will succeed. Change happens by altering behavior patterns and helping people understand how the new behaviors relate to performance improvements. Eventually these changes will be absorbed into the underlying norms, beliefs and mind-set.
- *Implementation is more about commitment than correctness*. Excellent implementation is based on shared understanding, continuing communication to all levels and teamwork that yields personal motivation. Once there is commitment the details will be refined and adjusted as the program evolves.
- *Action plans for teams are more about coordination than control*. Without accountabilities for results, schedules and resources allocated to priorities, the plans are only aspirations.
- *Measurement is essential to recognizable achievement*. Monitoring of progress against these measures allows learning and suggests where improvements are needed.

Obstacles to Overcome

As noted in the opening of this chapter, most change programs don't achieve their objectives. Post-audits of failed efforts have identified a variety of potential problems, including:

- *Absence of leadership*. Nothing will derail a program faster than absence of leadership. If the presumptive leaders lack credibility or credentials, demand politically acceptable solutions, or can't bring the rest of the management team to consensus, the whole effort is likely to be futile.

- *Initiative burnout.* A daunting obstacle is the weariness that settles on organizations that have been forced to change more or less continuously as strategic priorities change. Some managers will have seen five or six widely heralded change initiatives in their time with the company, each promising salvation and each soon supplanted by yet another initiative. This leads to a bewildering mix of approaches with distinct methods, vocabularies, deliverables and teams of outside consultants, and these compete for a shrinking share of the organizational mind. When this syndrome prevails the cynics refer dismissively to the "fad of the month" and conclude that if they just wait patiently the latest one will soon pass. The beleaguered cartoon character Dilbert is a master at this passive resistance.

- *Stifling cultures.* Cultures in which managers and employees are suspicious of ideas outside the status quo can quickly derail a change process. Often the rules of conduct and practice thought to be behind a firm's earlier success are codified into rigid operating standards and styles. A more subtle form of resistance arises when the employees or middle managers think they are doing well and regard the new program as an implicit criticism of their efforts.

- *Management turmoil.* Too many initiatives have stalled or failed during turmoil in management's ranks. Not only is the champion of the change program gone, but the new team may not have accepted the initiative or may want to make their mark by doing something different. If there is a lot of turnover at the top no one can remember why various initiatives were started, and the organization becomes progressively more confused and disenchanted. These signals strengthen the status quo. Those clinging to the past are encouraged by inconsistencies in the picture of the future. They are further encouraged when the picture changes rapidly and for no apparent reason.

- *Lack of urgency.* If managers and employees don't feel the change is urgently needed, other more pressing concerns (such as immediate sales results) will push it aside. This lack of urgency leads to the argument that "we're too busy now, and can't possibly spare the time." Others may protest that "we're already doing it," or "this is a waste of money." Furthermore, "we already know our customers and competitors, which should be obvious since we're doing well right now."

- *Poor implementation.* Implementation problems range from not allocating enough resources or time, to the benefits and goals not being clearly understood by the employees. It is also very hard to sustain enthusiasm if there is a lack of early success, or the successes aren't celebrated properly. There is an important difference between seeing early encouraging results from the program versus the impatience that tries to short-circuit key steps in building support or putting systems in place and can't see why it should take so long to reach the end of the change process.

THE SIX CONDITIONS

In the face of these obstacles, how did the change programs of Owens Corning, Sears and Eurotunnel succeed? For the remainder of this chapter we will examine their stories in more depth to see what these (and other) companies did to satisfy the six necessary conditions.

Condition 1. Demonstrate Leadership Commitment

Do we have a leader . . .

- *who sees the need to change the orientation?*
- *who is committed to making it happen?*
- *who makes market issues a priority?*
- *who is willing to invest time and resources?*
- *who sets aggressive goals for improvement?*
- *who has established a sense of urgency?*

How can top managers signal their commitment, and successfully persuade the entire organization that the firm's performance hinges on satisfying target customers better than the competition? The answer depends on the style of the CEO, the magnitude of the change in values and beliefs, and the past history of efforts to change. However, the following actions have been found to deliver a "customer first" message fluently through the organization:

- an enthusiastic emphasis on superior quality of service and customer relations, with occasional direct interventions to help solve a customer's problems.

- time spent visiting customers and listening aggressively for their point of view and an insistence that all senior managers spend time with these customers.
- an emphasis on customer and market issues—trends, needs, requirements, opportunities for advantage—during strategy reviews. This needs to be supported with a willingness to invest resources in deeper understanding of customers and competitors.
- an insistence on calibrating the performance of the business in serving the target customers against the "best of breed," and then understanding why these competitors excel.

All these moves signal the commitment of senior management. But how can a real sense of urgency be infused deep into the organization? One could argue that the performance problems of Owens Corning, Sears and Eurotunnel would be enough to galvanize their organizations. There was no need to invent a crisis—they were living with one. Unfortunately, as John Kotter observes, this is not enough:[8]

> In most organizations today, the sense of urgency is much too low. Ironically this can happen even in an organization where anxiety and anger are high. It is amazing how people can maintain a relatively high degree of complacency while they are either furious about the way things are going or they're scared to death. They think the problems are "out there," not within the organization or themselves. Angry or scared employees aren't going to try to figure out how to make major improvements.

The CEOs of all three firms gave direction and meaning to the sense of urgency by setting aggressive targets for improvement. Martinez of Sears posed five new strategic priorities—core business growth, customer focus ("make Sears a compelling place to shop"), cost reduction, responsiveness to local markets, and organizational and cultural renewal. He also set difficult goals. Within two years Sears would quadruple its margins to achieve industry parity, reverse the share decline and improve customer satisfaction by 15 percent. Glen Hiner was very explicit about his aspirations for Owens Corning. He signaled that raising cash to cut the debt was no longer the priority: it was time to grow. In 1993 he wanted the company to grow from $2.8 billion to $5 billion by 2000, by supplying everything needed for the "envelope" of the house. And he vowed that sales outside the United States would grow from 21 percent to 40 percent, with productivity growing at 6 percent a year and profits growing twice as fast as sales. Similarly, Eurotunnel management set ambitious targets for revenue growth by making the tunnel the natural choice for all segments, while also committing to aggressive cost cutting to address the big operating loss.

It is tougher to infuse urgency when the business has been doing well. In this case, it is even more important for top leadership to make the organization feel a compelling need to change. Recently Larry Bossiday explained why he felt Allied Signal[9]—the $15 billion defense and auto parts conglomerate—would have to be changed as much in the next five years as in the previous five years (a period when the stock quadrupled):

> We have a long way to go in terms of understanding our customer. I'm asked all the time "What worries you the most?" And the predominant worry is, Are we going to be able to satisfy ever more demanding customers? I was talking to somebody in the food business the other day. They deliver in ten-minute windows. In the aerospace industry you used to deliver in 30-day windows. Now it's overnight. Do we have the processes—the overnight processes—to deliver in ten-minute windows? Some of our competitors will have them someday, so we'd better be prepared. To meet these challenges, a company's people have to feel urgency and commitment.

Condition 2. Understand the Need for Change

Do the key implementers . . .

- *understand what it means to be market-driven, and what changes are needed?*
- *recognize the barriers to change?*
- *see how the change program will benefit them and the business?*

Companies have used two approaches to get deep understanding of the need for change to permeate the organization. The starting place is always with the customer—then the management team can make its own judgments of the orientation of the organization and identify priorities for change.

Exposure to customer judgments. Regardless of how the customer's views are injected into the process, two rules must be observed if the results are to have an impact. First, there is no substitute for firsthand contact with customers by all members of the management team: R&D, manufacturing, and field service. Until everyone has heard the complaints and frustrations, there will not be a pervasive sense of urgency. Second, there is nothing to be gained from collective delusion. This is an ever-present risk with managers who have grown up believing their firm excels, and refusing to acknowledge change. Customers may abet this tendency by holding back criticism so as not to offend. To minimize this risk, some form of objective information should be collected by a third party, who is not identified with the sponsoring client.

Sears established a customer task force that reviewed past survey data and conducted eighty focus groups to get direct feedback. They asked the participants why they shopped at Sears, what they wanted, what they expected and what they disliked. The findings were at odds with the avowed values: "Satisfaction guaranteed or your money back," and "Take care of the customer," which seemed to have lost their meaning. Instead the task force heard endless stories about how shoppers were disappointed with out-of-stock merchandise, nonexistent sales help, bad service and time-consuming returns.

It is not enough to interview current customers; many of the best insights will come from defectors, or attractive prospects in the target market who have never shopped or bought anything. Defectors are a particular gold mine because they pinpoint shortcomings and reveal what the competitors are doing to capture customers.

It is essential that lower-level employees also get involved during this stage. Many companies sponsor employee workshops to define customer expectations, reasons for defection and opportunities for change. The most energizing part of these workshops is sending multifunctional teams to visit the competitors' stores, outlets, branches or sales points to analyze how they deliver value to customers and create a different experience. The teams come back full of ideas, with a vivid appreciation of what they have to do better. These workshops work because they are very concrete and understandable, and confront employees with competitive realities.

Above all, employees must learn "to see things as the customer sees them, and then measure that." This is a lesson David Fuentes, CEO of Office Depot, the $9 billion office supplies retailer, has taken to heart. Ten years ago, they began putting green dots on any space where a customer would see a stock-out, regardless of where the product was in the store.

Today, they are recognized for their superiority in inventory control, and their number-one measure is still the total green dots accumulated.

Solicit management judgments of effectiveness. After confronting reality—as defined by target customers' expectations and competitors' abilities—the management team needs to candidly assess its relative standing in creating the culture, capabilities, structure and strategy of a market-driven organization. The assessment questionnaire found in the Appendix was designed to serve this purpose and help set priorities for improvement.

It is normal for members of the management team to disagree—sometimes quite sharply—on how well their organization is performing. This reflects differences in frames of reference, recent experiences with customers, functional backgrounds and level in the organization. Too much disparity in these judgments is a cause for concern because the sense of urgency is likely to be dissipated in a battle over details. It takes strong leadership to drive to an acceptable consensus.

Dow Chemical—the $20 billion chemicals giant—adopted the management survey approach in 1994. Executives had abundant reasons to believe they had to adopt a stronger market orientation: investors were complaining about the cyclical performance in commodity chemicals, new competitors with lean business models were challenging them and customers were signaling that they had new requirements that weren't being met by Dow. A standard survey was given to all levels of management.[10] This survey was used because it had benchmark results for peer companies.

As shown in the table below, while senior management had a high perception of a market orientation, middle managers gave the firm much lower marks and salaried employees came in even lower. According to its own managers, Dow was in the bottom third of peer companies, with an overall rating in the 32nd percentile for all companies in the benchmark survey. Given the spread in judgments across the levels, somebody had to be out of touch and it was probably senior management.

Percentile Score on Survey of Market Orientation

Senior management	65
Band 2 (middle management up to director level)	32
Band 1 (lower levels of salaried employees)	24

The reactions to the survey followed a familiar pattern: confusion at first, then resistance and denial including objections to the premise of the survey, followed by gradual acceptance of the findings and the need for deep-rooted change. The program of change was driven by the president, who signaled the seriousness of his intentions by bringing customers to board meetings and establishing multifunctional task forces to lead the change process.

Condition 3. Mobilize Commitment

Do the sponsors of the change . . .

- *have experience and credibility?*
- *recognize who else needs to be committed to the change to make it happen?*
- *know how to rally a coalition of supporters and overcome the expected resistance?*
- *have the resources they need?*

Companies need to create an effective management team to mobilize commitment for change efforts. This team can be drawn together from mavericks inside the firm or—often more effective in a crisis situation—may include outsiders to bring fresh perspectives to the problem. Wherever it is drawn from, the team must demonstrate the experience and credibility to gain the commitment of the entire organization.

A popular—but generally ineffectual—method for mobilizing commitment for a market orientation is to create a council or steering group. This is, more often than not, a charade. Firms use this approach when they feel they should do something, but aren't quite ready for deep-seated change. Commonly, the charter of the council is to elevate skills, share best practices, or understand what it means to be market-driven.

These groups as they are implemented in many organizations have little chance of success. With as many as 30 to 40 people involved and shifting faces, the groups are too large for real work and have little continuity. Meetings are carefully orchestrated set pieces with outside speakers, but no mandate for serious follow-up actions. Resources are usually limited—perhaps a staff person and a modest budget—and time commitment of members is also too limited, usually less than 10 percent of their attention.

Some companies succeed in overcoming these obstacles. When Monsanto created a council to drive the company toward "best of class" mar-ket orientation, it established a small leadership team of ten VPs and general managers that was given a mandate to change basic behaviors, build market-driven capabilities, and transfer best practices. They were expected to spend at least 30 percent of their time on this effort, and they agreed to partially tie their compensation to the results. The council was given all the resources it needed, including a full-time Director of Mar-keting Core Capability. They met at least two times a week as a group, and focused their efforts on only a few big issues—such as relationship management—that they felt would have the greatest leverage in chang-ing a culture that was very technology-driven.

When a company is in as deep a hole as Sears or Owens Corning, more drastic measures are needed. No amount of councils, consultants and conferences will yield fundamental and durable change. For the effort to be taken seriously, a new management team is needed, because the old one is likely short of credibility, energy and imagination.

Sometimes the right people can be found within the organization. They have the right instincts, and probably have been agitating for change for some time and been frustrated in their crusade. The advantage of insiders is that they know the prevailing culture. The disadvantage is that they may not be able to escape its deeply embedded values and assumptions, to envision a more open, externally oriented culture, and then orchestrate a change effort. Sometimes the agitators for change lack credibility and respect because they have been operating at the periphery of the organization. These people should be consulted but not asked to lead the change initiative.

One of the main reasons Arthur Martinez was able to change Sears is that he changed most of the senior executive team, and most of the new appointees had no prior experience in retailing. The executive vice pres-ident in charge of logistics was the three-star general who masterminded the supply chain in the Gulf War. The head of marketing had extensive experience in brand management with Pepsi and Procter & Gamble, and saw that the strong brands that Sears had developed had much more potential for building loyalty than was appreciated within the company.

The survivors from the old Sears team tended to be broad-minded, outspoken mavericks like Bill Salter. "We used to be so inbred, it's a won-der we all didn't have one eye in the middle of our foreheads," he says. "A number of us who are still here are almost ashamed we didn't figure out how to fix Sears ourselves. But our experiences were all the same: retailing. The most important thing Arthur has done is bring in specialists in their fields."

Unfortunately outsiders are often treated like foreign antibodies and rejected by the organization. This is a particularly common fate of successful marketing people who have been brought in from powerhouse marketing companies like Procter & Gamble, American Express or Coke to lead the change effort in an established firm in a very different industry—perhaps one that is deregulating such as banking or telecommunications. These people face two problems at the outset: they don't understand the technology, customer requirements or the key success factors in the new business, and they are separated from most of the support systems and cultural reinforcement that made them successful. When disenchantment sets in, these victims even lose the top-level support they once had. The usual advice is to follow one of these people, but never take on the thankless task of being the first stalking horse for change.

Condition 4. Shape the Vision

Do all employees . . .

- *understand how superior customer value will be created?*
- *see what they have to do differently?*
- *get excited about the promised results?*

The most uncomfortable moment for the change program at Sears was in November 1993 when Arthur Martinez asked his change team how the five strategic priorities announced in March were progressing. It became clear that the priorities set by top management weren't meaningful to the rest of the organization. One forthright senior manager finally stood up and said, "To be perfectly honest, I don't know what I'm supposed to be doing differently." The problem was that the five priorities lacked broad ownership and employee engagement.

An organization's members do best when there is a line-of-sight understanding between the strategy for delivering superior customer value and their individual contributions. Each of the three companies worked hard to convey the larger picture to their people and enable them to develop a vision and strategy for their domain that supported the overall effort. These bottom-up efforts also expanded the collective understanding of how much change was possible and what options were feasible.

One of the coalescing visions for Owens Corning was *system thinking* which pushed the notion that roofing, exteriors, insulation, and sound absorption are all systems that work together to solve customers' problems. The idea was that if buyers knew how shingles, vents, insulation and soffits worked together to make a better roof, if they could pick a reliable contractor who could provide financing and Owens Corning provided all the information there would be more sales of Owens Corning products. Under this umbrella, product developers have clear priorities, merchandising and advertising are easier to target, relationships with contractors are closer, and systems provide the integrating information.

Early in the change process Sears management articulated a vision of a "compelling place to work, to shop, to invest," which was then combined with the three values of "passion for the customer, our people add value, and performance leadership." As a guiding vision it had a lot of merit, being simple and to the point. It also fell on deaf ears, for the line employees had a completely different mind-set. When a large sampling of employees was asked what they were paid to do everyday, the answer was most likely "I get paid to protect the assets of the company." In short, they completely misunderstood their role. But how to shift the mind-set toward making Sears a compelling place to shop?

To help employees understand their proper role in the bigger picture, the company prepared learning maps,[11] which were discussed by teams of employees at "town hall meetings." A learning map is a large picture of a town, store or river that leads participants through a business or historical process. One map portrayed the shifts in the retail environment and the proliferation of competitors between 1950 and 1990. Another map asked employees to analyze the sources and uses of funds as they flowed from the cash register to the bottom line. Sears then asked the teams to apply what they had learned and recommend actions they could take immediately in their store, warehouse or office to improve customer service or simplify their activities. The strong signal was that front-line employees were going to be given more autonomy to do right by the customer—and help Sears win in an increasingly competitive retail market.

Eurotunnel management also used a team approach to overcome the suspicion of its employees that the change program was about cutting costs, and get them to focus on how they contributed to improving operations and satisfying customers. At the peak of the change activity, almost one-third of the 3,000 employees were participating in one of 87 multifunctional teams. Many of the teams that addressed the needs of a customer segment included a customer such as a lorry owner. These teams were given plenty of latitude in their activities but were held accountable for delivering a set of benefits. If no benefits were forthcoming, the team was likely to be disbanded or combined with another team.

The mobilizing vision was to make Eurotunnel the natural choice for crossing the channel. Each team had a defined role in supporting the vision. The vision and all the connecting elements of processes, systems and roles were communicated in dozens of meetings, newsletters and a wall chart that covered most of a large wall and showed each team where they fit. The team responsible for reducing unwelcome stops in the tunnel—caused by equipment failure—could readily see how their work could save money and improve customer satisfaction. Most people hate to be stopped in a tunnel, especially when they don't know why or for how long. The efforts of this team helped reduce the number of these stops from an average of thirty down to nine per week; but sometimes as low as five in a week.

Learning from experiments. Instead of assembling large, cross-functional teams to develop change initiatives and then pilot test, it may be better to start a number of hothouse experiments and then see what works. These could also be grassroots initiatives that were originally started without top-down direction as responses to a local problem. Either way, they are excellent learning vehicles.

The advantage of hothouse experiments is that they are not so initially disruptive to the entire organization. But if they work, they are an example everyone else can understand and follow. There is more of a bottom-up, market-back feel because it involves the very people who know the problems and how they might be handled. The box below describes a hothouse experiment in a major UK supermarket chain.[12]

The method can be applied in any industry that operates through a set of functionally identical units such as stores, call centers, bank branches or restaurants that can be geographically isolated.

HOT IDEAS FROM A HOTHOUSE EXPERIMENT

Store staff kept getting conflicting signals from the head office. Sometimes, the emphasis was on cutting the time customers spent in the checkout line. When they diverted resources from shelf filling to comply with this mandate, another directive would demand improvements in on-shelf availability. Because staff didn't feel they could win, morale suffered.

Given the counterproductive effect of these directives, managers decided to try another approach. One store was isolated as a hothouse, and a team was given free rein to experiment with solutions to the problem of balancing service and shelf stocking—and to track the results. When they started looking for a root cause, they found that the volume of incoming stock (held in cages) was too great to absorb and was causing serious congestion. This forced the staff to spend too much time off the floor, simply looking for line items. If they stopped looking, the resulting gaps on the shelves prompted customer complaints and led the management to berate the staff. The dispirited staff then allowed even more cages to clog the storage area.

The hothouse team was able to break this vicious cycle when they were asked to suggest ways to reduce stocks without increasing stock-outs. During the experiment, stock fell by 28 percent, there were 40 percent fewer cages in the back store, on-shelf availability rose 5 percent and customer satisfaction ratings for the store rose from 3.5 to 4.7 (on a 5-point scale). This was such a success that it became a model rolled out at another 500 stores, with the team moving to different stores in succession to transfer their know-how. If management had sent employees a directive to achieve these goals or change this process, it would have fallen on deaf ears. But a small-scale, hothouse experiment created a successful model that ultimately transformed the organization and increased morale.

Condition 5. Align Structures, Systems and Incentives

Is there a credible plan for . . .

- *modifying the organization structure and systems?*
- *recruiting, developing and deploying people in the new structure?*
- *developing the market-sensing and market-relating capabilities?*
- *changing the systems?*
- *encouraging and rewarding market-driven behavior?*

Once the change initiative is underway, attention soon turns to how to institutionalize it so the organization doesn't revert to its old ways. How can sustained market-driven behavior be encouraged and rewarded? The three most effective levers are organizational and process redesign, systems support, and incentives and rewards.

Organizational and Process Redesign. In Chapter 10, we proposed a hybrid organizational structure, with teams focused on managing distinct customer and consumer segment groups, for achieving closer alignment. Each customer-facing group is charged with creating a credible superior value proposition for its segment. Eurotunnel used this lever as a central part of its effort to get a functional organization to think about the distinct needs of tourist travelers versus business travelers as well as lorry drivers and international trains.

Crucial to an organizational redesign is "reengineering" the core value development and delivery processes and realigning them with the supporting processes such as human resources. This is reengineering in the proper sense of optimizing a sequence of activities. IBM used this approach to revamp its Customer Relationship Management (CRM) processes in 1994 and 1995. They began with a clear set of customer requirements—i.e., "understand me and my business . . . keep your promises . . . do business on my terms"—that were translated into objectives for each of the ten supporting processes such as opportunity management, customer satisfaction management and market management.[13]

The pivotal process was market management based on the familiar sequence of analyzing markets, identifying and selecting segments and devising strategies for each segment. The output of this tidy process fed all the other processes—and that's where the trouble started. For example, if a new target segment was identified, it was difficult to get the human resources/training department to pay attention, but without their contribution the right skills wouldn't be available to serve the new segment. The sales force was particularly resistant to changing its day-to-day activities. Their mind-set was that all business is good business, that all sales opportunities are good opportunities and that all revenue is good revenue. This clashed directly with the emphasis on attractive opportunities rather than diffusing energies across high and low priorities.

Incentives and Rewards. The best intentions of a market-driven change program will be thwarted if the compensation plan came from another era. No surprise that IBM people thought all revenue was good revenue—for that was how they were compensated.

The research here is unequivocal. If the change effort is to be taken seriously, the rewards and incentives have to be aligned. This may be as modest as ensuring that employee evaluation forms have explicit customer-contact metrics built into them. Sears has taken the concept as far as any company by basing long-term executive compensation on nonfinancial as well as financial performance—one-third on employee measures, one-third on customer satisfaction and retention measures and one-third on traditional investor measures. Their willingness to take this step is a measure of their confidence in the business model we described in Chapter 6. Since this is such a powerful signal and motivator, it has been extended to nearly all field managers, whose annual incentive is now based on targeted improvements in customer satisfaction. Even hourly associates can earn variable incentive pay based on improved customer satisfaction.

Systems. The hodgepodge of mismatched legacy systems that afflicts most companies makes it impractical for them to focus on the customers with the greatest life-time value or the segments that are most profitable, or to ensure widespread access to market and cost data, or presume to offer seamless service. This is why some of the biggest breakthroughs come from systems projects, and also why they are among the last steps in the process.

One of the centerpieces of the change process at Owens Corning was the realignment of systems to support its new strategy. The concept was to let customers enter their system to learn what inventory was available, find out when their order was shipped and pay electronically in a way that the multiplicity of products they sold looked like a coherent bundle. This required replacing all systems with SAP, the powerful and notoriously difficult enterprise software. But old systems and procedures couldn't simply be replicated on the new systems; they all had to be completely redesigned to mesh with the new processes that flowed information throughout the company rather than leaving it contained in separate silos. After paying $110 million to install SAP and train people, the company expects to save as much as $80 million a year by 2000. More important, they have achieved a vital alignment and integration of external information flows and internal processes and information.

Condition 6: Sustain the Change

Do those responsible for change . . .

- *know how to get started and ensure an early success?*
- *have benchmarks for measuring progress?*
- *have a plan to keep attention focused on the change program?*

Organizations beset with day-to-day internal concerns often backslide after their initial wins in becoming more market-driven. Managers need to be vigilant in sustaining the change process and driving the organization to higher levels of market orientation. This process is called "painting the bridge" in reference to the painters of large bridges who finish their job at one end and immediately start over. They need to continuously create wins and disseminate these best practices, measure and assess progress (and assess the metrics used to measure), and keep attention focused on the process.

Companies need to find ways to turn episodic efforts at improvement into a discipline that is embedded in the culture. Most successful change initiatives begin with an early, visible win that could be widely celebrated, and used as an exemplar by the rest of the organization. The message is, "This is what we expect, and here is how it should be done." Eurotunnel pushed hard in the early stages of the change program to launch a club class for business travelers, which showed the benefits of working in multifunctional teams. Pilot programs can also be used to fine-tune the change program and build enthusiasm.

The development of these wins, and the dissemination of the best practices created by them, need to be ongoing. Wal-Mart has mastered the rapid diffusion of best practices and winning programs to all stores. During regular Saturday morning merchandising meetings, the company celebrates outstanding achievements by managers. A manager of a department in one store with a very effective approach communicates her strategy to managers throughout the organization via satellite. These managers can then immediately implement this best practice in their own stores.

A sustained effort requires ongoing monitoring of performance against objectives for improvement in important market metrics. When Xerox launched its customer satisfaction program in 1990, it set a target of 90 percent ratings of "somewhat" or "very" satisfied by 1992. As the company moved closer to the goal, the bar was raised. Then the target measure was changed to customer retention, which reenergized the program. Whatever measure is chosen, it should be closely linked to financial performance, easily understood, and reliably measured so there is confidence in the results.

Overall, managers need to keep attention focused on the change process to sustain it. In addition to disseminating best practices and using measures, companies can use continuous benchmarking against competition, frequent inputs from customers and constant questioning of all processes to reinforce the effort to become market-driven.[14]

CONCLUSION: ANSWERING THE CALL TO THE MARKET

The stories of Owens Corning, Sears and Eurotunnel show that every organization follows a unique path to becoming more market-driven, shaped by its own past, competitive position and leadership team. But their experiences also demonstrate that the transformation is likely to be more effective if six conditions are met:

- there is demonstrated leadership commitment
- key implementers fully understand the need for change
- there is commitment at all levels
- all employees know what they are trying to accomplish
- structures, systems and incentives are aligned with the strategy
- those responsible for leading the change to a market orientation know how to sustain the change

The change process can stretch out over many months or even many years, depending on the breadth and depth of change required, the shared sense of urgency that change is needed and the willingness of senior management to stay the course without being distracted by other priorities. The aim in all cases is to have a market-facing culture, distinctive capabilities for market sensing, marketing relating, and strategic thinking, and a configuration that can stay in alignment with an increasingly unpredictable market. The payoff is an organization that can continuously create superior value for its chosen customers.

Being market-driven is not an end point, but rather an ongoing process. As markets become more volatile and less predictable managers need to stay alert that their organization doesn't calcify by staying too long with an obsolete strategy or by missing new requirements. There is no room for complacency.

But if the actions of rivals or market shifts can erode a firm's advantages from the outside, changes from the inside can create new advantages. As shown by the stories of Sears, Owens Corning and Eurotunnel, any organization has the opportunity to realign itself more closely to the market. And, given the proven profit and performance benefits of being market-driven, there are more compelling reasons than ever to do so.

The place to start is with the self-assessment in the Appendix. It will help you identify the weaknesses and strengths of your organization in market orientation. Then carry the tools and insights described in this book out to the widest possible group of managers within your organization, to create as broad as possible a movement for change. It is surprising what a small but motivated group can accomplish with the right knowledge.

The stories here of many successful firms that became more market-driven—and the benefits they derived from this shift—point the way for others to follow. They show that becoming market-driven is not only possible but profitable.

Is Your Organization Market Driven?

This assessment form was designed to be used by senior management teams to establish the orientation of their organization. The purpose is to illustrate the traits of market-driven organizations and to help teams set priorities for their change program.

Each question is designed so the right-hand side represents superior performance—if not best practice—while the left-hand side is deficient practice.

I. Overall Orientation: Values, Beliefs and Behavior

1. Who takes the customer's perspective?

Understanding and responding   ❑—❑—❑—❑—❑   All functions and activities
to customer requirements   are integrated in serving
is marketing's job.   the needs of our target customers.

2. Senior management priorities and interests?

Internal concerns take   ❑—❑—❑—❑—❑   Customer and competitor issues
precedence—time for   are of paramount importance.
customer visits is seldom   They schedule regular visits and
available.   actively solicit customer
   feedback.

3. Emphasis in orienting the business toward serving the needs and wants of chosen markets?

Emphasis is on selling to   ❑—❑—❑—❑—❑   All decisions start with
whomever will buy.   the customer and
   opportunities for
   advantage.

4. How is market knowledge sharing viewed?

The flow of information about customers is impeded by a silo mentality. ❑—❑—❑—❑—❑ We freely share information about customers and successful and unsuccessful customer experiences across all business functions.

5. Emphasis in strategy development?

Our business strategies are reactive and focused on the short term. ❑—❑—❑—❑—❑ Our business strategies are guided by our shared beliefs about how we can create value for customers.

6. Orientation to target competitors?

We are slow to respond to competitors. ❑—❑—❑—❑—❑ Everyone strives to outperform the target competitors.

7. Relationships with customers?

Emphasis is on one-time transactions. ❑—❑—❑—❑—❑ Emphasis is on building long-run relationships.

8. Attitudes toward channels?

Seen as passive conduits. ❑—❑—❑—❑—❑ Viewed as long-run partners with shared interests.

9. Willingness to innovate?

Existing products and technologies suppress thinking about changing market needs and opportunities. ❑—❑—❑—❑—❑ Continuous striving to find better solutions to customer's problems.

10. Management of quality?

Emphasis is on achieving conformance to internal standards. ❑—❑—❑—❑—❑ Achievement of superior market-perceived quality is a high priority for all functions.

11. How well is market thinking at the top communicated and implemented throughout the organization?

Poorly. ❑—❑—❑—❑—❑ Successfully.

II. Market Sensing Capability

1. How extensively does the business explore and understand its customers and channel partners?

Limited to publicly available information and informal sales force feedback. ☐—☐—☐—☐—☐ Strong commitment to thoroughly understanding the market as the basis for strategic decisions.

2. Extent of market monitoring?

Seldom done beyond tracing sales and share. ☐—☐—☐—☐—☐ Frequent and extensive—including post-transaction follow-ups, customer satisfaction and quality monitoring.

3. Willingness of customer contact employees to feed market information to management?

Poor—no incentives or mechanisms are available. ☐—☐—☐—☐—☐ Excellent—there is a continuous flow of information about customer needs and competitors' activities.

4. Extent of search for innovative product concepts?

Search is limited to copying competitors. No formal activity is undertaken. ☐—☐—☐—☐—☐ Continuous and thorough—including search for latent and unfilled needs in target markets.

5. Frequency that functions other than sales and marketing meet with customers and channels?

Seldom or never. ☐—☐—☐—☐—☐ Multi-functional teams make frequent visits.

6. Knowledge of market segments?

Limited—based on available data and industry classification. ☐—☐—☐—☐—☐ Extensive—considerable investments are made in identifying need-based segments and tracking emerging segment opportunities.

7. Knowledge of competitors?

Limited to readily available data on direct competition. ☐—☐—☐—☐—☐ Thorough insights into all those with an opportunity to serve the customer.

8. Use of customer complaints?

Complaints are evidence of ☐—☐—☐—☐—☐ Complaints are learning
failure. opportunities.

9. Knowledge of cost effectiveness of marketing programs?

Limited to readily available ☐—☐—☐—☐—☐ Extensive—based on careful
information. monitoring of experiments.

10. Willingness to undertake regular post-audits of unsuccessful programs and communicate results widely?

Post-audits are avoided ☐—☐—☐—☐—☐ Post-audits are systematically
because they usually amount undertaken and lessons for
to a search for the guilty. improvement are widely
recommended.

11. Adequacy of market information systems?

Incompatible databases and ☐—☐—☐—☐—☐ Systems make it easy for all
software difficulties make managers to retrieve
it impossible to extract comprehensive and timely
information. information.

12. Integration of customer and competitive information into the new product development process?

Poorly integrated. ☐—☐—☐—☐—☐ Extensively integrated in all
stages of the process.

13. Role of the market research function?

Limited to sales analysis and ☐—☐—☐—☐—☐ Widely recognized for expertise
occasional negotiation with in undertaking market studies
outside data suppliers. and developing useful strategy
recommendations.

14. Reliance on outsiders for market analysis and interpretation?

Most continuing market ☐—☐—☐—☐—☐ Limited reliance except for
studies are done by special one-time studies.
outside consultants with little
ongoing company involvement.

15. Sharing of lessons about market behavior and activity between functions and countries?

Marketing researchers are ☐—☐—☐—☐—☐ Excellent—there is ongoing
the experts in the market sharing of market insights at
and hoard their knowledge. several levels.

III. Market-Relating Capability

1. What is the prevailing mind-set?

Focus is on attracting customers, and emphasizes one-time transactions. ❑—❑—❑—❑—❑ Customers are viewed as partners and business assets to be managed for long-run profit.

2. Knowledge of individual customer loyalty and profitability?

Limited to occasional surveys of satisfaction; systems can't provide information on relative profitability. ❑—❑—❑—❑—❑ Information is widely available and used to estimate impact of increase in retention rate on overall profitability.

3. Ability to differentiate among customers?

Any differences in treatment are due to variations in current level of sales. ❑—❑—❑—❑—❑ Key accounts with long-run potential are targeted for special treatment and loyalty-building programs.

4. Relationships with key accounts?

Negotiations are usually adversarial and focus on short-run price concessions. ❑—❑—❑—❑—❑ There is close collaboration, extensive information sharing and integration of joint systems.

5. Role of sales force?

Act as gatekeepers that control all customer contacts and filter market signals to rest of organization. ❑—❑—❑—❑—❑ Act as leaders of multifunctional teams partnering with key accounts and coordinate level-to-level contacts.

6. Extent of efforts to align business systems toward increasing customer retention?

No systematic efforts are being made or contemplated; not a strategic priority. ❑—❑—❑—❑—❑ Appropriate systems, processes, measures, and incentives are designed to increase customer retention.

7. How are channel intermediaries viewed?

Seen as passive conduits to be bypassed whenever possible. ❑—❑—❑—❑—❑ Seen as close business partners with shared long-run interests.

8. *Utilization of advances in network technology?*

Limited to a Web site with ☐—☐—☐—☐—☐ Actively developing ways to
catalogs and advertisements. use information from customers
to modify the offering and
tighten relationships.

9. *Management of brand equity?*

Little attention paid to ☐—☐—☐—☐—☐ Organization is committed to
value of brand names or ways understanding and protecting
to exploit them. the basis of brand equity and
finding ways to exploit it.

10. *Measure of relationship effectiveness?*

Limited to usual measures ☐—☐—☐—☐—☐ Usual measures are subordinated
of revenue, profit and to measures of customer loyalty,
customer satisfaction. defections and employee loyalty.

IV. Strategic Thinking

1. *What is the orientation of the planning process?*

Process is adversarial and ☐—☐—☐—☐—☐ Process is collaborative with
control-oriented: each function emphasis on creating integrated
sees it as a zero-sum game. strategies.

2. *Design of the planning process?*

Routinized procedure that is a ☐—☐—☐—☐—☐ Real-time issues-oriented
prelude to the annual budget. approach that anticipates the
future.

3. *Participation in the strategic planning process?*

Limited participation— ☐—☐—☐—☐—☐ Broad participation in cross-
emphasis is on finding one functional teams and openness
satisfactory strategy. to alternatives enhances
creativity and commitment.

4. *Length of planning horizon?*

Focus is on next year's ☐—☐—☐—☐—☐ Focus is on long-term creation
profit and fast payback. of shareholder value.

5. *Quality of strategic analysis?*

Yields a laundry list of ☐—☐—☐—☐—☐ Used to identify key issues
generalized strengths, weaknesses, and competitive advantages
threats, and opportunities. that can be used to protect or
build the business.

6. *Knowledge of market?*

Limited to historical data on financial performance and generally available market statistics. Limited ability to anticipate competitor moves.   □—□—□—□—□   Deep and shared understanding of drivers of customer value, sources of profits, and competitor behavior.

7. *How are market initiatives evaluated?*

Short-term expense-oriented mind-set prevails.   □—□—□—□—□   Long-term investment-oriented mind-set focuses on future revenues.

8. *Adequacy of marketing resources?*

Resources are inadequate for the job to be done.   □—□—□—□—□   Resources are adequate and are deployed efficiently.

9. *Extent of contingency thinking and planning?*

Not required.   □—□—□—□—□   Management formally identifies the most important contingencies and develops contingency plans.

10. *Type of strategy review by senior management?*

Annual, with emphasis on financial projections and budget requests.   □—□—□—□—□   Periodic, with focus on quality of assumptions about strategic fundamentals, feasibility of strategy and management of risks.

V. Organizational Alignment

1. *Design of organization structure?*

Organization is structured around functions or large families of products.   □—□—□—□—□   Organization is structured around market segments so responsibilities for serving market needs are well-defined.

2. *Relations between departments and functional groups?*

Departments are isolated—vertical silos impede communication.   □—□—□—□—□   Departments willingly share information and participate effectively in multifunctional groups.

3. Understanding of business strategy?

Functions have different and conflicting assumptions, and lack a common understanding of the strategy.

☐—☐—☐—☐—☐

Excellent—there is a shared understanding and acceptance of the strategy.

4. Coordination and integration of functional groups and departments in serving customer needs?

Functional hierarchy with limited coordination by product or segment managers and national account managers.

☐—☐—☐—☐—☐

Coordination within multifunctional teams permanently assigned to core processes and guided by a strategic integration team.

5. Ability of information systems to support interfunctional coordination?

Each function has separate and incompatible systems and databases.

☐—☐—☐—☐—☐

Everyone has ready access to databases with complete customer and cost information, and can communicate with everyone else in the organization.

6. Interactions with customers, clients and channel members?

Strong sales group "owns" customer relations and cuts off market signals to rest of organization.

☐—☐—☐—☐—☐

All functions can and do interact with customers directly and share a deep understanding of their needs and usage situations.

7. Role of the marketing function?

Marketing people play a subordinate role in sales support activities or as participants in multifunctional teams.

☐—☐—☐—☐—☐

Marketing is seen as responsible for keeping the entire organization focused on the customer and providing the strategic logic for the value proposition.

8. How are executives rewarded?

For being safe, careful and conservative.

☐—☐—☐—☐—☐

For being innovative strategists and pursuers of new opportunities.

9. *Ability of management to react quickly and effectively to on-the-spot developments and new opportunities?*

Sales and market information is out of date and reaction times are slow. ❑—❑—❑—❑—❑ Systems yield highly current information and the organization can respond quickly.

10. *Emphasis of incentive systems?*

Most weight is given to short run sales results and capturing new accounts. ❑—❑—❑—❑—❑ Reward systems and recognition programs are designed to reward short- and long-term results consistent with strategic priorities.

Acknowledgments

Writing a book has many parallels to a voyage of discovery. Like any explorer, I accumulated many debts of gratitude to those who encouraged me to launch the project, shared their experience on the directions to take and pitfalls to avoid, guided me on in the right direction with their comments and helped me to finish. But, of course, none of them can be held accountable for the destination I reached with this book.

The sponsor of the voyage was surely the Marketing Science Institute. At the outset they had funded an influential stream of research by top scholars in marketing on what it meant to be market-driven. While executive director from 1989 to 1991 I became interested in the top research priority of 1990 which was "improving the utilization of market information." The member companies were generous in sharing their approaches to this issue, and helped me see that market-driven firms had a superior market-sensing capability. That insight became a critical element of this book. I'd like to especially thank Paul Root, Kathy Jocz, and Steve Haeckel for guiding this unique organization, influencing my thinking in more ways than they can appreciate, and providing support at critical junctures.

There is a large community of fellow explorers whose work provided invaluable guidance. Many were associated with the Marketing Science Institute during the time this book was in progress. Fred Webster, John Farley, Rohit Deshpandé, Ajay Kohli, Bernie Jaworski, John Narver, Vince Barabba and Gerald Zaltman each added important conceptual and empirical insights. It is also a pleasure to acknowledge the intellectual stimulation provided by Tom Robertson, Jagdish Sheth, Rajan

Varadarajan, Ben Shapiro, Adrian Ryans and Ken Roering who were raising the same issues that led to this book. This recognition is inadequate recompense for all their contributions.

At several critical junctures during the voyage, I was aided by my colleagues here at Wharton. Jerry Wind has tackled many of the same issues in his broad inquiry into the twenty-first century organization. Ian MacMillan, Rita McGrath, Bruce Kogut, John Kimberly, Sid Winter, Harbir Singh, Jitendra Singh, and Paul Schoemaker were especially helpful by sharing the latest thinking of the strategic management field, and helped me understand what capabilities set market-driven organizations apart. My students—especially Adam Fein—brought me many insights. I want to pay special tribute to Ned Bowman whose wisdom has shaped my thinking in many ways. Sadly, he passed away as I was finishing this book. All these colleagues were part of the stimulation I gained from being a part of this world-class institution which in its own way is working hard to become a market-driven organization.

My greatest intellectual debt is to the friends and colleagues who sailed with me at least part of the way, and were always willing to share their advice and experience while challenging me to clarify my thinking. Liam Fahey and Dave Reibstein were especially helpful in shaping my thinking about the role of a competitor orientation. Paddy Barwise provided insightful comments at critical points in the development of the book, and Robin Wensley helped me to separate the truly important from the merely interesting.

During my journey, many valuable lessons came from thoughtful practitioners who shared their experience in piloting their own organizations toward a marketing orientation. Some were clients who invited me to work with them over a number of years to test my ideas. A number of consulting firms shared their thinking with me. I'd like to single out the London office of Gemini Consulting for helping me to understand the deep challenge of changing organizations. Lastly, I have deep appreciation for the feedback I gained from hundreds of senior executives in dozens of executive development programs. Their enthusiasm for the ideas, and continuing challenges to sloppy thinking kept me digging further to explain why and how organizations had to be market-driven to prosper.

Many books are started, but few finish the journey. I had the good fortune to have many people help me reach the destination. Robert Wallace, my editor for over twenty years here at the Free Press, was the first to see the possibilities for this book and kept urging me to take the plunge. Robert Gunther provided invaluable editorial help. In many respects, he was like a ship's pilot who took the reader's point of view to rewrite and reorganize the ideas so they were persuasive. Throughout the project, I had the good fortune to have the assistance of Michele Klekotka. She exercised unfailing good cheer and good judgment in managing the essential details of the venture. John Carstens and his staff provided an exceptional level of word-processing support in turning my scribbles into readable text.

This book is dedicated to my wife and the light of my life. Marilyn has been an unfailing source of support, enthusiasm and inspiration. Had she not shared this voyage with me, it might not have been started or finished.

George Day
Bryn Mawr, Pennsylvania
January 1999

Notes

Chapter 1. What It Means to Be Market Driven

1. Delphine Parmenter, Jean-Claude Larreché and Christopher Lovelock, *First-Direct: Branchless Banking*, INSEAD, 1997, Fontainebleau, France.

2. Ron Winslow, "How a Breakthrough Quickly Broke Down for Johnson & Johnson," *Wall Street Journal*, September 18, 1998.

3. Peter F. Drucker, *The Practice of Management* (New York, Harper & Row, 1954).

4. Roger O. Crockett, "How Motorola Lost Its Way," *Business Week*, May 4, 1998, p. 140; Daniel Roth, "Burying Motorola: From Poster Boy to Whipping Boy," *Fortune*, July 6, 1998, pp. 28–29, and "Mr. Internet," *The Economist*, March 28, 1998, p. 98.

5. Danny Miller, "Configuration of Strategy and Structure: Towards a Synthesis," *Strategic Management Journal* 7 (1986): 233–249 and "Configurations Revisited," *Strategic Management Journal* 17 (1996): 505–512.

6. This description of Saturn draws from David A. Aaker, "The Saturn Story: Building a Strong Brand," *California Management Review* 36, Winter 1994, pp. 114–133.

7. Henry Mintzberg, Bruce Ahlstrand and Joseph Lampel, *Strategy Safari: A Guided Tour Through the Wilds of Strategic Management* (New York: Free Press, 1998).

8. Bernard Jaworski and Ajay K. Kohli, "Market Orientation: Antecedents and Consequences," *Journal of Marketing* 57 (July 1993): 53–70; John C. Narver and Stanley F. Slater, "The Effect of Market Orientation on Business Profitability," *Journal of Marketing* 54 (October 1990): 20–35. For a recent synthesis of this work, see Rohit Deshpandé and John U. Farley, "Measuring Market Orientation," *Journal of Market-Focused Management* 2 (1998): 213–232; and John Narver and Stanley Slater, "Additional Thoughts on the Measurement of Market Orientation: A Comment on Deshpandé and Farley," *Journal of Market-Focused Management* 2 (1998): 233–236.

9. These results were derived from George S. Day and Prakash Nedungadi, "Managerial Representations of Competitive Advantage," *Journal of Marketing* 58 (April 1994): 40, by applying the results of subjective judgments of relative financial performance to the distributions of return on investment results in the PIMS database. We caution that the performance differences do not control for differences in the competitive market environment or strategic choices. These profitability results are in line with results for John C. Narver and Stanley F. Slater, "The Effect of a Market Orientation on Business Profitability," *Journal of Marketing* 54 (October 1990): 20–35, using a different procedure for measuring market orientation.

10. Judy A. Siguaur, Gene Brown and Robert E. Widing II, "The Influence of Market Orientation of the Firm on Sales Force Behavior and Attitudes," *Journal of Marketing Research* 31 (February 1994): 106–116.

11. Steven E. Prokesh, "Competing on Customer Service: An Interview with British Airways' Sir Colin Marshall," *Harvard Business Review*, November–December 1995, p.103.

12. Hermann Simon, "Lessons from Germany's Mid-Size Giants," *Harvard Business Review*, March–April 1992, pp. 115–124.

13. Frederick F. Reichheld and W. Earl Sasser, Jr., "Zero Defections: Quality Comes to Services," *Harvard Business Review*, September–October 1990, pp. 105–111.

14. This section draws from Adrian Slywotzky and Benson P. Shapiro, "Leveraging to Beat the Odds: The New Marketing Mind-Set," *Harvard Business Review*, September–October 1993, pp. 97–107.

15. Ken Iverson, *Plain Talk: Lessons from a Business Maverick* (New York: John Wiley & Sons, 1997).

16. George S. Day, "Strategies for Surviving a Shakeout," *Harvard Business Review*, March-April 1997, pp. 92–104.

17. Stephan A. Haeckel, *Adaptive Enterprise: Creating and Leading Sense-and-Respond Organizations*, (Boston: Harvard Business School Press, 1999).

Chapter 2. Misconceptions About Market Orientation

1. For insights into IBM see C. Ferguson and C. Morris, *The Computer Wars: The Fall of IBM and the Future of Global Technology* (New York: Random House, 1993); D. Quinn Mills and G. B. Friesen, *Broken Promises: An Unconventional View of What Went Wrong at IBM* (Boston: Harvard Business School Press, 1996); Ira Sager, "How IBM Became a Growth Company," *Business Week*, December 9, 1996, pp. 154–162; and Brent Schlender, "Big Blue Is Betting on Big Iron Again," *Fortune*, April 29, 1996, pp. 103–112, and "The Rebirth of IBM," *Economist*, June 6, 1998, pp. 65–68.

2. Raju Narisetti, "Too Many Choices: P & G Seeing Shoppers Were Being Confused Overhauls Marketing," *Wall Street Journal*, January 15, 1997, pp. A1, A8.

3. Gary Hamel and C. K. Prahalad, *Competing for the Future* (Boston: Harvard Business School Press, 1994).

4. Justin Martin, "Ignore Your Customer," *Fortune*, May 1, 1995, pp. 121–126.

5. Jerry Flint, "Company of the Year: Chrysler," *Forbes*, January 13, 1997, p. 84; and Robert A. Lutz, *Guts: The Seven Laws of Business That Made Chrysler the World's Hottest Car Company* (New York: John Wiley & Sons, 1998).

6. This discussion draws from Vincent Barabba, *Meeting of the Minds: Creating the Market-Based Enterprise* (Boston: Harvard Business School Press, 1995).

7. Joseph L. Bower and Clayton M. Christenson, "Disruptive Technologies: Catching the Wave," *Harvard Business Review*, January–February 1995, pp. 43–53.

8. Glenn Bacon, Sara Beckman, David Mowery and Edith Wilson, "Managing Product Definition in High-Technology Industries," *California Management Review* 36, Spring 1994, pp. 32–56.

9. John P. Workman, Jr., "Marketing's Limited Role in New Product Development in One Computer Systems Firm," *Journal of Marketing Research* 30 (November 1993): 405–21.

Chapter 3. Market Driven Cultures

1. This discussion of culture draws on David DeLong and Liam Fahey, "Building the Knowledge Based Organization: How Culture Drives Knowledge Behaviors," The Ernst & Young Center for Business Innovation, May 1997.

2. Andy Grove, *Only the Paranoid Survive* (New York: Doubleday, 1996).

3. The value of demanding buyers in the home market in providing a window into advanced customer needs and setting high standards for product quality, features and service, as a determinant of national competitive advantage was established by Michael Porter, *The Competitive Advantage of Nations* (New York: Free Press, 1990).

4. Other terms for mental models are conventional wisdom, "genetic code," or paradigm. See Gary Hamel and C. K. Prahalad, "Strategic Intent," *Harvard Business Review*, May–June 1989; and James Walsh, "Managerial and Organizational Cognition: Notes from a Trip Down Memory Lane," *Organizational Science* 6 (May–June 1995): 280–321.

5. This section draws from the work of Rohit Deshpandé, John U. Farley and Frederick E. Webster, Jr., in "Corporate Culture, Customer Orientation, and Innovativeness in Japanese Firms: A Quadrad Analysis," *Journal of Marketing* 53 (January 1993): 3–15 and "Factors Affecting Organizational Performance: A Five-Country Comparison," Marketing Science Institute Report, 97–108 (May 1997). Their model is adapted from Robert E. Quinn and J. Rohrbaugh, "A Spatial Model of Effectiveness Criteria: Toward a Competing Values Approach to Organizational Analysis," *Management Science* 29 (1983): 363–377, and is described in Richard W. Woodman and W. A. Pass-

more, eds., *Research in Organizational Change and Development*, Vol. 5 (Greenwich, CT: JAI Press, 1991). We also employed some of the concepts in Paul McDonald and Geoffrey Gandz, "Getting Value from Shared Values," *Organizational Dynamics* (1994): 64–77.

6. Rohit Deshpandé, John U. Farley and Frederick E. Webster, Jr. (1997), *op cit.*

7. Peter Drucker, *The Practice of Management* (New York: Harper & Row, 1954).

8. Benjamin Schneider and David E. Bowen, "The Service Organization: Human Resources Management Is Crucial," *Organizational Dynamics* (Spring 1993): 39–52.

9. Adam Bryant, "What Price Efficiency: Focus on Costs May Have Blurred Delta's Vision," *New York Times*, July 25, 1997, pp. D1–D2; and Alex Taylor III, "Pulling Delta Out of Its Dive," *Fortune*, December 7, 1998, pp. 156–164.

Chapter 4. Configuring Around Capabilities

1. The concept of capabilities is not new, dating back to Edith T. Penrose, *The Theory of the Growth Firm* (London: Basil Blackwell, 1959). The recent popularity can be traced to C. K. Prahalad and Gary Hamel, "The Core Competencies of the Corporation," *Harvard Business Review*, May–June 1990, pp. 79–91. For our purposes, the concepts of competency and capability are interchangeable, although we prefer to reserve the notion of core competencies for cross-corporation purposes and capabilities for within business unit purposes. See George S. Day, "The Capabilities of Market-Driven Organizations," *Journal of Marketing* 58 (October 1994): 37–52.

2. David J. Collis and Cynthia Montgomery, "Competing on Resources: Strategy in the 1990's," *Harvard Business Review*, July–August 1995, pp. 118–128.

3. Dorothy Leonard-Barton, *Wellsprings of Knowledge: Building and Sustaining the Sources of Innovation* (Boston: Harvard Business School Press, 1994).

4. Kevin P. Coyne, Stephen J. D. Hall and Patricia Gorman Clifford, "Is Your Core Competence a Mirage?" *The McKinsey Quarterly* (1997): 40–54.

5. These tests were developed by Gary Hamel and C. K. Prahalad, *Competing for the Future* (Boston: Harvard Business School Press, 1994).

6. George Stalk, Philip Evans and Lawrence E. Shulman, "Competing on Capabilities: The New Rules of Corporate Strategy," *Harvard Business Review*, March–April 1992, pp. 57–69.

7. David A. Garvin, "The Process of Organization and Management," *Sloan Management Review* 39, Summer 1998, pp. 33–50.

8. This basic distinction was first suggested by Frederick E. Webster, Jr., "The Future Role of Marketing in the Organization," in Donald R. Lehmann and Katherine E. Jocz, eds., *Reflections on the Future of Marketing* (Cambridge, MA: Marketing Science Institute, 1997), pp. 39–66.

9. Andrew Parsons, Michael Frisser and Robert Wartman, "Organizing Today for the Digital Marketing of Tomorrow," *Journal of Interactive Marketing*, forthcoming, 1999.

10. Michael Hammer, *Beyond Reengineering: How the Process-Centered Organization Is Changing Our Work and Our Work Lives* (New York: Harper Business, 1996).

11. Michael E. Porter, "What Is Strategy?" *Harvard Business Review*, November–December 1996, pp. 61–78.

12. This analysis of Virgin Atlantic Airways draws heavily on INSEAD Case 4323, Fontainbleu, France (1995).

Part II. Building the Capabilities

1. Richard Teitelbaum, "The Wal-Mart of Wall Street," *Fortune*, October 13, 1997, and "The Best and Worst Full-Service Brokers," *Smart Money*, October 16, 1997.

Chapter 5. Market Sensing

1. Although researchers have had difficulty defining and studying organizational learning, there is reasonable acceptance of the information processing view of learning that is adopted here. See Barbara Levitt and James G. March, "Organizational Learning," in R. Scott and J. Blake, eds., *Annual Review of Sociology* 14 (1988): 319–340; K. Imai, I. Nonaka and H. Takeuchi, "Managing the New Product Development Process: How Japanese Firms Learn and Unlearn," in K. Clark, R. Hayes and C. Lorenz, eds., *The Uneasy Alliance* (Boston: Harvard Business School Press, 1985), pp. 337–376; and George Huber, "Organizational Learning: The Contributing Processes and Literature," *Organization Science* 2 (1991): 88–115.

2. This discussion draws from John Case, "Customer Services: The Last Word," *Inc.*, April 1991, pp. 89–93; Jim Heskett, Earl Sasser and Len Schlesinger, "Listening to Customers" Harvard Business School Video Tape (1993); and Eryn Brown, "Is Intuit Headed for a Meltdown," *Fortune*, August 10, 1997, pp. 200–202.

3. This final stage in the process is the key idea behind double-loop learning, in which efforts are directed beyond solving immediate problems to addressing the underlying reasons for the problem. See Chris Argyris, *On Organizational Learning* (Cambridge, MA: Blackwell, 1993).

4. Gerald Berstall and Denise Nitterhouse, "Looking 'Outside the Box': Customer Cases Help Researchers Predict the Unpredictable," *Marketing Research* (Summer 1997): 5–13; and Ronald D. Lieger, "Storytelling: A New Way to Get Close to Your Customers," *Fortune*, February 3, 1997, pp. 102–110.

5. Dorothy Leonard and Jeffrey Rayport, "Spark Innovation Through Emphatic Design," *Harvard Business Review*, November–December 1997, pp. 102–115.

6. The dedication to continuous experimentation and improvement is epitomized in the Japanese philosophy of "kaizen" that embraces everyone in the organization. See

M. Imai, *Kaizen: The Key to Japan's Competitive Success* (New York: Random House, 1986).

7. Leonard M. Lodish and Dwight R. Riskey, "Expanding the Role of the Chief Learning Officer: Balancing the Costs and Value of Generating and Using New Marketing Knowledge," unpublished working paper, The Wharton School (July 1997).

8. A growing body of research suggests persuasively that it is the structure and content of these simplified cognitive portrayals of environments (mental models) that actually drives strategic decisions. Useful references are Karl Weick and R.L. Daft, "The Effectiveness of Interpretation Systems," in K.S. Cameron and D.A. Whetten, eds., *Organizational Effectiveness: A Comparison of Multiple Models* (New York: Academic Press, 1983), pp. 71–93; Joseph Porac and Howard Thomas, "Taxonomic Mental Models in Competitor Definition," *Academy of Management Review* 15 (1990): 224–240; James P. Walsh, "Managerial and Organizational Cognition: Notes from a Trip Down Memory Lane," *Organizational Science* 6 (May–June 1995): 280–321; and Kim Warren, "Exploring Competitive Futures Using Cognitive Mapping," *Long Range Planning* 28 (1995): 10–21.

9. Arie P. de Geus, "Planning as Learning," *Harvard Business Review*, March–April 1988, pp. 70–74.

10. George S. Day and Prakash Nedungadi, "Managerial Representations of Competitive Advantage," *Journal of Marketing* 58 (April 1994): 31–44. These mental models are sensible adaptations to present realities, as reflected in the pressure points on the market on the emphasis of their strategy.

Chapter 6. The Shared Knowledge Base

1. L. Ealey and L. Soderburg, "How Honda Cures Design Amnesia," *The McKinsey Quarterly*, Spring 1990, pp. 3–14.

2. Peter R. Peacock, "Data Mining in Marketing: Parts I and II," *Marketing Management* (Winter 1998 and Spring 1998): 8–18 and 14–25.

3. Ikujiro Nonaka and Hirotaka Takeuchi, *The Knowledge-Creating Company: How Japanese Firms Create the Dynamics of Innovation* (New York: Oxford University Press, 1995).

4. A similar example is reported by Hermann Simon, "Pricing Opportunities—And How to Exploit Them," *Sloan Management Review* (Winter 1992): 55–65.

5. For a more thorough discussion of segmentation concepts and approaches see Chapter 5 of my earlier book, *Market Driven Strategy* (New York: Free Press, 1990).

6. These (disguised) data were reported in Rodger Boehm and Cody Phipps, "Flatness Forays," *McKinsey Quarterly* 3 (1996): 128–143.

7. This structural model is a composite of the sources—position—performance framework in George S. Day, *Market Driven Strategy* (New York: Free Press, 1990), the service-profit chain in James L. Heskett, Thomas O. Jones, Gary Loveman, W. Earl

Sasser, Jr., and Leonard A. Schlesinger, "Putting the Service-Profit Chain to Work," *Harvard Business Review*, March–April 1994, pp. 164–174, and the model reportedly used by Sears, Roebuck, as described in Anthony J. Rucci, Steven P. Kirn and Richard T. Quinn, "The Employee-Customer-Profit Chain at Sears," *Harvard Business Review*, January–February 1998, pp. 82–98.

8. Rucci, et al., p. 91.

9. These two examples are taken from Daniel Finkelman, "Crossing the Zone of Indifference," *Marketing Management* 2 (1993), pp. 22–31.

10. These data were reported by James McCormick of First Manhattan in 1995.

11. Linda Grant, "Why FedEx Is Flying High," *Fortune*, November 10, 1997, pp. 156–160.

12. See Benson P. Shapiro, Adrian Slywotzky and Richard S. Tedlow, "How to Stop Bad Things from Happening to Good Companies," *Strategy & Business* (First Quarter 1997): 25–41, and Adrian Slywotzky, *Value Migration* (Cambridge, MA: Harvard Business School Press, 1995).

13. The distinction between an expense versus an investment mind-set is made by Adrian J. Slywotzky and Benson P. Shapiro, "Leveraging to Beat the Odds: The New Marketing Mind-Set," *Harvard Business Review*, September–October 1993, pp. 97–107.

Chapter 7. Market Relating

1. The first reports appeared in Frederick F. Reichheld and W. Earl Sasser, Jr., "Zero Defections: Quality Comes to Services," *Harvard Business Review*, September–October 1990, pp. 105–111. Subsequent work is described in Frederick Reichheld, *The Loyalty Effect* (Cambridge, MA: Harvard Business School Press, 1996).

2. Thomas A. Stewart, "A Satisfied Customer Isn't Enough," *Fortune*, July 21, 1997, pp. 112–113.

3. This example is adapted from a story told by Regis McKenna, *Relationship Marketing* (Reading, MA: Addison Wesley, 1991).

4. Leonard L. Berry, *On Great Service—A Framework for Action* (New York: Free Press, 1995).

5. Philip Kotler elevated relationships to a new paradigm in a speech to the November 1990 trustees meeting of the Marketing Science Institute, "From Transactions to Relationships to Networks." Many others were making similar arguments: Stan Rapp and Tom Collins, *The Great Marketing Turnaround* (Englewood Cliffs, NJ: Prentice-Hall, 1990); and Regis McKenna, *Relationship Marketing: Successful Strategies for the Age of the Customer* (Reading, MA: Addison-Wesley, 1991).

6. The role of reciprocity is well explained by Richard P. Bagozzi, "Reflections on Relationship Marketing in Consumer Markets," *Journal of the Academy of Marketing Science* 23 (Fall 1995): 272–277.

7. Leonard L. Berry, "Relationship Marketing of Services—Growing Interest, Emerging Perspectives," *Journal of the Academy of Marketing Science* 23 (Fall 1995): 236–245.

8. The idea of a continuum of exchange relationships was introduced by Barbara B. Jackson in *Winning and Keeping Industrial Customers* (Lexington, MA: Lexington Books, 1985); and elaborated by James C. Anderson and James A. Narus, "Partnering as a Focused Market Strategy," *California Management Review*, Spring 1991, pp. 95–113.

9. This discussion draws from Baxter International annual reports and Rahul Jacob, "Why Some Customers Are More Equal than Others," *Fortune*, September 19, 1994, pp. 215–224.

10. William Gurley, "Seller Beware: The Buyers Rule E-Commerce," *Fortune*, November 19, 1997, pp. 234 and 236.

11. "In Search of the Perfect Market," *The Economist*, May 10, 1998, special survey on electronic commerce; and Gene Bylinsky, "Sales Are Clicking on Manufacturing's Internet Market," *Fortune*, July 7, 1997, pp. 136c–t.

Chapter 8. Competing for Customer Relationships

1. Rahul Jacob, "How One Red Hot Retailer Wins Customer Loyalty," *Fortune*, July 10, 1995, pp. 72–79.

2. Peter Child, Robert J. Dennis, Timothy C. Gokey, Tim I. McGuire, Mike Sherman and Marc Singer, "Can Marketing Regain the Personal Touch?" *The McKinsey Quarterly*, 3 (1995).

3. Frederick F. Reichheld, "Learning from Customer Defectors," *Harvard Business Review*, March–April 1996, pp. 56–69.

4. See Graham R. Dowling and Mark Uncles, "Do Customer Loyalty Programs Really Work?" *Sloan Management Review*, Summer 1997, pp. 71–82, and letter in response by Erik Muller in *Sloan Management Review*, Winter 1998, p. 4.

5. This is adapted from Sean Meehan and Patrick Barwise, "Do You Value Customer Value?" *Financial Times*, September 14, 1998, p. 10.

6. Lawrence A. Crosby, Kenneth R. Evans and Deborah Cowles, "Relationship Quality in Services Selling: An Interpersonal Influence Perspective," *Journal of Marketing*, 54 (July 1990): 68–81.

7. The concept was introduced by Fred Wiersema, *Customer Intimacy: Pick Your Partners, Shape Your Culture, Win Together* (Santa Monica, CA: Knowledge Exchange, 1996). Details on Calyx & Corolla come from Harvard Business School Case 9-592-035 (revised January 1995).

8. Leonard L. Berry, "Relationship Marketing of Services—Growing Interest, Emerging Perspectives," *Journal of the Academy of Marketing Science*, 23 (Fall 1995): 236–245.

9. David A. Aaker, *Building Strong Brands* (New York: Free Press, 1996).

10. John Deighton, "The Future of Interactive Marketing," *Harvard Business Review*, November–December 1996, pp. 4–15, and Robert C. Blattberg and John Deighton, "Interactive Marketing: Exploiting the Age of Addressability," *Sloan Management Review*, Fall 1991, pp. 5–21.

11. See B. Joseph Pine, *Mass Customization: The New Frontier in Business Competition* (Boston: Harvard Business School Press, 1993); James H. Gilmore and B. Joseph Pine II, "The Four Faces of Mass Customization," *Harvard Business Review*, January–February 1997, pp. 91–101; and Barbara E. Kahn, "Dynamic Relationships with Customers: High Variety Strategies," *Journal of the Academy of Marketing Science*, 26 (1998): 45–53.

12. Kenneth Hill, "Electronic Marketing, the Dell Computer Experience," in Robert A. Peterson, ed., *Electronic Marketing and the Consumer* (London: Sage Publications, 1997), pp. 89-100.

13. Bruce H. Clark, "Welcome to My Parlour . . ." *Marketing Management*, Winter 1997, pp. 11–25; and Donna L. Hoffman and Thomas P. Novak, "Marketing in Hypermedia, Computer-Mediated Environments: Conceptual Foundations," *Journal of Marketing*, July 1996, pp. 50–68

14. Robert D. Hof, "Amazon.com: The Wild World of E-Commerce," *Business Week*, December 14, 1998, pp. 106–114.

Chapter 9. Collaborative Partnering

1. James C. Anderson, "Relationships in Business Markets: Exchange Episodes, Value Creation, and Their Empirical Assessment," *Journal of the Academy of Marketing Science*, 23 (Fall 1995): 346–350.

2. Fred Wiersema, *Customer Intimacy: Pick Your Partner, Shape Your Culture, Win Together* (Santa Monica: Knowledge Exchange, 1996).

3. Frederick E. Webster, *Market-Driven Management* (New York: Wiley, 1994).

4. These attributes are adapted from James C. Anderson and James A. Narus, "Partnering as a Focused Market Strategy," *California Management Review*, Spring 1991, pp. 95–113.

5. Abstracted from Anderson and Narus, *op cit.*

6. Robert D. Buzzell and Gwen Ortmeyer, "Channel Partnerships Streamline Distribution," *Sloan Management Review*, Spring 1995, pp. 85–96.

7. Adapted from Thomas A. Stewart, "The Information Wars: What You Don't Know Will Hurt You," *Fortune*, June 12, 1995, pp. 119–120.

8. George S. Day, "Assessing Advantage: Frameworks for Diagnosing the Present and Prospective Competitive Position," in George S. Day and David Reibstein, eds., *Wharton on Dynamic Competitive Strategies* (New York: John Wiley, 1997), pp. 48–75.

Chapter 10. Reshaping the Organization

1. Gary Hamel and C. K. Prahalad, *Competing for the Future* (Cambridge: Harvard Business School Press, 1994).

2. Adapted from V. Kasturi Pangan, "Managing Market Complexity: A Three-Ring Circus," *Harvard Business School*, May 10, 1994. Unpublished paper.

3. Frederick E. Webster, Jr., "The Future Role of Marketing in the Organization," in Donald R. Lehmann and Katherine E. Jocs, eds., *Reflections on the Future of Marketing* (Cambridge, MA: Marketing Science Institute, 1997).

4. The diagram and the related discussion are drawn from Philip B. Evans and Thomas S. Wurster, "Strategy and the New Economics of Information," *Harvard Business Review*, September–October 1997, pp. 70–83.

5. Michael Hammer, *Beyond Reengineering: How the Process-Centered Organization Is Changing Our Work and Our Lives* (New York: Harper Business, 1996).

6. In July 1998, Astra Merck was combined with Astra USA. This discussion benefited from the insights of Matt Emmens, then CEO of Astra Merck. Other sources included Frank V. Cespedes, *Astra Merck Group*, Harvard Business School Case 9-594-045 (revised March 1, 1995); and Wayne Koberstein, "Wayne Yetter: Astra Merck Turns Model to Reality," *Pharmaceutical Executive* 15 (March 1995).

7. The study was conducted by the Boston Consulting Group, and was reported in *Vision of the Future: Role of Human Resources in the New Corporate Headquarters* (Washington, DC: The Advisory Board Company, 1995).

8. Rodger Boehm and Cody Phipps, "Flatness Forays," *McKinsey Quarterly* 3 (1996): 128–143; Arthur G. Armstrong, Helene Enright, Elizabeth C. Lempres and Stacey Rauch, "What's Wrong with the Consumer Goods Organization?" *McKinsey Quarterly* 1 (1996): 126–135; and Nora Aufreiter, Mike George and Liz Lempres, "Developing a Distinctive Consumer Marketing Organization," *Journal of Market-Focused Management* 3, 1 (1996): 199–208.

9. Ikujiro Nonaka and Hirotaka Takeuchi, *The Knowledge-Creating Company* (New York: Oxford University Press, 1995).

10. For useful perspectives see Thomas W. Virden, "Can This High-Tech Product Sell Itself?" *Harvard Business Review*, November–December 1995, pp. 24–40; and John P. Workman Jr., "Marketing's Limited Role in New Product Development in One Computer Systems Firm," *Journal of Marketing Research* 30 (November 1993): 405–421.

11. This argument has benefited greatly from the insights of Frederick E. Webster Jr., "The Future Role of Marketing in the Organization," in Donald R. Lehmann and Katherine E. Jocz, eds., *Reflections on the Future of Marketing* (Cambridge, MA: Marketing Science Institute, 1997).

12. Marni Clippinger, "A Conversation with Carl Gustin, Kodak's Chief Marketing Officer," *MSI Review* (Fall 1997), 7.

13. John P. Workman Jr., Christian Hamburg and Kjell Gruner, "Marketing Organization: An Integrative Framework of Dimensions and Determinants," *Journal of Marketing* (July 1998), 21–41.

Chapter 11. Setting the Direction

1. This strategy is described in George S. Day, "Strategies for Surviving Shakeouts," *Harvard Business Review*, March–April 1997, pp. 92–104.

2. Justin Martin, "Are You as Good as You Think You Are?" *Fortune*, September 30, 1996, pp. 142–143.

3. For a sampling of the recent debate on this question see John Kay, *Foundations of Corporate Success* (London: Oxford University Press, 1993); Gary Hamel, "Strategy as Revolution," *Harvard Business Review*, July–August 1996; Henry Mintzberg, *The Rise and Fall of Strategic Planning* (New York: Free Press, 1994); and Kevin P. Coyne and Somu Subramanian, "Bringing Discipline to Strategy," *The McKinsey Quarterly* 4 (1996).

4. Michael Treacey and Fred Wiersema, *The Discipline of Market Leaders* (New York: Addison-Wesley, 1995).

5. Mark Fuller, "Strategic Planing in an Era of Total Competition," *Strategy & Leadership*, May/June 1997, pp. 22–27.

6. Kathleen M. Eisenhardt, "Making Fast Strategic Decisions," *Academy of Management Journal* 32 (1989): 543–576.

7. Useful sources are Liam Fahey and Robert Randall, *Learning from the Future: Competitive Foresight Scenarios* (New York: John Wiley, 1998); Paul J. H. Schoemaker, "Scenario Planning: A Tool for Strategic Thinking," *Sloan Management Review*, Winter 1995, pp. 25, 40; and Peter Schwartz, *The Art of the Long View* (New York: Currency Doubleday, 1991).

8. Reproduced with permission from Adam J. Fein, *Consolidation in Wholesale-Distribution: Understanding Industry Change* (Washington, DC: National Association of Wholesaler-Distributors, 1997).

9. Gary Hamel, "Strategy Innovation and the Quest for Value," *Sloan Management Review* 39, Winter 1998, pp. 7–14.

10. Shelly Branch, "What Is Eating McDonald's?" *Fortune*, October 13, 1997, pp. 122–125.

Chapter 12. Guiding the Change

1. Nitin Nohria, "From the M-Form to the N-Form: Taking Stock of Changes in the Large Industrial Corporation," *Harvard Business School*, Working Paper 96-054.

2. John P. Kotter, *Leading Change* (Cambridge, MA: Harvard Business School Press, 1996).

3. Peter Drucker, "Not Enough Generals Were Killed," *Forbes ASAP,* April 8, 1996.

4. This change model is adapted from one used extensively within the General Electric Company, as described by one of the developers in Dave Ulrich, "A New Mandate for Human Resources," *Harvard Business Review,* January–February 1998, pp. 124–135.

5. This description draws heavily from Thomas A. Stewart, "Owens Corning: Back from the Dead," *Fortune,* May 26, 1997, pp. 118–126.

6. Sources include Patricia Sellers, "Sears: The Turnaround Is Ending; The Revolution Has Begun," *Fortune,* April 28, 1997, pp. 106–118; and Anthony J. Rucci, Steven P. Kirn and Richard T. Quinn, "The Employee-Customer-Profit Chain at Sears," *Harvard Business Review,* January–February 1998, pp. 82–98.

7. This is a central premise of the market-back approach to guiding the change process. See John C. Narver, Stanley F. Slater and Brian Tietje, "Creating a Market Orientation," *Journal of Market Focused Management* 2 (1998): 241–255.

8. "Interview with John Kotter," *Strategy and Leadership,* January/February 1997, pp. 18–23.

9. "Larry Bossiday Won't Stop Pushing," excerpts from his appearance at the 1996 *Fortune* 500 Forum.

10. The Dow change program was described in a presentation by David Fischer and Ajay Kohli to the MSI trustees in April 1995, "Enhancing Market Orientation: Lessons from Recent Efforts." The survey was based on an empirical model developed in Ajay K. Kohli, Bernard J. Jaworski and V. Kumar, "MARKOR: A Measure of Market Orientation," *Journal of Marketing Research* 30 (November 1993): 467–477.

11. These learning maps are described in Rucci et al., pp. 92 and 93.

12. This example is drawn from Sue Grist, "Hothousing: A Faster Way to Grow," *Transformation* 15 (Summer 1998): 6–12.

13. Donna Carmichael, "IBM's Journey Towards a Market-Driven Process-Managed Business Model," *Journal of Market-Focused Management* 2 (1997): 99–103.

14. Richard Pascale, Mark Millemann and Linda Gioja, "Changing the Way We Change," *Harvard Business Review,* November–December 1997, pp. 127–139.

INDEX

About the Author

GEORGE S. DAY is the Geoffrey T. Boisi Professor, Professor of Marketing, and Director of the Huntsman Center for Global Competition and Innovation at the Wharton School of the University of Pennsylvania. He has taught at Stanford University, IMD (International Management Development Institute) in Lausanne, Switzerland, and the University of Toronto. He has also held visiting appointments at MIT, Harvard Business School, and the London Business School. Prior to joining the Wharton School, he was Executive Director of the Marketing Science Institute, an industry-supported research consortium.

A member of the Board of Directors and Chairman of the Audit Committee of Footstar Corporation, Dr. Day has directed and participated in numerous senior-management development programs in the United States, Canada, Europe, Japan, Singapore, Latin America, Australia and Africa. His consulting clients include such corporations as AT&T, Eastman Kodak, General Electric, IBM, US West, Metropolitan Life, Marriott, Whirlpool Corporation, Molson Companies, Unilever, E. I. du Pont de Nemours, W. L. Gore and Associates, and Northern Telecom.

The author of fourteen books, including *Market Driven Strategy*, Dr. Day has written more than 125 articles for leading journals, including *The Journal of Marketing, Harvard Business Review, Sloan Management Review,* and *Strategic Management Journal.* He is also the recipient of numerous awards, including two Alpha Kappa Psi Foundation Awards, two Harold H. Maynard Awards, the 1994 Charles Coolidge Parlin Award, the 1996 Paul D. Converse Award, and the 1999 Outstanding Marketing Educator Award.